William Henry Locke

The Story of the Regiment

William Henry Locke

The Story of the Regiment

ISBN/EAN: 9783743312531

Manufactured in Europe, USA, Canada, Australia, Japa

Cover: Foto ©ninafisch / pixelio.de

Manufactured and distributed by brebook publishing software (www.brebook.com)

William Henry Locke

The Story of the Regiment

THE STORY OF THE REGIMENT.

BY

WILLIAM HENRY LOCKE, A M.,
CHAPLAIN.

PHILADELPHIA:
J. B. LIPPINCOTT & CO.
1868.

Entered, according to Act of Congress, in the year 1867, by

J. B. LIPPINCOTT & CO.,

In the Clerk's Office of the District Court of the United States for the Eastern District of Pennsylvania.

In compliance with current copyright law, U. C. Library Bindery produced this replacement volume on paper that meets ANSI Standard Z39.48-1984 to replace the irreparably deteriorated original

1998

TO THE LIVING OF THE

OLD PENNSYLVANIA ELEVENTH,

AND TO THE

MEMORY

OF ITS MANY GALLANT DEAD,

THIS VOLUME

Is Inscribed.

PREFACE.

The first object sought in this volume is to put on permanent record the deeds of a brave and noble regiment—an effort that will be fully appreciated by its numerous friends. The author also designs that it should be a contribution to the general history of the war. To secure such a history, the story of each separate regiment must first be known.

The duties of the writer did not require him to carry either sword or musket, and the story he here tells is made up from a note-book never absent from him, whether in camp or on the march. When the original record—sometimes made during a halt along the roadside, and sometimes in the midst of battle—better tells the story, that record is inserted, day and date.

Everything promising to throw light upon the campaigns of the Army of the Potomac has been carefully read and freely used, in giving the reasons for certain movements and the ends to be secured. It was the fortune of the Eleventh Regiment to be connected with most of the principal operations of the army to which it belonged. Enough of general information is therefore given to form a continuous narrative of events; and to the ordinary reader perhaps the book will be found to serve the place of a larger and more pretending history of the Army of the Potomac.

W. H. L.

PITTSBURG, October 1, 1867.

CONTENTS.

I.

CHAPTER I.

Rebellion armed and defiant—Call for troops—Eleventh Regiment organized.. 13

CHAPTER II.

The offensive—Guarding the railroad—Patterson on the Upper Potomac—March into Virginia—Battle of Falling Waters—Pennsylvania's first killed—Martinsburg........ 16

CHAPTER III.

McDowell and Patterson to co-operate—Army delayed— The runaway slave —Reconnoissance to Winchester— Charlestown—Battle of Bull Run............................. 26

II.

CHAPTER I.

The rebellion in a new phase—Re-enlistment—From citizen to soldier—Filling up regiments—Quarrel about the number—Governor's order—Field and staff................. 35

CHAPTER II.

From Pennsylvania to Maryland—Through Baltimore— Annapolis—Northern arguments—Master and slave...... 42

CONTENTS.

CHAPTER III.

Side issues of the conflict—The iron-clad Merrimac—The subdued domestic—Washington—Review by the President............ 51

CHAPTER IV.

From Maryland to Virginia—Manassas—Midnight alarm—Clerical captive............ 57

CHAPTER V.

Manassas and environs—Bull Run battle-field—White Plains—Absconding darkies............ 65

CHAPTER VI.

Marching southward—Hartsuff's Brigade—Falmouth—McDowell's Corps—Fredericksburg—A night march—Alexandria—Pursuit of Jackson—Front Royal—Belle Boyd—Escape............ 72

III.

CHAPTER I.

Pope's campaign—Warrenton—Waterloo—Arrival of Pope—Review—Army of Virginia—Culpepper—Battle of Cedar Mountain—Advance to the Rapidan............ 82

CHAPTER II.

An opportune capture—Retreat to the Rappahannock—Culpepper greetings—Fight at Rappahannock Station... 93

CHAPTER III.

Pope retreating northward—Company G—Battle of Thoroughfare Gap—Hospital at Manassas............ 100

CHAPTER IV.

Second Bull Run—Porter disobeys orders—Longstreet unites with Jackson—Division on the left—Losses in the Eleventh—Retreat to Centerville—Battle of Chantilly—Within the fortifications—Pope and McDowell............ 106

IV.

CHAPTER I.

Hall's Hill—Colonel Martin—Maj. Frink—Colonel Fletcher Webster—Invasion of Maryland—McClellan—Feeling of troops—March through Washington—Recruits from Harrisburg—Battle of South Mountain............................ 115

CHAPTER II.

McClellan and Lee on Upper Potomac—Rebel chaplain—Keedysville—Battle of Antietam—Hartsuff's Brigade—Fighting on the right—Scenes in hospital—Antietam after the battle.. 123

CHAPTER III.

Army in repose—Walnut Grove camp—Foraging for the mess—Louisiana vs. Virginia—Sermon in camp............ 134

CHAPTER IV.

Tent life in Maryland—Night experiences—Stuart's cavalry raid—Dreams and visions............................... 146

V.

CHAPTER I.

McClellan superseded by Burnside—Feeling in the army—Campaign begun—On the Rappahannock—Bombardment of Fredericksburg—Across the river.................. 152

CHAPTER II.

Fredericksburg—Night before the battle—December 13th—Operations on the left—Pollock's house—Burying the dead... 161

CHAPTER III.

After the battle—Wounded in Washington—Excitement in the city—Burnside—Camp near Fletcher Chapel—Notes from diary—Virginia schoolmaster—Northern claim on Virginia.. 168

CHAPTER IV.

Burnside to cross the Rappahannock—Troops in motion—Winter storm—Army in the mud.................................. 178

VI.

CHAPTER I.

Burnside gives place to Hooker—Organized desertion—A new bill of fare—Army kept employed—Improved condition of the troops—Preparations to march................. 184

CHAPTER II.

Chancellorville campaign—First Corps on the left—Into the Wilderness—Jackson's flank attack—Death of Jackson—First Corps on the right—Retreat from the Wilderness.. 193

CHAPTER III.

After the battle of Chancellorville—Feeling among the troops—Revelations of old letters—Division reorganized—General Baxter—Marching northward—Across Manassas plains... 205

CHAPTER IV.

Hooker and Lee—Moseby—Parting with Virginia—First Corps at Emmettsburg... 215

VII.

CHAPTER I.

Hooker displaced by Meade—Impression on the Army—Enemy in front of Gettysburg—First day of July—Rebels quartered in the town.. 223

CHAPTER II.

Armies concentrated at Gettysburg—Second day of July—Third day of July—July Fourth.............................. 233

CONTENTS. xi

CHAPTER III.

Gettysburg under rebel rule—A rampant quartermaster—First Corps on Cemetery Hill—Pickett's charge—A bold pioneer.. 240

CHAPTER IV.

Retreat and pursuit—Bulletins of victory—Vandals—The lost found—Lee across the Potomac......................... 247

CHAPTER V.

Marching through Loudon Valley — Battle-field of Antietam—An unamiable lady—Fording Goose Creek—White Plains—Bealton Station—Fight at Brandy Station—Eleventh on Hartsuff's knoll..................................... 255

CHAPTER VI.

Occupying the line of the Rapidan—Substitutes—Raccoon Ford—Execution of a deserter—Reading the enemy's signals—Kelly's Ford—Raid on the sutlers—Retreat to Centerville—Mysterious movements............................ 267

CHAPTER VII.

From the Rapidan to Centerville—First Corps at Bristow—Bull Run—Reprieved deserter—Bull Run battle-field—Detected conscript—Thoroughfare Gap—Camp rumors.. 277

CHAPTER VIII.

Back to the Rappahannock—Eleventh at Morrisville—Across the river—Bivouac on Auburn farm—Alarm—Camp near Liberty — Guerrillas—Adventures of the wounded—An outside patient....................................... 288

CHAPTER IX.

Mine Run Campaign—South of the Rapidan—In position on Mine Run—Marching back—Short rations—Kelly's Ford.. 303

CHAPTER X.

Another campaign completed — Faith of the army — Re-enlisting—Veteran furlough.. 314

VIII.

CHAPTER I.

Lieutenant-General U. S. Grant—Furlough ended—Promotions—Farewell to First Corps—Campaign begun—Battle of the Wilderness—Longstreet on the left—Rebel successes on the right—Race for Spottsylvania—Death of Major Keenan 318

CHAPTER II.

In front of Spottsylvania—Laurel Hill—Moving to the left—Grant marching southward—On the North Anna—Chickahominy—Bethesda Church—Cold Harbor—Harrison's Landing 334

CHAPTER III.

South of the James—In front of Petersburg—Mine explosion—Fight for the Weldon Railroad 351

CHAPTER IV.

Advances and retrogrades—Changes in the Eleventh—Hicksford raid—Burning ties—Successful ambush—In camp 362

CHAPTER V.

Extending the left to Hatcher's Run—Consolidation of Eleventh and Ninetieth—Opening of the campaign—Battle of Hatcher's Run 371

CHAPTER VI.

Final Concentration—Army incredulous—Boydton plankroad—Reinforcing Sheridan 379

CHAPTER VII.

Fifth Corps with Sheridan—Getting into position—Battle of Five Forks—Captures and losses 386

CHAPTER VIII.

Last march of the Fifth Corps—General Warren relieved of command—Bivouac at Deep Creek—Appomattox Court House—Lee surrenders 391

CHAPTER IX.

Homeward bound—Through Richmond—Across the Peninsula—Hall's Hill—Grand review—Army disbanded—Harrisburg—Eleventh Regiment living and dead—End .. 398

STORY OF THE REGIMENT.

I.

CHAPTER I.

REBELLION ARMED AND DEFIANT.

The roar of Sumter's guns, as it rolled northward along the Atlantic coast, and westward across the prairies, awakened the nation from its peaceful dream of half a century, to the startling reality of armed and defiant Rebellion.

A dissolution of the Federal Union, at first darkly hinted, and afterward openly avowed, toward the close of the year 1860 became a fixed purpose with leading Southern statesmen,—a purpose to which they gave masterly energies, entailing upon the country four years of calamitous war.

Following close upon the surrender of Fort Sumter, came the call from Washington, not less startling than the report of the first cannon shot, for volunteers to defend the rightful authority of the Government. Every Northern State sent back the same enthusiastic response.

Party lines were obliterated, and political differences forgotten in the common danger. Cities and towns and villages rivaled each other in their patriotic offers of men and means. It was the uprising of an indignant and insulted people. The South had taken the sword; and though reluctant to begin the strife, the North accepted the issue.

The State capital became the military rendezvous of Pennsylvania; and to Harrisburg her sons hastened, from their farms and their workshops; from offices and stores and counting-rooms. Rapidly as the troops arrived they were organized into regiments and sent to the front, each regiment distinguished by the number that marked the order of its organization.

One week later than the President's call for troops, ten companies, representing six different counties, and containing in all nearly a thousand men, were united and formed into the Eleventh Regiment. Co. A, Captain J. C. Dodge, Co. D, Captain W. B. Schott, and Co. G, Captain J. N. Bowman, represented Lycoming County; Co. B, Captain Phaen Jarrett, and Co. C, Captain H. M. Bossert, Clinton County; Co. E, Captain John B. Johnson, Luzerne County; Co. F, Captain C. J. Brunner, Northumberland County; Co. H, Captain W. M. McLure, Montour County; Co. I, Captain Richard Coulter, and Co. K, Captain W. B. Coulter, Westmoreland County. These brave men, meeting as strangers, but drawn together by the same noble impulse of love of country, were now united, for life or for death, in strong and enduring bonds.

The election for field officers that followed this union of companies resulted in the choice of Captain Phaen Jarrett for Colonel; Captain Richard Coulter, Lieutenant-Colonel; and W. D. Earnest, Major. To complete the regimental organization, Lieutenant A. F. Aul was appointed Adjutant; W. H. Hay, Quartermaster; Dr. W. F. Babb, Surgeon, and H. B. Beuhler, Assistant Surgeon.

The ELEVENTH REGIMENT OF PENNSYLVANIA VOLUNTEERS was thenceforth a corporeal reality. From the 23d of April, 1861, to the surrender of General Lee at Appomattox Court House, the history of the "Old Eleventh"—so designated to distinguish it from the Eleventh Regiment of the Pennsylvania Reserve Corps—is the history, in part, of all the grand movements of the Army of the Potomac.

CHAPTER II.

NATIONAL FORCES TAKE THE OFFENSIVE.

The secession of Virginia, on the 17th day of April, made the National Capital the main point to be defended; and to Washington each State sent its first available troops. But the Government soon discovered that there were other enemies to provide against than those openly in arms in Virginia. Traitors walked abroad in the guise of peaceful citizens; and since the wanton attack upon the troops passing through Baltimore, and the destruction of the railroads leading to that city, all the lines of travel communicating with Washington were closely guarded.

Three days after its organization, by order of General Patterson, commanding the Department of Pennsylvania, the Eleventh Regiment, then at Camp Wayne, West Chester, was assigned to duty on the Baltimore and Wilmington Railroad, occupying the territory between Havre de Grace and Elkton. The instructions issued to Colonel Jarrett, defining the nature of the service required of his regiment, indicated, even at that early day, the conciliatory spirit that ever animated the Government throughout the entire rebellion.

"The Major-General understands that along the line of railway placed under your charge, and more particularly in the neighborhood of Newark, inoffensive citizens have been molested by the troops lately removed. He wishes you to instruct your men that this must not be; and that the object of being where you are is to make friends of the inhabitants, and not enemies. * * You will instruct the officers stationed at Newark to be careful to allay the angry feeling which has been excited at that point."

The railroad was well guarded; and without any compromise of integrity, the other object—making friends of the inhabitants along the line—was also secured. At Havre de Grace, Cos. A and B, and Co. K at Newark—where persons had been arrested on idle and ill-founded charges—were made the recipients of the confidence and good will of the citizens, expressed in the most substantial manner.

Into the brief hours of those unusual days were crowded events for whose maturity a quarter of a century had been necessary. Harper's Ferry, evacuated by the Federal troops in the evening, was occupied next morning by a large rebel force that marched down the Shenandoah Valley, under command of General J. E. Johnson. An attack upon Washington, by way of Alexandria, was hourly expected; and the appearance of the enemy at Harper's Ferry and along the banks of the Upper Potomac, looked as though an attempt was to be made to invest the city by overrunning the borders of Maryland and Pennsylvania. With something of the spirit that characterized later army movements, all the troops that could be spared from the actual defense of Washington were placed under command of General Patterson, and hastened to the border. The Eleventh Regiment, relieved of guard duty on the railroad, and marching by way of Baltimore and Washington, reported to the commanding general at Hagerstown, and was assigned to Colonel Abercrombie's Brigade of Keim's Division.

The army of General Patterson, as it was the largest single column acting against the enemy, was an object of national interest. It was preparing to march against twenty thousand rebels, whose leader expressed a determination to hold Harper's Ferry at all hazard, as the key of the Shenandoah Valley. General Scott counseled Patterson that it would not be enough simply to sustain no reverse. "A check, or a drawn battle, would be a victory to the enemy, filling his heart with joy, his ranks with men, and his magazines with voluntary contributions," telegraphed the veteran commander at the moment the troops took their first forward step.

Filing out from the numerous camps around

Hagerstown, with the rising of the sun of June 1st all the brigades and divisions of Patterson's column were moving in splendid order toward the Potomac. The army thus marching to the attack of Harper's Ferry, embraced within itself names since become of household familiarity in the military records of the nation. Major-General Burnside was then known as Colonel Burnside, in command of a Rhode Island regiment; Major-General George H. Thomas was simply Colonel Thomas, commanding a brigade in Keim's Division; Major-General John Newton was only Captain Newton, of the Engineer Corps.

The rebel general did not wait for the near approach of Patterson's forces. Drawing in the two regiments of Texan riflemen that picketed the Potomac as far up as Sheppardstown, the day after our movement began Harper's Ferry was evacuated, Johnson falling back to Martinsburg. The unexpected retreat of the enemy was received with demonstrations of delight. It was regarded as an omen of good, promising a successful issue to all succeeding undertakings.

Full of confident enthusiasm, the pursuit of Johnson was commenced the following morning. Seven or eight thousand troops had already crossed into Virginia, and were marching down the south bank of the Potomac, when a sudden halt was ordered by a telegram from Washington, announcing that the city was threatened from the direction of Alexandria, and calling on Patterson for immediate reinforcements.

The troops required by General Scott left the army on the Upper Potomac without either artillery or cavalry, and so greatly reduced in the number of its effective men as to make a further advance impossible. The regiments that had crossed the river were recalled; and a movement, that at the first promised the most complete success, ended in days of wearisome inaction — as full of monotony to the soldier, as they were of impatience to the entire North.

Meanwhile the rebels, reassuring their courage at Patterson's unavoidable delay, again approached the Potomac. Scouts reported that a large Confederate force occupied the country between Dam No. 4 and Sheppardstown, under command of Stonewall Jackson; and that Johnson was at Bunker Hill, with a reserve of not less than five thousand men.

Toward the latter part of June, a battery of six guns and a small force of cavalry having been sent to him, General Patterson prepared to resume his forward movement. A reconnoissance in force was to be made into Virginia, the troops moving in two separate columns. The Sixth Brigade, Colonel Abercrombie, under the guidance of Captain John Newton, of the Engineer Corps, was to cross the river near Dam No. 4, supported by the First Brigade, Colonel Thomas, and four pieces of artillery. The Second and Fifth Brigades, Generals Wynkoop and Negley, were to remain within striking distance of Abercrombie and Thomas. These troops constituted the first column, under command of Major-General Keim. The second column consisted of the Third and Fourth Brigades, a squadron of cavalry, and one section of Perkin's Battery, under Major-General Cadwallader. The second column was to cross at Williamsport.

The night preceding the contemplated movement, Lieutenant-Colonel Coulter and thirty men of the Eleventh Regiment, were detailed to explore the fordings of the river near the proposed place of passage for the first column. Marching quietly down the left bank, their movements concealed from the enemy's pickets by the intense darkness and the heavy falling rain, the exploring party carefully surveyed the river, crossing and recrossing at several different points. Everywhere high water rendered the fordings impassable.

It was then decided to cross the entire force at Williamsport in the following order: Colonel Abercrombie's Brigade, with one section of artillery and a squadron of cavalry. Colonel Thomas's Brigade, with one company of cavalry and two pieces of artillery. General Negley's Brigade, with one section of artillery and a company of cavalry, forming General Keim's Division. General Cadwallader's Division was to follow close in the rear.

One day was lost by the change in the order of march. But early on the morning of July 2d the army was in motion. An advance guard of one hundred and fifty men of the Eleventh, and McMullin's Philadelphia Rangers, was thrown across the river to carry the fording. A small rebel force, stationed on the Virginia shore to watch our movements, received the vanguard with a brisk, though entirely harmless, volley of musketry. Nothing daunted by a reception so purely Southern in all its characteristics, our men continued to advance, and the enemy retiring from the river, the army crossed the Potomac without further opposition.

The first column marched southward along the main road, except Negley's Brigade, that diverged to the right, a short distance from the river, to protect our flank. The smooth pike leading to Martinsburg had not then received the impress of a tramping army; nor were the green fields, on either side of it, transformed into fields of blood and carnage. Yet there was a sound of battle in the air. Skirmishers were kept thrown out well to the front, and an occasional rebel vedette could be seen, falling slowly back before our cautious advance.

Six miles from Williamsport, toward the middle of the forenoon, the army reached Falling

Waters. Broad acres of wheat flanked the road right and left, and on a slight elevation in front stood the residence of the proprietor. At the moment of advancing through a skirt of woods, and in turning a short angle in the road, our skirmish line suddenly developed a force of the enemy posted in a clump of trees, while the main body of the Confederates appeared in sight, sheltered behind breastworks of fence rails and fallen timber. It was the Brigade of Stonewall Jackson by which we were thus confronted, since celebrated as the "Stonewall Brigde," consisting of the Second, Fourth, Fifth, and Twenty-seventh Virginia Regiments, J. E. B. Stuart's cavalry regiment, and Captain Pendleton's battery of four guns.

The disposition of the Federal troops was quick and judicious. Abercrombie deployed the Eleventh Pennsylvania and First Wisconsin to the right and left of the pike. Hudson's battery, supported by McMullin's Rangers, was placed in the middle of the road, and a general advance ordered against the rapid fire of the rebels, drawn up in battle-line behind Porterfield's house. With shouts and cheers, that ran along the whole column of troops hurrying forward at the sound of cannon, the leading brigade obeyed the word of command.

The enemy's artillery was admirably posted to sweep the Martinsburg pike; but, fortunately,

Pendleton's range was too high, and the shot passed harmlessly overhead. While thus engaging the rebel infantry and artillery in front, Stuart brought up his cavalry, and riding swiftly from the opposite direction, was seen to make threatening demonstrations on the right of the Eleventh. Repulsing two separate efforts on the part of Stuart to charge our line, Colonel Jarrett detached Cos. A, B, and C as skirmishers, to take the cavalry on the flank; while the left wing of the regiment was pushed forward to turn the rebel cannon planted in the middle of the road.

The unusual excitement of battle now extended to the remotest file of the army, and footmen and horse were pressing with eager haste toward the front. Thomas's Brigade, marching behind Abercrombie, and the next to reach the ground, quitting the pike, and moving in compact lines through the fields, extended its right toward the enemy's left flank. Closely pressed by Abercrombie in front, and threatened on the left by Thomas, further resistance was useless; and after a spiteful encounter of nearly an hour, Jackson reluctantly abandoned the field.

The purple tide, that has since reached its flood height, has effaced almost every mark of the battle of Falling Waters. Yet the features of war are ever the same. Those fields of wheat, just ripe for the harvest, were trodden down and destroyed. The elegant farm-house, whose white front could be seen through overhanging trees and climbing vines, was shattered by artillery, and the peaceful scene of rural felicity marred and ruined.

Stonewall Jackson's first engagement with our troops did not promise the success of later exploits. Eight of his dead were left unburied on the field, and a large number are known to have been wounded. The Union loss was two killed and fifteen wounded. Of these the Eleventh lost Amos Sappinger, Co. H, killed. Wounded — William Hannaker, Co. B; James Morgan, D. Stiles, Nelson Headen, Co. E; Christian Shawl, Co. F; Russel Levan, John De Hass, Co. G; John Reed, Wm. G. Kuhns, Co. K.

Amos Sappinger was Pennsylvania's first life offering on the battle-field, in the war for the Union. He deserves a more enduring monument than these pages.

The pursuit of the retreating foe was kept up as far as Hainesville, four miles from Martinsburg, where the army bivouacked for the night. Resuming the march with the earliest dawn of next day, on the 3d of July Patterson occupied Martinsburg, Stonewall Jackson falling back on the reserve force at Bunker Hill.

CHAPTER III.

M'DOWELL AND PATTERSON TO CO-OPERATE.

The duty first assigned to General Patterson was the capture of Harper's Ferry. Now he had another and more important task to perform. A column from Washington, under command of General McDowell, was to move against the rebel army concentrated at Manassas Junction; and Patterson was to co-operate with that column either by directly attacking Johnson at Winchester, or by threats and a well sustained show of opposition, prevent him from leaving the Valley to reinforce Beauregard.

The term of service for which the three months' troops had volunteered would soon expire. Anticipating an easy victory, and regarding the whole affair very much in the light of a holiday excursion, every man was greatly solicitous that before returning home, his regiment should be brought into actual conflict with the insurgents.

But there was a serious delay of several days at Martinsburg. The rebels had utterly destroyed the railroad from thence to Harper's Ferry, leaving behind them, in their retreat from the town, nothing but the smouldering ruins of the spacious depot and the charred remains of forty-eight locomotives. No reliance could be placed on foraging from the adjacent country, as the hungry Southerner had already eat it bare. The Quartermaster's Department did not know how to provide for an army of eighteen thousand men as expeditiously as in later days. Wagons were scarce, and as all the supplies for Patterson's troops were hauled from Williamsport, to collect rations for more than two days in advance was next to impossible.

On the 8th of July orders were issued to the army for an advance on Winchester early next morning. But before midnight, and in the midst of active preparations by each regiment and brigade for the expected movement, the order was countermanded. A part of the reinforcements arrived on that day was reported unable, without rest, to bear the fatigues of a further march, and be in proper condition to meet the enemy.

In consultation with some of his principal officers, General Patterson found decided opposition to the advance on Winchester; and before renewing the order to march, a council was called, composed of the division and brigade commanders, the officers of the engineers, and the chiefs of the departments of transportation and supply. There was great unanimity of opinion that the army was on a false line; that it could more certainly hold Johnson at Winchester, and cooperate with McDowell at Manassas, by taking a position at Charlestown, than by remaining at Martinsburg, or advancing further down the Valley.

As a result of this council, the abandoned picket lines around Martinsburg were again established; and officers who did not spend their evenings at the gay mansion of minister Faulkner, enjoying the polite society of his accomplished wife and daughters, detailing to them all the probable movements of the Federal army—only to be faithfully reported to the rebel commander—went about discharging the duties assigned to them.

Every one coming into Martinsburg from the direction of Bunker Hill or Winchester, supposed to be able to give any information respecting the movements of the enemy, was at once taken before General Patterson. Our pickets were familiar with this custom, and when they arrested the runaway slave of Mr. Byerly, living at Darksville, some distance beyond Bunker Hill, they knew that he would be welcome at army headquarters.

The colored man had not yet arrived to the estate of a contraband; but his information was always regarded as more reliable than that of any other. If he sometimes told more than he knew, the fact was no disparagement to the negro. It only proved that in one point at least he was very much like his white master.

All the knowledge possessed by the slave was soon imparted. Johnson and Jackson often came to his master's house. He had heard them say that the principal part of the Southern force was at Winchester, throwing up intrenchments in expectation that the Yankees were coming; and that many of the colored people had been sent there to help on the work. Jackson was at Bunker Hill, with Colonel Stuart and Captain Pendleton. He knew these officers, because they often visited at his master's house.

"Did you ever hear your master say how many soldiers Johnson has?"

"No, sah; but he always shakes his head when he talks about it, and says: 'jist let de Yankees come on!'"

The colored man's face was turned toward the Potomac, and when the general and his staff had ceased to question him, he begged to be permitted to pursue his journey. But in reward for revealing what he knew, he was sent to the guard-house, and confined as a runaway slave.

"How did you get off at last, George?" we asked of him a year or two later, in the interior of Pennsylvania.

"Well, sah, dey kept me in de guard-house until de army moved to Bunker Hill. Den I got away from de guard, and went right back to my ole massa. I was afeard ob de Yankees after dat, and when dey come again into de Valley I staid close at home. But one mornin', jist about daylight, your army begin to come back along de road from Winchester, marchin' very fast. My ole massa rubbed his hands and shook his head. 'I know'd it,' says he; 'Jackson is arter Banks, and he'll cotch him yit.'

"I watch'd 'em comin' back for two or three hours; and I seed among de wagons an' de hosmen a good many colored people dat I know'd. Den I says to my wife: 'Mary, I feel as if I ought to go too.' 'Jist do as you like, George,' says she; 'but don't forgit to come back arter me.' Ole massa was settin' out on de poach; so I goes down behind de barn and up through de orchard. If I could only git through de orchard, den I know'd I would be out ob sight. But it seemed as if I'd never git to de top ob de hill; my feet felt so heavy I couldn't run. Bime-by I got out to de road among de soldiers, den safe across de Potomac, and at last into Pennsylvany. Arter awhile I goes back for Mary. Somebody told massa I was in de neighborhood, and he watched all night wid a gun to shoot me when I come round de house. But Mary got away safe too, and now I 'spect we'll jist stay whar we is."

The movement from Washington, under General McDowell, was to commence on the 16th of

July. To keep up a threatening attitude in front of Johnson, and by every possible means retain him in the Valley, on the day preceding that date General Patterson advanced his entire force from Martinsburg to Bunker Hill.

Despite the example of the Faulkners, and others of like sympathies, there was a strong Union sentiment in Martinsburg; and when the army left the town on that fair summer morning, the Eleventh Pennsylvania Regiment and the First Wisconsin each carried a beautiful national flag, the gift of the loyal ladies of the place, in acknowledgment of our first victory over the rebel forces at Falling Waters.

The ashes of Jackson's camp fires were still warm and smouldering as our troops stacked arms on the ground recently occupied by the Southrons, and bivouacked for the night. Next day Gen. Patterson made a reconnoissance from Bunker Hill toward Winchester. The roads were strongly barricaded at every available point, causing frequent halts to remove the trees that had been felled across the highway, and to fill up the ditches, with which Johnson hoped to impede the passage of artillery. Four miles from Winchester the column came to a final halt. The enemy occupied the town in large numbers, and without waiting for him to come out from his intrenchments, Patterson returned to Bunker Hill.

The same day General McDowell began his

movement against Manassas. On the 17th, General Scott telegraphed to Patterson that McDowell's first day's work had driven the enemy beyond Fairfax Court House, and that in all probability Manassas Junction would be carried on the following morning.

Up to that time, General Patterson had implicitly obeyed the orders of his superior officer. Feeling himself unable to attack the rebel general in his strong position, by a well-maintained show of opposition, Johnson was kept in his front, and could not reach Manassas, even if disposed to move in that direction, in less than three days. There was no longer any seeming occasion for keeping his troops on a false line, or of maintaining communications running through a country in active sympathy with the rebellion, and at any moment liable to interruption; and on the morning of July 17th Patterson retired from Bunker Hill to Charlestown.

From the fording of the Potomac at Williamsport to Bunker Hill, the enemy had retired before us; and when the troops began to move on that Wednesday morning, ignorant of the plans of the commander, a battle in front of Winchester was not only desired, but confidently expected by the rank and file of the Federal army. The first five or six miles of the march looked as though we were threatening to fall on the enemy's right flank, but toward noon the column changed front, and moved in the direction of Charlestown. From Bunker Hill to Winchester is thirteen miles—from Charlestown to Winchester is twenty miles; and without knowing the relative geographical positions of the different places, the soldiers looked upon the movement as a retreat without a pursuing foe. Murmurs of discontent, audible to every ear, ran along the line, and the reproach visited upon the commanding general was without stint or measure.

The Army of the Upper Potomac presented a woe-begone appearance on its arrival at Charlestown. The vanguard that entered the place might well have been taken for the ghosts of John Brown's raiders, had they carried pikes in their hands instead of bristling muskets. Entire regiments were without shoes and without coats, while the nether garments of many of the men were out at the knees and out at the seat, flaunting their shoddy fragments in the breeze, or else presenting the rents closed up with patches of canvas torn from dilapidated tents.

The Federal occupation of Charlestown broke up the innocent business of a band of secession militia, engaged in pressing into the rebel service the young men of the surrounding district. It also had the good effect of sending many of its principal citizens on a reluctant pilgrimage further South. From this securer base, and on a line far more advantageous as it was supposed,

General Patterson began at once active preparations to attack Winchester.

In one week the term of enlistment of eighteen regiments—full three-fourths of the army—would expire. An appeal was made to the troops to remain ten days longer, and from the spirit thus far manifested by them, a hearty response was anticipated. But the men had become dissatisfied, and only three Pennsylvania regiments—the Eleventh, the Fifteenth, and the Twenty-fourth—declared their willingness to stay. Patterson was now powerless to do anything, and the army lay idle at Charlestown awaiting orders from Washington.

While these delays and disappointments in the Army of the Upper Potomac were causing heart-burnings and bitter criminations, the nation was nearing the first great calamity of the war. McDowell did not carry Manassas Junction on the 18th of July, as General Scott had so confidently expected; and the battle of Bull Run was not fought until the 21st. Meanwhile, in answer to an urgent call from the rebel government to hasten to the assistance of Beauregard, Johnson quietly withdrew his forces from Winchester, and marching toward Manassas, arrived on the afternoon of the engagement at the moment to turn the tide of battle, and change what promised a victory to the Federal arms into defeat and disastrous rout.

II.

CHAPTER I.

THE REBELLION IN A NEW PHASE.

THE rebellion assumed a different shape in the eyes of the country after the battle of Bull Run. The huge proportions to which it afterward grew, began then to be distinctly foreshadowed. Its leaders, flushed with victory, and expecting a speedy conquest of the North, did not hesitate to reveal, undisguised, the spirit of prejudice and hate that conceived and inaugurated the whole secession movement.

The three months' campaign accomplished comparatively little; and closing with the defeat of Bull Run, seemed scarcely anything else than a total failure. Yet there was no abatement in the enthusiasm of the people; and nowhere was this enthusiasm greater than among the men who had passed through this first campaign. Whole regiments, with hardly any change in their organization, re-enlisted for the long term of three years, or during the war.

On the 24th of July, the Eleventh Regiment

left Harper's Ferry for Baltimore, en route for Harrisburg, where the men were mustered out of service. General Patterson's order for transportation was accompanied by a commendation of the regiment, carefully preserved among its papers.

"It gives the commanding general great satisfaction to say, that the conduct of this regiment has merited his highest approbation. It had the fortune to be in the advance at Falling Waters, where the steadiness and gallantry of both officers and men came under his personal observation. They have well merited his thanks."

Before the first term of enlistment had altogether expired, steps were taken to reorganize the Eleventh for the three years' service. Colonel Jarrett submitted to General Patterson a complete regimental organization, headed by the name of Richard Coulter, as Colonel. The recommendations were heartily indorsed by the general, and referred to Governor Curtin for commissions.

Under date of July 25th, Simon Cameron, Secretary of War, telegraphed to Colonel Coulter that his regiment was accepted for the long term of service. A few days later, the colonel was directed, by the same authority, to enter his men in Camp Curtin and hold them ready for marching orders, leaving an officer behind to recruit the several companies to the maximum standard.

With the many hands into which it was divided, it was only the work of a moment to transform the peaceful citizen into a soldier, of martial look and mien. Finely polished boots were exchanged for a pair of substantial brogans, often without finish, and oftener without fit. Pantaloons of sable black, or demure brown, or sprightly gray, gave place to a pair of unmixed blue. The head that supported a luxuriant growth of chestnut curls, and nodded gracefully under a shining beaver, first closely shorn of all capillary superfluities, was incased in a cap of the smallest pattern; while a blue coat, with an economically short tail, took the place of the neatly fitting frock.

When the quiet citizen, thus attired, had a knapsack strapped upon his back, and a haversack thrown across his shoulders, with gun, canteen, and cartridge box, the transformation was complete. He was thenceforth prepared to enter upon a mode of life, as different from his former self, as though he had entirely changed his personal identity.

Early in the month of August, Co. B, under command of Captain William Shanks, arrived at Camp Curtin. To this first company others were quickly added; and by the 1st of September, the regiment might have gone to the front with its full complement of men.

In those days of intense excitement, twenty-four hours in camp reached the limit of any one's patience. Officers and men were alike clamorous to be sent to Washington, or anywhere else out of the State that danger threatened. Each one acted as though in fear that the rebellion might be crushed, and the war closed up, without giving him an opportunity of striking a single blow for the Union.

Perhaps it was well for the Cause that it could not then be known how much of the dark and angry-looking war-cloud, that appeared above the Southern horizon, hung below concealed from human eyes.

At no time, from August to November, were there less than five to ten thousand men in camp. But the work of assigning to regiments the innumerable squads and companies into which the number was divided, was a slow process; too slow, indeed, for the active spirits with which the State authorities had to deal. As a result, regimental officers took the matter of filling up their commands into their own hands; and as men were in demand, not he who knew most of Jomini's Art of War, or Cassey's Tactics, but that one who could bring with him the largest force of recruits, might secure any position from a field officer down through all the grades to a second lieutenant.

Then, again, some valiant captain, anxious to have his favorite doctor or parson transformed into a surgeon or a chaplain, or his patriotic friend made quartermaster or sutler, in consideration of one or the other of these positions, would agree to transfer his company to the regiment where such a place could be secured. Patriotism had gone up beyond fever heat; and the excessive desire to be among the foremost of the country's defenders must apologize for all questionable practices. Especially as it happened, that when the times came that tried men—as come they did—the unfit stepped aside, and the right men gravitated into the right places.

Though among the first of the three months' troops to be accepted for the long term of enlistment, and by the 4th of August sent its first recruits into camp, the Eleventh did not leave the State until late in November. The authorities at Harrisburg shared somewhat in the feelings of the citizen-soldiers. There was a possibility that the work of putting down the rebellion would not require all the men called into service, and that each regiment might alike enjoy the fame to be achieved in actual conflict with the rebels, four companies, at several different times, were taken from the Eleventh, and given to other regiments that had exhausted all their resources for recruiting, and still remained below the maximum number. The grave reason for such official partiality was in the fact that the Eleventh had already the distinguished honor of being the only Pennsylvania regiment that had participated in a battle during the three months' campaign, and it could therefore afford to wait a longer time than some others for its complement of men under the new enlistment.

But there was another cause for our long delay at Camp Curtin. All connected with the regiment desired to retain the old regimental number—Eleventh. The men had learned to love it; and, besides, there was true soldierly pride in wishing to be known as the Eleventh Regiment, —the name under which they had defeated Stonewall Jackson,—won the first congratulatory order issued by the commander of the army of which they were a part, and by which the Secretary of War had so early accepted them for the second term of enlistment.

For some reason, this very natural desire on the part of the regiment was strenuously opposed by a few of the dignitaries of the State capital. Early in October a flag was prepared, designating the regiment as the Fifty-first, but the flag was refused; and by way of punishing the officers for their obstinacy in not yielding the point, they were kept longer in camp than would probably have been the case had there been less devotion to the old number.

The dispute was at last settled by an order from Governor Curtin, dated Harrisburg, October 26th, 1861:

"The Regiment of Pennsylvania Volunteers, commanded by Colonel Coulter, will continue to be known as the Eleventh Regiment Pennsylvania Volunteers. It is just to the officers and men, that the regiment should have future opportunities of displaying the courage and gallantry of Falling Waters, which is now a part of the military history of the State, under their original designation."

In everything relating to soldierly efficiency, our stay at Camp Curtin was beneficial. The drills were regular and complete. Its discipline was the happy medium between the liberty of the citizen and the strict military rule of active service, preparing each man gradually to forget the one and submit to the other.

It also introduced us to the active sympathies of a band of noble women in Harrisburg, principal among whom were Mrs. George H. Small, Mrs. James Denning, and Mrs. Lile Cornyn. The constant care of these ladies for the sick of the regiment in the camp hospital, and when the disease became serious removing the patients to their own houses, entitles them to our lasting gratitude.

The organization of the field and staff officers had undergone some change in the interval of six months, compared with that first recommended by Colonel Jarrett. Colonel Coulter had associated with him, as Lieutenant-Colonel, Thomas

S. Martin, formerly of the Twenty-third Pennsylvania Regiment; Henry A. Frink, of Philadelphia, was commissioned Major; Lieutenant Israel Uncapher, of Co. F, Adjutant; Lieutenant G. W. Thorn, of Co. B, Quartermaster; Dr. R. M. S. Jackson, of Cresson, Surgeon; Dr. James W. Anawalt, of Greensburg, Assistant Surgeon, and William H. Locke, of Pittsburg, Chaplain.

CHAPTER II.

FROM PENNSYLVANIA TO MARYLAND.

On the 20th of November, in the presence of a large concourse of spectators, Governor Curtin presented to the regiment the stand of colors provided by the State, bearing on its graceful folds, in bright gilt letters, "ELEVENTH REGIMENT PENNA. VOLS." Side by side with this cherished gift of the State was carried the flag presented by the ladies of Martinsburg, both alike to be shielded from dishonor with nothing less sacred than our lives.

One week later, Colonel Coulter was ordered to report his regiment to General Dix, at Baltimore. Co. A, Captain Christian Kuhn; Co. B, Captain William Shanks; Co. C, Captain Jacob

J. Bierer; Co. D, Captain John Knox; Co. E, Captain James C. McCurdy; Co. F, Captain David M. Cook; Co. H, Captain Edward H. Rauch; Co. I, Captain George A. Cribbs; and Co. K, Captain John B. Keenan, took cars at the Northern Central depot the same evening, leaving Co. G to follow next day.

It was hard to realize, as we marched through the streets of Baltimore in the early morning of November 28th, on our way to the wharf where the regiment was to take shipping for Annapolis, that we were treading the same thoroughfares in which Union soldiers, but a few months before, had been stoned to death. A very different reception awaited the Eleventh. Subsistence committees met us at the cars, ready to escort us to the Soldiers' Home; smiling faces and waving handkerchiefs everywhere greeted us, as though Baltimore would erase all recollection of the hateful 19th of April.

Late at night we disembarked at Annapolis, and marched to the old St. John's College. Ever since General Butler landed his troops at the mouth of the Severn River, and marched from thence to Washington, Annapolis had been an important point to the Government. At the time of our arrival it was an immense depot of military supplies, besides the rendezvous of the Burnside expedition, whose unknown destination lent a romantic charm to everything connected with it.

In the midst of the formidable array of ships and men that crowded the harbor and thronged the streets of the antique city, we found ourselves surrounded by associations inexpressibly dear to the heart of every American. We were in one of the oldest cities of the Union. Here was the State House, with a history running back to the days of the Revolution, in which the treaty of peace with Great Britain, acknowledging our independence, had been ratified by Congress. Here Washington resigned his commission as commander-in-chief of the American army, and retired to Mount Vernon. The room has been preserved unchanged; and to stand upon the spot where Washington stood at that hour of his life, to look upon the same objects on which he had gazed, seemed to place one in close communion with the spirit of the mighty dead. It was indeed singular that upon such hallowed ground the demon of treason should dare to manifest itself.

St. John's College—in which were found excellent quarters for men and officers, the former occupying the three large school edifices and the latter the several dwelling-houses of the professors—was scarcely less venerable and venerated than the State House itself. The main building had been erected more than a hundred years, and was at first designed as the Executive Mansion of the State. But the General Assembly of Maryland, in 1784, incorporated St. John's College, and conveyed to the trustees the building and four acres of land, known as College Green.

College Green was used in the revolutionary war as the camping-ground of the French army; and also by the American troops assembled in the war of 1812. Now, for the third time, it became a military encampment. It was not a foreign foe that threatened us, but those of our own household. Violent men were seeking to destroy the integrity of the republic, and the troops then drilling on soil already consecrated by the footsteps of the patriots who established the Government, had before them the not less glorious work of preserving that Government intact to those who should come after.

During the several beautiful Sabbaths that followed our arrival at Annapolis, as the chaplain stood beneath the overhanging branches of a venerable tree, whose age can certainly be counted back two hundred years, and in the midst of the historical associations alluded to, speaking to officers and men in the name of JESUS, and remembering that our fathers had only succeeded in their struggle through the blessing of GOD, how necessary it seemed that our cause should be sanctified by prayer, and that our hope of success be placed alone in HIM.

It would have accorded better with the inclinations of all concerned had the Eleventh been selected to make a part of the Burnside expedition, then nearly ready to sail. But the order of General Dix assigned us to duty in Annapolis. The duties were onerous, and more than should have been required of any one regiment. The city was furnished with a provost guard, twenty-one miles of railroad were protected, besides performing a large share of fatigue duty at the Naval Academy, the commissary depot of the sailing expedition.

A contraband trade had been kept up between Baltimore and Virginia through the lower counties of Maryland, upon which we were also to keep an eye; as well, possibly, by our presence, protect the Maryland Legislature, then about to assemble, in its expressions of loyalty and denunciations of treason.

Companies B, E, I, and K were sent out on the railroad, while the other five companies (Co. G having failed as yet to report) made up the provost guard, and all the details for duty elsewhere. The guard-house was in the old city ball-room, one of the historic places of Annapolis. Older than the State House, it had been used as the legislative hall during the erection of that building; while the supper-room was formerly the revenue office of the province. The walls were still decorated by portraits of Lord Baltimore and several of the former Governors of Maryland. Those gentlemen of the olden time seemed strangely out of place in the crowd of unruly soldiers that the Provost Marshal, Captain Jacob J. Bierer, almost nightly provided with lodgings in that room.

Everything looked as though the regiment would pass the winter in Annapolis, and our plans were made with a view to patient submission. The men guarding the railroad were apparently satisfied with their part of the contract, and those in quarters had no more complaints than are usual to a soldier. The trustees of the Methodist Episcopal Church kindly offered us the use of their house, where religious services were held every Sabbath afternoon, a hospital tent, then out of use, serving as a chapel for week-night meetings.

Nor was the service required entirely devoid of the kind of excitement so essential to the volunteer. The companies on the railroad found ample exercise for all their vigilance in the number of passing trains, and in the travel in private conveyance to and fro along their lines. The guard in town was not less active, keeping a sharp lookout that no suspicious craft or contraband cargo was permitted to escape from the harbor.

Governor Hicks, Speaker Berry of the House of Delegates, Judge Brewer, and other prominent citizens, gave us special personal attention, and contributed greatly to our social enjoyment. Through the efforts of such men as these, who nobly breasted the tide of disloyalty and treason, at one time setting in hard against her, Maryland escaped the desolation and ruin that have swept over her sister State of Virginia.

Western boys, such as composed the Eleventh, had no sympathies in common with those who could find apologies for secession and rebellion. Maryland had not then accepted the logic of events, nor declared herself a free State; and occasionally a rampant Southron was to be met, whose zeal for the South was greater than his discretion. The Articles of War forbade political discussions by any in the service. But more than one of those blatant apologists of wrong found that Union soldiers had a way of their own of settling disputed points, without violating the letter of military law; and that the hard fist of a Northern yeoman struck out from the shoulder was an argument by no means easy to oppose.

The chaplain was in duty bound to be less demonstrative, even at the risk of being less convincing. But as a compensation, he had opportunities of learning the true sentiments of many leading citizens. One gentleman, himself a slaveholder, who frequently visited at regimental headquarters, though heartily condemning the rebellion, could not but blame the North for an impertinent interference in the affairs of the South. Servitude, in his opinion, was the normal condition of the black man, and it was only a false philanthropy to attempt to place him anywhere else.

"But why not hire the negro, and pay him stated wages?"

"Because it won't do, sir. I have been in public life for more than twenty-five years, and pretend to know something about this matter; and I give it to you as my decided opinion that the scheme is not practicable. Hired blacks, or free blacks, are too lazy to work, and you cannot coerce them. We must either have absolute control of them, such as ownership gives, or dispense with their labor altogether. Take the cultivation of tobacco, for instance. There are particular times when a delay of two hours would ruin the crop. How could we then go round gathering up hands? And knowing him as we do, who would trust to a hired negro in such an emergency? No, sir; it will not do. And we find fault with you men of the North, because you will meddle with a thing you do not understand."

We ventured the remark, that there were men at the North who did not so much oppose the peculiar institution of slavery, as the many and great evils connected with it; and to mention no other, the breaking up of the family, in the separation of husband and wife, and of parent and child.

"Well, sir, we have nothing of that kind in Maryland, except in very rare cases. I have had some experience in settling up estates; and where negroes are to be sold in this State, they almost invariably select their own masters. Let me give you an illustration. A friend of mine owned a black man, whose son belonged to another part of the estate. A death occurring, the estate was to be sold, servants and all. Some time before the sale, the boy came to my friend with the request that he would buy him. The gentleman did not need him at the time, and so gave an evasive answer. But when the day of sale came round, of the several persons who really wanted Jack, not one of them could get him to say he would go to live with him. 'Massa Judge Duvall is gwine to buy me,' was the negro's reply; and as no one else would bid for him, the Judge was obliged to take him. So, in almost every instance, they select their own masters, and very rarely, in this State, are families divided by sale."

New ideas have been developed since the conversation of that afternoon in March, 1862. Maryland is a free State; and upon her own soil the practicability of free black labor has been clearly demonstrated.

CHAPTER III.

SIDE ISSUES OF THE CONFLICT.

Many bright days visited us during that winter in Annapolis, when a ride to the camp of the Ira Harris Cavalry, or along the South River, or wherever else inclination might suggest, was a charming relief from the monotony of life in quarters. Nor were we so far from the front as to be undisturbed by the passing events of the great conflict.

It was on a Sunday afternoon, just after religious services had commenced, that an order was received at the church from General Hatch, commanding the post, requiring one company, fully armed and equipped, to report at headquarters for special duty. It was well that all the facts in the case did not come out at once, or the chaplain could scarcely have kept the attention of his remaining audience.

The iron-clad Merrimac, with which the rebels had been threatening our navy for months, had actually encountered and sunk the frigates Congress and Cumberland, and was reported to have passed Fortress Monroe with a fleet of gunboats. Great excitement prevailed throughout the city, every one supposing the vessel would sail direct to Annapolis, for the purpose of capturing the extensive commissary stores in depot.

Company A was sent down the bay on the steamer G. A. Warner to watch the movements of the iron-clad, and to give notice of her first approach. All the steamers in port were ordered to Baltimore, as in case of attack the harbor of Annapolis was without adequate defense; while many of the citizens were preparing to fly at the moment of certain danger. But most opportunely, a new opponent appeared in the shape of a Monitor, to contest the further advance of the formidable adversary. After a severe struggle of three hours, the Merrimac gave up the fight, and in a disabled condition returned to Norfolk.

When the alarm had ceased, and all things once more assumed their quiet ways, one family at least, found itself greatly benefited by the threatened visit of the rebel iron-clad. Among the domestics of that household is one who bears the not very poetical name of Jane. She is decidedly hard to manage, and a source of great vexation to the female portion of the family. Various and novel have been the ways resorted to in order to bring her to terms. A year or two before, a negro man was hanged for some crime, and among those sent to see the sight, for the good it might do, was Jane. But strange to say, not the least impression was made upon the incorrigible colored girl. Hanging is not an everyday affair, and it is hard to tell whether, in course of time, the effect on Jane might not be all that is desired. Up to that eventful Sunday afternoon, the only thing that subdued the unruly and wayward domestic, was to sing:

"Hark from the tombs, a doleful sound."

Whenever coaxing and driving and the whip failed in their efforts, some one of the family struck up the notes of this funeral hymn.

With what imaginary terrors Jane had invested the Merrimac, the family did not care to inquire. But it was soon discovered that a threatened visit from the hideous monster, whatever the terror might be, was a source of alarm as potent as that of singing the hymn; and as the new remedy admitted of an easier application than the old one, it was ever after adopted to quiet into obedience the obstreperous Jane.

Attachment to place does not belong to the volunteer soldier. No matter how comfortably he may be quartered, or what advantage the locality may possess, a few days satisfy him; and an order to strike tents, though full of uncertainty as to where they shall be pitched again, is received with joy. When the Second Maryland Regiment relieved us of duty on the railroad, and the men were ordered to prepare for a speedy move, there were no regrets expressed in parting with the fine accommodations and numerous advantages of Annapolis.

General Burnside was to be reinforced. Already several spirited engagements had taken place, achieving important victories for the Union cause on the North Carolina coast. Much remained yet to be done; and though not permitted to take part in the first operations, there was every prospect that we should be in time for these later movements. But after days of expectation and waiting for the order to embark for North Carolina, the regiment was sent back to guard the Annapolis railroad.

To make matters still more unsatisfactory, the Second Maryland at once took shipping for Fortress Monroe, General Burnside having especially named it as the regiment at Annapolis he desired to have sent to him. The general fell fully one-half in our estimation. We forgot our early association with him on the Upper Potomac, and seriously doubted the abilities of an officer having so little discernment as to prefer the Second Maryland to the Eleventh Pennsylvania.

When the whole truth came out, it was found that at the personal request of a number of prominent citizens, who preferred to have a Pennsylvania rather than a Maryland regiment quartered among them, the order for the removal of the Eleventh had been countermanded. Cos. C, D,

F, and H took the stations B, E, I, and K had formerly occupied on the railroad, while Co. A was sent to do guard duty at Friendship, twenty-five miles down the Chesapeake Bay.

Several changes occurred among the commissioned officers during our sojourn in the capital of Maryland. The vacancy occasioned in Co. B, by the appointment of Lieutenant G. W. Thorn Regimental Quartermaster, was filled by promoting Second Lieutenant B. F. Haines to be first lieutenant, and Sergeant George Tapp to be second lieutenant. Captain Knox, of Co. D, while absent on recruiting service, died at his home in Jersey Shore. Governor Curtin commissioned W. E. Sees, of Harrisburg, to fill the vacancy, who proved himself an officer every way worthy and competent.

In Co. F, Sergeant Michael J. Kettering was promoted to be first lieutenant, in place of Israel Uncapher, appointed adjutant; Sergeant-Major Edward H. Gay to be second lieutenant, in place of Lieutenant W. McCutcheon, who died in camp of disease contracted in the service.

The evacuation of Centerville and Manassas Junction by the rebels, and the landing of a large Federal force on the Yorktown peninsula, caused new combinations of troops to be made throughout the whole theater of war; and during the afternoon of April 9th, the cars that were to transport us to Washington switched off in front of our quarters.

The embarking of eight hundred men, with tents, baggage, and quartermaster's stores, consumed what was left of daylight. With night came the most violent snow-storm of the season, blocking up the railroad, and holding us fast on the track a few miles from the place of starting until the next morning. It was a freak of the weather never before known in that latitude. But the warm April sun soon melted the snow, and by the time we reached Washington every vestige of the winter storm had disappeared.

Soldiers' Home, as the large white-washed buildings at the railroad station were called, good enough in itself, was but a poor substitute for the excellent quarters vacated in St. John's College. But every day was so full of conflicting rumors that the style of our quarters, and even the quality of the rations, were forgotten in the uncertainty of our destination.

The one event that gave character to our short stay in Washington was the review of the Eleventh by President Lincoln. A special invitation was sent to Colonel Coulter to march his regiment to the White House. An hour later, donning the new clothes issued to them by the quartermaster, our boys were marching up Pennsylvania Avenue. Standing on the steps of the Executive Mansion, as we then saw him in the clear light of that 15th of April, with head uncovered, and a kindly smile playing over his face, bowing to the ranks of men that passed in review before him, is associated our most vivid recollection of Abraham Lincoln.

The next day the regiment took boat for Alexandria, and from thence was transported by rail to Manassas Junction.

CHAPTER IV.

FROM MARYLAND TO VIRGINIA.

MANASSAS was the name formerly given to a small village and railroad station at the junction of the Alexandria and Orange and the Manassas Gap Railroads. Now it is applied indiscriminately to a section of country several miles in extent. Nothing was left of the village but confused heaps of bricks and mortar, while either side of the railroad, for miles in extent, was blackened with the charred remains of camp equipage, baggage and stores, that the rebels, for want of transportation, had been compelled to destroy.

The Manassas Gap Road extends from its intersection with the Alexandria and Orange Road, through Front Royal to Strasburg, in the Shenandoah Valley. Important co-operative movements were in contemplation from all points upon Richmond, making it necessary that this line of communication should be kept open. The construction corps was already at work repairing damages and rebuilding the bridges across the Shenandoah River, while a guard sufficient to protect the road from guerrilla attacks extended along its entire length.

The Eleventh was placed on duty between Manassas Junction and White Plains, a distance of twenty-two miles. Major Frink, with Cos. B, C, and D, was stationed at White Plains; Co. E at Broad Run; Co. K at Thoroughfare Gap; Co. I at an intermediate point between K and H; Co. H at Haymarket; Co. F at Gainesville, and Co. A between F and the Junction. Regimental headquarters were at Manassas, as here a general depot of supplies had been established, and direct telegraphic communication with the department at Washington.

White Plains, Haymarket, and Gainesville are small villages, rescued from oblivion by the fierce engagements associated with their names. Thoroughfare Gap is a rocky chasm in the Bull Run Mountains. Through this natural cut the railroad passes, and Broad Run, a limpid stream on whose banks are several valuable mills, also finds a passage through the gap to the Potomac.

The companies at all the several points had the same instructions issued to them: "To prevent the destruction of the track, or any property or stock belonging to the road; to see that the track is kept clear, and bridges fully protected; to prevent depredations on the private property of citizens; all suspicious persons to be carefully examined, and if circumstances warrant, to be sent to headquarters, especially all mounted men found with arms near the road or any of the pickets."

The duty required on the Manassas road, though the same in kind as that performed at Annapolis, was more exciting because demanding greater vigilance.

We had passed from comparatively loyal Maryland into positively disloyal Virginia, where the most peaceable citizen was ready to strike a blow secretly, when he could not do so openly. Guard duty assumes a very different character under such surroundings. It loses every feature of monotony; and if the ears of the picket do not put on the dimensions of those of the rabbit, he has at least all the acuteness of hearing accredited to that watchful little quadruped. The gentlest zephyr does not loosen from its stem a solitary leaf without arresting his attention, while his eye possesses such magic power that many times a moss-grown stump, or a stray horse, has been metamorphosed into an armed rebel.

Co. H was stationed at Haymarket. It was known that several of Ashby's Cavalry had resided in the town, and a strict guard was kept over all the inhabitants. Toward twelve o'clock of a particular night, when quiet reigned throughout the quarters of Co. H, and all were wrapped in soundest sleep save the trusty sentinel, whose duty it was to watch for danger, an unusual commotion was observed throughout the village. The bright light in one house, that had first attracted the notice of the guard, was soon seen in several others. The captain was aroused, and having satisfied himself that *something* more than ordinary was going on, the men were ordered to fall into line with the utmost dispatch and quiet. In a moment sixty men, with guns and cartridge-boxes, stood in their places. All could now see lights flickering in half a dozen windows, and even the fast trotting of horses was distinctly heard.

It was enough. Either Ashby meditated an assault on Co. H, or else some of his bold partisans were on a visit to friends. But, in the present state of affairs, a visit could not be allowed, and an assault must be resisted. The plan of attack was to surround the town, and then close in toward that point where suspicion seemed the strongest.

By the time these arrangements were completed, all the lights had disappeared, except in the windows of a single house, and at this one the several squads into which the company had been divided at last met. The captain boldly entered, demanding the surrender of the impertinent foe

THE MIDNIGHT ALARM. 61

who had dared to plot mischief at such an unseasonable hour. A small man, with spectacles on his nose, and of demeanor far too quiet for a soldier, made his appearance. In answer to the captain, he announced himself a physician, called on professional business; and that the good people of the house were rejoicing in a *small* addition to the male department of the family.

Early in the month of May, a citizen brought information to White Plains that two deserters from the Union army had taken possession of a forsaken residence, some miles distant in the direction of Warrenton, and were threatening the lives of all around them.

It was feared that the story might be intended to entrap our men; but a detachment sufficiently strong to protect itself, was sent out under command of Captain Sees. When the party came near the house, a squad of cavalry, drawn up in line of battle, was in full view. Selecting the best possible position of defense, Captain Sees awaited the result of what he now felt certain to be a scheme to capture himself and men. In a little while, two horsemen rode out from the line, waving their hats. At first no attention was paid to the movement; but as the cavalrymen continued to advance, the captain stepped forward to meet them, when they were found to be a part of Colonel Geary's command, stationed at Salem, and out on the same errand as himself.

Coming up to the house, the cavalry discovered that a party of citizens had anticipated them; and in their attack upon the deserters, one of them had been killed, but at a loss of two of their own number, of whom was Mr. Scott, a prominent citizen of Warrenton and a leading member of the bar. The surviving deserter made good his escape.

The next day after the affair, the reported deserter came to Captain Keenan's quarters at Thoroughfare Gap, and gave himself up. He and his companion belonged to the Seventh Wisconsin Regiment. While on picket duty, they had been captured by Ashby's cavalry; but making their escape in a few days after, were leisurely getting back to Warrenton to join their regiment. The only depredations committed were for something to eat. When attacked by the party of citizens, only one of them was in the house, the other being some distance from it. The man on the outside was without arms of any kind, and surrounded by half a score of men. But instead of attempting to secure him as a prisoner, and return him to his regiment, he was shot dead, three balls entering the body. His companion witnessed the whole scene, and having both guns in his possession, and anticipating a similar fate, fired each from an open window with fatal effect.

The prisoner was retained in our possession until we reached Falmouth, and then sent to General McDowell's headquarters.

A CLERICAL CAPTIVE.

Colonel Coulter's stringent order to arrest all mounted citizens, found with arms near our lines, was not based entirely upon suspicion. Several men of Colonel Geary's command had already been murdered on picket; a fact that fully revealed the animus of the people around us. Some of the arrests may have caused great personal inconvenience; but the convenience of the few had to be sacrificed to the safety of the many.

A clergyman of the Southern Methodist Church, named Williams, and in charge of Warrenton Circuit, was among those arrested and brought to headquarters at Manassas. He was quite indignant that our pickets should molest *him;* but when questioned as to the propriety of carrying a loaded revolver in his saddle pockets, he could give no satisfactory answer. In respect for his profession, the clerical captive, instead of being placed in the guard-house, was handed over to the charge of the chaplain, who tried to make him feel that he had fallen into the hands of generous captors. We gave him supper, shared with him our blankets when night came on, and breakfast in the morning. The colonel having assured himself, by telegraphing to Warrenton, that Mr. Williams was practicing no imposition, he was at once released, and furnished with a pass through our lines; leaving his carnal weapons in the hands of the soldier who made the arrest.

No class of men did more to embitter the Southern feeling, and urge on to open rebellion, than the ministers of the Southern Methodist Church. Mr. Williams was present at the conference that met in Norfolk. The iron-clad Merrimac was nearly finished, and the entire conference, by special invitation, paid a visit to the vessel as she lay in her moorings. Speeches were made in the highest style of secession eloquence; hopes were expressed, and prayers offered up for the success of the huge monster in her work of ruin and death. Many of these men, forsaking the peaceful calling of the gospel, took the sword, and by the sword they perished. Others of them, through the madness of rebellion, drifting away from the principles and practices of the religion of Christ, are now moral wrecks, stranded on the shores of time.

CHAPTER V.

MANASSAS JUNCTION AND ITS ENVIRONS.

At Manassas we were in the vicinity of the Bull Run battle-field. Not curiosity only, but such an interest in that event as nearly related us to the actors, prompted an early visit.

Near regimental headquarters was Fort Beauregard, a large and formidable earth-work; while at different points on the Manassas plain, and in commanding positions, were several other works of lesser magnitude. Two miles distant, on the road to Centerville, stood the large brick mansion of Mr. Weir, Beauregard's headquarters. Here the Confederate general and his staff remained during the attack at Blackburn's Ford, July 18th, which so greatly deranged the plans of McDowell, who intended that General Tyler should make a mere feint movement at that point, while the main force was making the transit of Bull Run at the Stone Bridge and further up to the right.

Crossing Bull Run at Blackburn's Ford, where the stream is perhaps fifty yards wide, we rode to Centerville. The whole intermediate space of territory was a chain of breast-works and fortifications. Everything that industry and skill could devise to make Manassas impregnable was done; and if General McClellan had marched from Washington direct upon those works, in the opening of the spring of 1862, after having allowed the rebels so long a time to perfect them, it would have been a disastrous undertaking.

Turning from Centerville, we continued our ride along the Warrenton pike to Stone Bridge. It is the highway across Bull Run, the northern bank of which is a steep, rocky bluff. In that direction our forces were retreating on the 21st of July; and standing on the spot, one could easily imagine how the blockading of the bridge by broken-down wagons and abandoned gun-carriages, would worse confound the scattered ranks of a retreating army.

On the south side of the bridge, and ascending a gentle slope, we were in full view of every point of the battle-field, from right to left. Near by is the dwelling of Henry Robinson. The old negro man remained in his house during the engagement of July 21st, though it was struck several times, and in one instance a cannon ball passed directly through its walls. When asked why he did not leave and seek a safer place, he replied:

"You see, massa, dey had no safe places dat day. Ole Henry 'spected to git killed anyhow, and he tink he jist as lief die in de ole house as anywhare else."

After the defeat of the Federal army, Manassas became a spot of great interest to Southerners, who visited it in large numbers. The old man's house stood so near where the principal engagement took place that no one came to the battle-field without making him a visit. He entertained us for a long time with the opinions and remarks of rebel officers, as he had often heard them express themselves, in reference to that battle. All agreed that early in the day Beauregard acknowledged himself defeated, and would have retreated but for Johnson, who, arriving on the ground some hours before his army, urged him to hold on until his forces should come up. The arrival of several thousand fresh troops was more than our exhausted men could endure. Still, at the first, they retired in good order; the panic which resulted so disastrously having occurred far in the rear of that part of the army actually engaged with the enemy.

In the sickening details of a hundred battles, the country has not forgotten the indignities offered to our killed and wounded on this first field. Many of its dead were left unburied, as the bleached human bones lying on the surface too plainly declared, while of those buried, arms and limbs and heads were seen projecting from the shallow graves.

Every available spot of the country over which we passed had been used as a camp. The quarters were comfortable log cabins with clap-board roofs, indicating that a large army, well cared for, had spent the winter at Manassas.

The village of White Plains escaped, in a great measure, the devastation of Manassas. It was the location of the rebel general hospital, and the numerous graves on the hillside above the town truthfully told how severely the enemy suffered in his first great battle, and that fell disease, during the long winter months, had almost decimated entire regiments.

Several brothers by the name of Foster, the owners of valuable estates, resided in the village. Colonel Ashby lived at Markham, some miles distant up the railroad, but his famous cavalry troop, that afterward degenerated into Moseby's guerrillas, was made up of the best young men of this and the adjoining neighborhoods. For a number of years tournaments, with Col. Ashby at their head, pronounced the best equestrian in Virginia, were among the chief attractions of Warrenton Springs. The young men of the vicinity became most expert horsemen, and when the war broke out, the Colonel had a troop of unequaled riders ready at hand.

In company with Dr. Jackson and Captain Shanks, the chaplain found a home for several days at the house of Thomas Foster, the Quartermaster of Ashby's Cavalry. The family consisted of the wife, two daughters, and an elderly uncle, their only male protector. It was to be expected that there would be more or less restraint in our social intercourse with those whose dearest friends we could only regard as our bitter enemies. But underneath all the studied politeness of which we were the recipients in that elegant residence, there was a stratum of the old Virginia hospitality that nothing but the actual existence of war could keep from coming to the surface.

Whatever was once said of the masses of the South not understanding the questions at issue between the two sections of the country, at no time could it ever apply to the more intelligent portions. The doctrine of State rights had been thoroughly studied and as heartily believed. In their libraries and on their tables were to be found the works of Nott and Gliddon, and Morton, plausible theories, all going to prove that the white man and the negro are of distinct races; that the negro belongs to an inferior order of beings, and finds his proper condition only in subjection to the superior. With this class of persons the war was a contest of ideas, thoroughly understood because thoroughly studied.

At an early period in the war Alexandria came to be regarded as the negro's paradise. Without newspapers or telegraph, he soon learned that to reach that point was to be no longer a slave. White Plains was the general rendezvous of absconding negroes for a large section of country, and scarcely a train of cars passed down the road without its complement of human freight. Sometimes they came to the station in pairs, and again in squads, big and little, old and young, carrying all their worldly possessions, rolled up in bundles, on their heads, or slung across their shoulders, having little conception of where they were going—except to some wonderful place called Alexandria—or what they would do. They knew they would be *free*, and that fact answered every question.

On one particular day a motley group of them, not less than twenty in all, came to White Plains in an ox-cart. Scarcely had they unloaded themselves on the platform, when a panting and foaming horse, carrying an excited-looking rider, stopped in front of headquarters. The man on horseback eagerly demanded where he might find the commanding officer, as he had special business with him. Every one was on the *qui vive*, and with the hope that he might be the bearer of such stirring news as would cause a speedy move, the rider was directed to Major Frink. But his business was altogether of a personal nature.

"Major," said he, "those people out there, who have just arrived in that ox-cart, belong to me, and I want you to compel them to return home."

"Well, sir," replied the major, "that kind of work is not exactly in my line. If your people wish to return home, not a man of my command will interfere; but if they do not desire to return, so far from compelling them myself, I cannot even allow their owner to compel them."

The Virginian was not satisfied with the major's decision, and inquired where he might find the commander of the regiment. He was informed that regimental headquarters were at Manassas Junction, and as his slaves had already got aboard of the train, which in the mean time had come up to the station, their owner took a place near them.

But it so happened that while conductors of trains were directed to allow all negroes free passage to Alexandria, without let or hinderance, no white person could travel over the road, to any point whatever, without a pass from the nearest post commander. In the hurry to keep in sight of his property, the white man had forgotten this salutary arrangement. When the train was ready to start the conductor politely told him that he could not carry him to Manassas without a pass from Major Frink. Enraged beyond endurance, and too haughty to ask permission to ride where his slaves could go with impunity, he left the train, people and all, swearing bitter vengeance against the whole North.

Many furtive glances, mingled with evident

fear and dread, had been cast by the fugitives at their old master. But when they saw him standing on the platform, and felt the train moving on the iron track beneath them, the comical shrug of the shoulder, and the laugh-provoking grin that spread over their ebony faces, were silent expressions of joy at the sudden breaking of life-long bonds.

CHAPTER VI.

MARCHING SOUTHWARD.

An order from General Hartsuff, directing Colonel Coulter to report his command at Falmouth, indefinitely postponed several proposed expeditions from different company stations in search of Ashby's Cavalry.

The march from Manassas, on the 12th of May, was our first going afoot. Hitherto the regiment had been transported in cars or on steamboats. During the campaigns that followed, the men repeatedly traveled twenty to thirty miles a day, but the sore feet, and the weary lengths to which those ten miles of that *breaking in* march stretched themselves, are remembered to this hour.

The route over which we passed—by way of

Catlett's Station, Bristersburg, and Hartwood Church—became the track of the army in its after surges back and forth between Washington and the Rappahannock. Then but few troops had marched that way, and the country was luxuriating in the undisturbed beauties of early spring. Handsome residences lined the roadside, while the first view of Fredericksburg, and those hights that are now historic, was enchanting. In three days after leaving Manassas Junction the Eleventh reported to General Hartsuff, and was permanently assigned to Hartsuff's Brigade of Ord's Division, McDowell's Corps.

The dingy little village of Falmouth was the gathering place of McDowell's troops, intended to co-operate with McClellan against Richmond. Large details of men were engaged in repairing the railroad from Aquia Creek, and in rebuilding the bridge across the Rappahannock. An extensive foundery located in Fredericksburg, where shot and shell were cast for the rebel army, was turned into a Union workshop, as artisans of every kind, from the master mechanic to the youngest apprentice, helped to swell the ranks of the great Federal army.

Fredericksburg is one of the ancient towns of Virginia. Walking leisurely through its clean and shady streets, filled with sauntering soldiers dressed in blue, there was an air of peaceful quiet strongly in contrast with the noisy and bustling camps across the river. It was in this place that the mother of Washington lived during the war of the Revolution, and here, too, is the burial place of that illustrious woman.

More than thirty years ago, a gentleman of New York proposed, at his own expense, to erect a monument to the memory of Mary Washington. The corner stone was laid near her grave with appropriate ceremonies by Andrew Jackson, President of the United States. But after the work had progressed to the completion of the pedestal, commercial reverses overtook the patriotic designer, and the monument has never been finished. To show their utter contempt for everything *Northern*, the chivalry of Fredericksburg, in the preparations to defend themselves against the ruthless Yankee invaders, made of this pedestal a target for their rifle shots. With its face marred and indented, and the corners broken off by glancing balls, we could only regard it as a monument of the ingratitude and hate possible to the human heart.

The denizens of the old town were amazed, not only at the versatility of the Yankee genius, but at the dreadful earnestness with which Northern soldiers went to work. It was almost too much to believe, though seen with their own eyes, that in five days a railroad bridge could be built across the Rappahannock River. An old Virginia esquire, who could be seen every day closely watching the rapid progress of the busy workmen, was conquered by the first locomotive that went puffing and screaming over the new and substantial structure.

"Don't burn any more bridges," said he. "It is all of no use. You might just as well attempt to keep rats out of a meal chest, as to keep back these Yankees. If there is no other way of getting over rivers, they will invent a plan to fill their knapsacks with wind, and cross on them!"

Everything was now in readiness for the advance of McDowell's Corps to Hanover Court House, where it was to form the right wing of the Peninsular army. Surplus baggage had been sent to Washington; immense depots of supplies established at Falmouth; and when, toward sundown of that Sabbath afternoon, May 25th, the order to march was received, officers and men had marked out the course as across the Rappahannock and through Fredericksburg.

But the head of the column turned in the opposite direction. The bright afternoon was succeeded by a cloudy night; and as we moved along in silence over those unknown Virginia roads, a thousand conjectures as to where we were going, and why we were going, floated through the mind.

An hour or two after midnight the troops bivouacked, as morning revealed, near Aquia Creek. It then began to be known that Stonewall Jackson had driven General Banks through the Shenandoah Valley, and across the Potomac, and rumor added that the rebels were threatening an attack on Washington, for whose defense Ord's Division had been ordered northward with all possible haste. Transports were already at the wharf to convey us to Alexandria, and at an early hour the troops began to embark.

Aquia Creek enters into the Potomac River forty miles below Washington. The banks are high and precipitous; and for a long time during the fall and winter of 1861, the rebel guns, mounted on fortifications at the mouth of the creek, completely blockaded the Potomac. The position was well chosen, having command of the river up and down for several miles.

It was three o'clock in the afternoon before our vessel steamed out into the channel; four or five hours later, we were safely moored at the Alexandria dock.

Neither the sail up the river, delightful in itself, nor the several points of interest to be seen,—among others Mount Vernon and Fort Washington,—could keep awake troops tired and fatigued by the long march of the preceding night. All were in the proper state of body and mind to hear, with great complacency of feeling, when the steamer reached Alexandria, that we should remain on shipboard until morning, and each one adjusted himself for an undisturbed night's sleep.

Alas, for human expectations. In the midst of peaceful dreams, the command—"fall in"— aroused every sleeping soldier. Half an hour later we were moving toward the railroad depot. It was believed that the rebels, successful in driving Banks across the Potomac, were concentrating large forces at Manassas Junction for an attack on Alexandria and the capital.

The city was wrapt in slumber, and the only sound that awoke the midnight stillness was the measured tread of the men marching through its deserted streets. Long trains of cars, filled with soldiers, were soon moving out from the station, and proceeding cautiously along the road, sending out skirmishers from Union Mills, Fairfax Station, and Bull Run, the Division reached Manassas Junction a little after daylight.

Banks had retreated before the advancing forces of Stonewall Jackson; and Washington City was in a state of feverish excitement, lest the next hour would bring the impetuous rebel thundering at its gates. But not a foe was to be seen near Manassas. The wily Jackson had no intention of coming in that direction. His flank movement was successfully executed. McDowell had been diverted from Hanover Court House,— a movement General Lee greatly feared,—and the rebel army, with all possible speed, was making its way down the valley toward Richmond.

The authorities at Washington, supposing that

Jackson might be intercepted in his homeward march, ordered McDowell to move on to Strasburg. While one column was approaching from the east, Fremont was to cross the mountains from the west, and between the upper and the nether mill-stone the rebel general was to suffer for his temerity.

Our line of march, that commenced on the morning of May 29th, lay along the Manassas Gap Railroad. We bivouacked the first night at Thoroughfare Gap, and on the second night at Oak Hill, the birthplace and residence of Chief Justice Marshall. The house is in the old style of architecture. Antique furniture, the product of a past century, filled the rooms, whose walls, wainscoted from floor to ceiling with polished oak panels, were adorned with many choice paintings. Here was written Marshall's Life of Washington. The estate is in possession of a grandson; but the numerous descendants of the chief justice residing in the neighborhood, forgetting the virtues of their illustrious ancestor, gave all their influence to break down the government that Marshall labored to render firm and enduring.

It was nine o'clock on the third night before we reached Front Royal. The march of the last day was long and wearisome, and for several hours during the latter part of it, through a violent rain-storm. A black cloud shut out moon and stars, and when the halt was ordered, we were lighted to our bivouac, in a thicket of pines, by vivid flashes of lightning that followed each other in quick succession. But much of the weariness of the march was forgotten in the striking beauty of the country through which we passed. The Blue Ridge was in sight from early morning, and toward evening the hills began to close us in on every side. An hour before sundown the head of the column entered Manassas Gap, a break in the Blue Ridge Mountains, which looks like one of nature's efforts to help man. Without it the mountain would be an insuperable barrier against railroad or stage-coach. Unequaled for its wild sublimity, it was rendered doubly impressive by the army of men and horse crowding its way through the narrow defile.

Front Royal was the scene of the gallant resistance made by Kenly's Maryland Regiment against Jackson's advance guard. But before assistance could be sent from Strasburg, they were overcome by numbers, and most of the regiment fell on the battle-field, or into the hands of the enemy.

Belle Boyd, whose subsequent career as a rebel spy has made her name notorious, appeared first at Front Royal. For several days prior to the attack she had been a visitor in the town, and through her information of the isolated position of Kenly's command was communicated to the rebel general.

The long roll of the drum early next morning brought each man from his hiding-place in the pines, and the march was continued toward Strasburg. The clouds had all cleared away, and a bright sun shone upon mountain and valley. Ord's entire division had now come together. The beautiful morning—the picturesque surroundings—the fine appearance of the troops—all conspired to make a scene full of spirit and animation.

The sight must have been as inspiring to General McDowell, who had accompanied the division from Falmouth, as to others; for not more than three miles from our bivouac the troops were drawn up in line for a grand review. But Stonewall Jackson did not choose to wait several hours on our parade. While we were thus amusing ourselves, he was pushing rapidly southward through Strasburg, Fremont's advance coming up barely in time to exchange a few shots with the Confederate rear-guard.

Next day Hartsuff's Brigade was advanced across the South Fork of the Shenandoah, and again, on the day following, across the North Fork, to Water-lick Station, two miles from Strasburg. It had rained incessantly for forty-eight hours. The Shenandoah was rapidly filling up its banks, and no longer fordable. The only bridge across the North Fork was a railroad bridge; and this, together with the temporary structure across the South Fork, was yielding to the pressure of the angry waters.

On the 4th of June, the brigade, then the advance of the division, was ordered back to Front Royal. To cross the several pieces of artillery and the wagons that had accompanied the troops, over the railroad bridge, was not thought possible, and orders were given to abandon them. But a little practical good sense, acting outside of the usual routine of military operations, easily overcame the apparently insurmountable difficulty, saving to the government a battery of four guns and ten or twelve wagons, and securing the troops, already greatly chagrined at the escape of Jackson, from further mortification. A detail of men from the Eleventh Regiment, with the colonel to direct operations, denuded an adjacent mill and several extensive out-houses of every available piece of timber. In a few hours the railroad bridge had a substantial flooring, over which artillery and wagons crossed in perfect safety.

Stonewall Jackson succeeded in evading the combined forces of Fremont and McDowell to intercept his retreat; and after severe engagements at Cross Keys and Port Republic, united his forces with those of General Lee before Richmond in time to bear a conspicuous part in the defeat of McClellan on the Peninsula.

General Fremont concentrated his army in the Shenandoah Valley, and McDowell's Corps returned to Manassas.

III.

CHAPTER I.

POPE'S VIRGINIA CAMPAIGN.

For the third time we pitched our tents on the wide-spreading plain of Manassas. But not too familiar did we become with the famous locality for the service there required of the Eleventh Regiment two months later.

The last week of June was full of exciting rumors. At one time we were to take shipping for the Peninsula, whither the eyes of the nation were now turned; the next day's rumor returned McDowell to Fredericksburg by the overland route. Marching orders were received on the 4th of July morning, not for the Peninsula, nor for Fredericksburg, but for Warrenton. By an order from Washington, read to all the troops, the three corps of Fremont, Banks, and McDowell were constituted the Army of Virginia, under command of General John Pope; and the march to Warrenton was the beginning of Pope's campaign in Virginia.

Never before was there so much opposition to marching orders. And not much wonder, when the march so interfered with the grand 4th of July celebration, for which there had been becoming preparation. Camps were decorated with arches, and festooned with evergreens, in honor of the day Our friends of the Ninetieth Pennsylvania sent North for fire-works to enliven the evening. But instead of the proposed jubilee, came a sweltering march of ten miles over dusty roads, and a bivouac at night near the little village of Gainesville.

On the evening of the second day the troops encamped in sight of Warrenton. It had seen none of the ravages of war, and was a handsome Virginia town of broad, clean streets, containing many elegant private residences, hid in groves of oak and maple, or surrounded by tasteful lawns, ornamented with shrub and flower.

General Blenker's troops passed through the place some time previous, leaving a mortal dread behind them of everything clad in Yankee blue. The general did not wait for Pope's order to subsist off the country, but supplied his men with whatever the merchants happened to have on hand. When they entered the drug stores, his directions were to take only the fullest jars on the shelves, without respect to what they contained. The general was always noted for having a well-stocked hospital.

What with our shaded encampment, on a farm adjoining the town, and the easy duty required of the men, the stay at Warrenton, though of nearly three weeks' continuance, was without the usual monotony of camp life. We had very little intercourse with the citizens. Now and then a gentleman was to be met who seemed disposed to exchange courtesies; but the bitterest of all rebels were the women. Our lady readers, however, must be informed that brass buttons and shoulder straps were as potent in reaching the female heart at the South as they were at the North, and many a Southern damsel, with strong disunion proclivities, has been brought to a better state of mind by the polite attentions of some gallant Yankee soldier.

On the 22d of July, Ricketts's Division (General J. B. Ricketts having succeeded General Ord) was moved from Warrenton to Waterloo, eight miles distant, on the Luray pike, where the road crosses the Upper Rappahannock. Waterloo was the site of an extensive woolen mill, manufacturing large quantities of cloth for the Southern army. The establishment was destroyed by General Banks because the proprietor, who claimed to be an English subject, insisted upon prosecuting his contraband trade.

Camp near Waterloo is remembered for the beauty of its location, and the abundant supply of pure cold water. When an army bivouacs for a night only, little attention is paid to the selection of grounds. But it is very different when the stay is to be protracted for days or weeks. The selection once made, streets are laid out with the nicest of regularity, on either side of which the tents of the men are pitched in double rows, each row facing a street. Trenches are dug for purposes of drainage, unsightly objects are removed, and a neat city, with perfect uniformity in its buildings, both as to shape and color, springs up in a day.

The picture would not be complete without a night scene. Each tent is then illuminated with the nightly allowance of two inches of candle. Those myriads of little lights, twinkling and dancing all around, often play fantastic tricks with the imagination of the beholder. As the shadows of evening hide all outward objects from view, how easy for the soldier to trace in those camp lights the streets of his own native town, and the very street in which he lives, and his own house—

"——with its light in the window,"

sure sign that the loved watcher is waiting for him. A loud blast from the bugle awakens the volunteer from his reverie. It is the signal to put out lights, and a moment later the beautiful vision has faded into darkness.

WEDNESDAY, July 30.—Spent most of the day in Warrenton, looking after the sick of the regiment, left there in hospital when we marched to Waterloo. Shedron, a member of Co. C, died last night, and was buried this morning. Poor fellow. In my possession are several letters addressed to him from home. What words of tenderness and affection they contained, that might have cheered his heart, came all too late.

General Pope arrived in town this afternoon, much to the displeasure of all seceshdom, but greatly to the joy of the whole army. We are hoping that he will make good the promise of a vigorous prosecution of the war throughout this Virginia valley.

While in Warrenton, and as a member of the board of appraisers appointed by General Hartsuff, whose business it is to assess damages done to the grounds upon which the brigade encamps, called on the proprietor of our late encampment adjoining the town. He is a gentleman of fine social qualities, who made us welcome to his house; but, like all the rest of the prominent men of this State, violently opposed to the Federal Government. The gentleman complained that any damages we might assess could not be recovered unless he took the oath of allegiance, in which case he would be an alien from the State of Virginia, and in the event of the success of the South, must lose all.

In the case of Mr. Horner, the damages assessed were larger than usual. We were three weeks on his estate, and one of the tenant houses, in which a colored man lay sick with small-pox, and where he died, before the body was removed was ordered to be burned, to prevent the spread of the infection.

FRIDAY, August 1.—General John Pope, accompanied by Generals McDowell and Ricketts, and their respective staff officers, reviewed Hartsuff's Brigade at seven o'clock this morning. It was a very quiet review. The men do not like the tone of the recent orders issued by General Pope, nor the covert reflections on the courage of the eastern army, which they think those orders contain. As he sat on horseback, the general seemed of manners so unassuming as to make one wonder whether he or his adjutant, who appeared far more important than his superior, had written the objectionable orders.

The Peninsular campaign was at an end. General McClellan had effected a change of base from the York River to the James, concentrating the remnant of his army at Harrison's Landing. It now became apparent what was expected of the Army of Virginia. Washington was to be protected, the Valley of the Shenandoah guarded, and by operating on the enemy's lines of communication toward Gordonsville, it was intended to draw off a large part of Lee's forces from Richmond, thus enabling the Army of the Potomac to escape from Harrison's Landing.

On the morning of August 4th, Ricketts's Division broke camp at Waterloo, and marched for Culpeper, the first step toward Gordonsville. The country through which we passed was of rare natural beauty. Many stately mansions were here and there to be seen, but a Northerner failed to discover the taste so apparent at home in the surrounding grounds and out-buildings. The straggling and inferior negro quarters, always near the main residence, are an insuperable barrier to neatness in external arrangement, or taste in appearance.

The old South Fork Church, near Robertson River, where we bivouacked after the first day's march, was an object of curiosity. Erected in the days of the colonies, the internal structure, of the style of a century ago, remains unchanged, even to the high-back pews and lofty pulpit. Here was to be seen the Yankee propensity for recording autographs on prominent places, and from the walls of the old church one might almost have made a muster-roll of the entire army.

The march was resumed at four o'clock of the following morning, and toward sundown of August 6th we encamped near Culpeper. Two days' marching, with the thermometer indicating a hundred degrees, was hard work, and the troops enjoyed the succeeding day of rest and quiet.

Already the ubiquitous Stonewall Jackson had

arrived at Gordonsville, and scouts from the front reported that the enemy was crossing the Rapidan River at several different points. Late on Friday afternoon Ricketts's Division was quickly formed, and moved through Culpeper to a point two miles beyond, where the road from Madison Court House intersects the road from Culpeper to Cedar Mountain. General Banks was three miles distant to the right, near Cedar Mountain. If the enemy was moving on Culpeper from Orange Court House, he would first strike Banks's line, but if he came from Madison, Ricketts's Division lay across his track.

The night passed without alarm; but with the morning of August 9th came authenticated reports that Jackson was showing himself in front of Cedar Mountain. Some hours later there was heard an occasional artillery discharge, and, as the day wore away, the firing increased in nearness and rapidity. From a knoll, near where the troops had rested on their arms from early morning, batteries could be seen getting into position and opening fire.

The greatest impatience was manifested by the men of Ricketts's Division, and when the forward command was given, about five o'clock in the evening, no time was lost in getting into line. We moved directly toward Cedar Mountain, and soon began to see evidences of the battle that had been fought so near us. Those of the wounded able to walk were moving slowly to the rear. Others, again, were supported by the arm of a companion, and at last they came in long lines of ambulances. As the Eleventh drew nearer to the battle-field, the men halted for a moment to be relieved of knapsacks, and then pushed on with a quickened step.

It was quite dark when Ricketts's Division reached the position held by Banks's right during the day. A renewal of the engagement was hardly expected before morning. But as Banks withdrew to give place to McDowell, concealed under cover of the night, the enemy had followed after; and while Ricketts was getting into position, opened upon us a furious cannonade. The suddenness of the attack, and the surrounding darkness that hid the enemy from view, save as the flash of the guns revealed his presence, was to many an experience strange and startling.

Moving forward through the heavy fire, Hartsuff's Brigade was placed under shelter of a stretch of rolling ground. Batteries were now got into position, and the answers returned from the Federal lines were as savage as the messages received. In the comparative safety the rising ground afforded, we could distinctly trace, by the burning fuse, the shells from our own and the rebel batteries, as they went hissing overhead through the heavy night air. The firing was kept up until after midnight, the enemy expending most of his shell on a dense woods some distance to our right.

The losses in the brigade were confined to the Twelfth Massachusetts and Eleventh Pennsylvania. The former had one commissioned officer killed, and ten men wounded. The Eleventh reported three wounded.

A little before daylight of next day, the regiment moved from the open ground where it lay in line of battle all night, to the rear of the woods so lately shelled by the enemy. We were in the front line, in momentary expectation of the renewal of yesterday's conflict.

Conscious that the chaplain, non-combatant and unarmed, ought to escape harm, perhaps it was easy for the men to believe that he would escape. On that morning one and another of officers and men, who well knew the rapacious character of the foe, and his intense hatred of everything belonging to Pope's army, came to commit to the chaplain whatever of value was about their person.

"This is for my wife, if I am killed or taken prisoner," said one.

"This is for my mother," said another.

Placing a valuable ring on our finger and a folded paper in our hand, a young man said: "If I do not come out of this day's fight, please send the ring as therein directed."

But the enemy did not attack; and the day

passed in unlooked-for quiet. Under a flag of truce, the 11th of August was spent in caring for the wounded left on the field, and in burying the dead. On the 12th, our scouts reported that Jackson was falling back across the Rapidan River. The Union loss in killed, wounded, and missing was fifteen hundred. If General Banks wanted to test the fighting qualities of his corps, he must have been greatly elated at the result of the battle of Cedar Mountain. But it was a useless and wicked sacrifice of life, to contend for half a day with double his number, when thousands of troops, impatient to assist, were within an hour's march.

Three days after the rebel army retired across the Rapidan, Pope's entire force was posted along its north bank. From Cedar Mountain we followed in the track of the retreating enemy. The road was strewed with tattered garments, abandoned equipments, and here and there a broken-down wagon, the *debris* of battle. Graves were everywhere, and of a size to indicate that large numbers of the dead had been buried together.

Leaving the advancing column for a time, we rode over the battle-field, and to the top of Cedar Mountain. Here was the residence of Mr. Slaughter, the owner of the estate, and from whom the hill is sometimes called Slaughter Mountain—a name by which it should evermore be known. The proprietor is an Episcopal clergyman, and his house among the most homelike we had seen in Virginia. But everything was in ruins; and over the yard were strewed fragments of elegant furniture, and valuable books and papers, the collection probably of two or three generations. Several books were brought away from the deserted mansion, that we retain in our keeping to be restored to their rightful owner.

CHAPTER II.

FROM THE RAPIDAN TO THE RAPPAHANNOCK.

At that opportune moment, and by one of those little events which men call accidents, for want of faith in an overruling Providence, the plans and intentions of the enemy became fully known. The adjutant-general of Stuart's cavalry was captured by our scouts, having on his person a letter from General Lee, dated at Gordonsville. It was therein revealed that the whole Confederate force was coming against Pope; that the Army of Virginia was to be overwhelmed before reinforcements could reach it from the James River.

The authorities at Washington had declared

that if the two armies of Pope and McClellan could only be united, the country was saved beyond a doubt. To secure a union so desirable, Pope's first move was to abandon the line of the Rapidan for the more defensible one of the Rappahannock.

August 19th, as we lay near Mitchell's Station, orders came to prepare to march. The wagon trains moved toward Culpeper soon after the receipt of the order; but it was eleven o'clock at night before the troops began filing off on the same road taken by the trains. Nothing in soldier life was so much to be dreaded as a night march. The sullenness of such vast bodies of men in motion—itself oppressive—is strangely increased by the absence of all genial sunshine.

The frequent halts, to allow the lumbering wagon trains to clear the road, detained the infantry until long after daylight in passing through Culpeper. Rank and file well understood that the rebels were in close pursuit, and that everything depended upon the crossing of the Rappahannock. The heat was intense, and the dust almost suffocating. At any season of the year that part of Virginia is only poorly supplied with water; but in the parching August month the springs are nearly dried up, and pure, cold water a rare luxury. Yet through heat and dust, and almost famishing with thirst, the army pushed heroically forward. Many there were, indeed, whose physical endurance was not equal to the trial; and throwing themselves down on the roadside, the very picture of despair, we were compelled to abandon them to their uncertain fate.

As we hurried through the town, a little dark-eyed girl, standing near the street, and swinging aloft a jaunty bonnet, inflated her lungs with the morning air to cry out after us:

"Good-by, Yankees. I'm glad you're gone! Good-by, Yankees."

But it was not thus with all our Culpeper friends. Crossing the deep bed of Mountain Run, at the northern extremity of the village, with ambulances and artillery, and officers on horse, was an old negro man, driving a yoke of oxen fastened to a rickety wagon, on which were piled women and children, bedding and boxes, in wonderful confusion.

"Halloa, uncle, where are you going with that load of darkies?"

"Gwine wid you all," was the satisfactory reply.

Whether it was a like preference for the Yankees, such as that possessed by their master, or the goad of the earnest driver that urged them forward, the oxen kept up with the quick pace of the troops, and crossed the Rappahannock at the fording below, while the footmen marched over the railroad bridge at Rappahannock Station, a short distance above.

It was nine o'clock at night, and no couch of

down invited to a sounder repose than did the grassy hillock of our bivouac, on the north side of the river, after that wearying march of twenty-five miles.

Wednesday morning, huge columns of dust, stretching away in the distance, indicated the approach of the enemy. An hour later, his cavalry emerged from the woods, three-quarters of a mile from the river, ready to carry the railroad bridge by a gallant charge. But a strong line of our own horsemen, sent across to support the infantry pickets, confronted him, and gave a different turn to his intentions.

Toward noon, Matthews's Pennsylvania Battery, supported by the Eleventh Regiment, was ordered to occupy a commanding elevation on the south side of the Rappahannock. Three hundred yards further in advance was another slight elevation, and, later in the day, a section of the battery occupied this new position, the Eleventh moving forward with it. These movements gave us possession of the best defenses on the enemy's side of the river, completely covering the bridge and the fording, though bringing us quite near to the position taken by the Confederates.

There have been few more daring and determined undertakings than that now made by the Army of Virginia. With a greatly inferior force, it had stretched itself along the Rappahannock

FIGHT AT RAPPAHANNOCK STATION. 97

in face of an opposing host, bold in the consciousness of superior numbers and elated at the total failure of the Peninsular campaign. It was not intended that Pope's army, unaided, should take the field against Lee. The present movements were all designed to gain time, that the hundred thousand veterans from Harrison's Landing might join their strength to the fifty thousand on the Rappahannock. To accomplish this object we were keeping close connections with Fredericksburg and Aquia Creek, the route by which many of those troops were to reach us. To break that line of defense, and intercept expected reinforcements, was, for the time being, the principal object of General Lee.

The Eleventh passed the night on the south side of the river without molestation, though every man slept with his hand on his musket, and was aroused by the breaking of a twig, or the chirp of a cricket. Thursday morning the rebels opened a furious fire from several batteries wheeled into position during the night. But the defenses thrown up by our men were ample protection from shot and shell; and though the attack lasted for more than an hour, the casualties in the regiment were only one killed and two or three wounded.

Simultaneously with the attack at Rappahannock Station, a determined effort was made to break the Union lines at Kelly's Ford, six miles below, but with no better success. All day of Friday comparative quiet prevailed in our front. Several attempts were made by the enemy so to place his artillery as to enfilade our position; but Thompson's Battery and the rest of Hartsuff's Brigade moved across the river, and every such effort was anticipated and defeated. The principal engagement was far to the right near Sulphur Springs. Through the latter part of the fight a heavy rain-storm prevailed, and the booming of cannon below was answered by the deep pealing thunder above.

Saturday morning dawned full of intense excitement. The heavy rain of the night before began to be seen in the rapid rising of the river. Shortly after midnight, a temporary bridge, built to facilitate the crossing of reinforcements, or the retreat of Hartsuff if need be, was washed away by the flood; and lodging against the railroad bridge, threatened to carry it down also. Every moment the river was swelling higher and higher, and every moment increasing the danger to the bridge.

The other three regiments composing the brigade were ordered across to the north side of the Rappahannock, carrying all the batteries with them but the two guns that remained with the Eleventh on the advance knoll. Some moments later, orders came for the Eleventh also to retire, excepting Cos. I and K. These two com-

FIGHT AT RAPPAHANNOCK STATION. 99

panies, with the guns of Thompson's Battery, took the first position of Wednesday. At the same time Co. B recrossed to the south side, and was placed to guard the approach to the bridge.

Now came on the rebels, cavalry, artillery, and infantry, crowding toward the river, and jostling each other for the position so lately evacuated by the Eleventh. But too surely did death meet the few, braver than their companions, that first made the ascent of the vacated hill for others to try it, until the little squad of two companies, whose guns were never silent, should be routed from their stronghold. Against our last position the whole rebel fire was concentrated. The men increased the hight of the breastworks by piling up their knapsacks, and thus, in close quarters with the enemy, awaited the signal to retire. At last it came, and under cover of our guns on the north bank, the companies crossed the river without the loss of a man. The batteries were then turned against the bridge, and in ten minutes not a timber remained standing.

The Rappahannock was at flood hight; the fordings were all sunk, and withdrawing from the river and marching toward Warrenton, the Eleventh bivouacked Saturday night in sight of the town.

CHAPTER III.

POPE RETREATING NORTHWARD.

For two days the enemy was reported in large force, moving up toward the right of the lines. Sunday morning Ricketts's Division was sent in the direction of Sulphur Springs, where it was supposed Lee might attempt a crossing. Monday we were pushed still further to the right; and on Tuesday afternoon, the division was thrown across the Warrenton pike, near Waterloo Bridge.

In the midst of this last shifting of position, fifty men, the first installment of Co. G, commanded by Lieutenant A. G. Happer, joined the regiment. They came to Warrenton by railroad, loaded down with heavy overcoats, blankets, and extra clothing, that some dishonest quartermaster had imposed upon them. But though only raw recruits, unskilled in the ways of war, and without training either in the manual of arms or in marching, they soon learned to adapt themselves to the exciting surroundings. Knapsacks were emptied of their contents along the roadside; and thus relieved of the one striking peculiarity — a John Bunyan load on their shoulders — the recruits of Co. G were lost in the rapidly moving column.

Scouts continued to say that the Confederates were marching toward our right, and by Wednesday evening it was known that Jackson had passed through Thoroughfare Gap, and was concentrating his corps at Manassas Junction. So confident was General Pope that troops from the Peninsular army would be at the points assigned to them, and at the time designated, that Jackson's movement in the direction of Salem and White Plains had given no uneasiness, as his passage through Thoroughfare Gap would not have been possible. But on the night of the 26th of August, telegraphic communications with Washington were interrupted, and Pope knew that reinforcements, from the quarter expected, had failed him. The Federal commander now determined to abandon the line of the Rappahannock, and throw his whole force upon the enemy that had passed through the Gap, hoping to destroy Jackson before the rest of Lee's army could come to his support.

Wednesday night McDowell's Corps bivouacked near Gainesville. Thursday morning had a promising look for the capture of Jackson. He could not retrace his steps toward Thoroughfare, because the sudden and unexpected movement of Pope placed Sigel and McDowell between him and retreat in that direction. No other course was left to Jackson but to retire toward Centerville; and as that carried him still further from Lee, it increased the probabilities of his capture.

Everything depended upon quick and energetic work. Reinforcements must first reach the rebel general by way of Thoroughfare, and General McDowell ordered Ricketts's Division to march direct for that point, while the rest of the corps moved on to Manassas Junction. Hartsuff's Brigade, under command of Colonel Stiles of the Ninth New York (General Hartsuff having been left sick at Warrenton), was in the advance of the division; and the Eleventh Pennsylvania, more familiar with the country than any other regiment, led the brigade.

At Haymarket, couriers reported that our cavalry held the Gap, but the enemy was advancing in strong column from White Plains. If the rebels could be kept in check two hours at Thoroughfare, McDowell had assured General Ricketts that Jackson and his whole force would be captured. Heavy and rapid firing was heard in the direction of Manassas. The other divisions of the corps were evidently performing their part of the great work then to be done, and every man in Ricketts's Division was anxious that we should do the part assigned to us. Within a mile of the Gap the cavalry were met retiring toward Haymarket. They had been driven back, and the enemy held the pass. A quarter of a mile further brought our own skirmish line in sight of that of the rebels.

It was now the middle of the afternoon, and until the sun went down did the contest continue for possession of that mountain Gap. The enemy could not bring his artillery into position, and such was the nature of the ground, that for our own batteries there was little use. It was a musketry fight, but the Bull Run Mountain, in whose face was the firing, seemed to catch each distinct volley, and in returning it again, the echoes were so loud and long as to remind one only of booming cannon and bursting shells.

Gradually the Confederates were pressed back to the entrance of the pass, where they were found to be in possession of Chapman's Mill, within the Gap, and of the hights on either side. Every foot of those hills was as familiar to the men of the Eleventh as a residence of several weeks could make them, and though nobly supported by the rest of the brigade, the brunt of the battle was met by the Eleventh Regiment gallantly leading the way. Pushing up the hill to the right of the Gap, against a severe fire from the enemy concealed behind the mills, our men finally succeeded in establishing a strong line on the summit of the ridge. The steep and rugged character of the ground over which they were contending rendered a further advance impossible. But if the Eleventh could not advance, neither could it be driven back, and the colonel maintained his position until ordered to retire.

For more than four hours the enemy was held in check. But it cost the regiment eighteen men killed and thirty-seven wounded. Among the killed were Captain Shanks, of Co. B, and Lieutenant Saxton, of Co. D. Among the severely wounded were Captain Keenan, of Co. K, and Lieutenant Tapp, of Co. B. Our killed and many of the wounded were left on the field. Those brought off were made as comfortable in hospital as the one solitary house near by would allow. When the division retired, the wounded were all placed in ambulances and brought off with the troops, rather than leave them to the tender mercies of the rebels.

The men of the Eleventh and other regiments of the brigade, as well as the few wounded Southerners that fell into our hands, had occasion to remember the kindness and unselfish devotion of Surgeon Anawalt, in charge of the regiment, and of Assistant Surgeon Phelps, who, two weeks before, had reported for duty.

The division fell back to Gainesville, and halted until morning. Less than a quarter of a mile distant was the entire force of Longstreet, neither commander knowing of the nearness of the other until the order of General McDowell, directing Ricketts to move at once to Manassas Junction, revealed it. The aid-de-camp lost his way, and did not reach our bivouac until the day had dawned. But a veil-like mist was between the two armies, and, marching by way of Bristow Station, the division came up with the rest of the corps at Manassas.

During the night two of the men died in the ambulances. On a little knoll near Bristow we placed them side by side in a single grave, in that sleep which neither the tramp of advancing or receding armies, nor the din of battle so often heard around that spot, has ever disturbed.

Scarcely had the division rested half an hour at Manassas until it was again ordered to Gainesville. Pope's plans had not been fully carried out by all the corps, and a break in the line was then discovered that might, as indeed it did, defeat everything.

It was now noon of Friday, August 29th. We had in our ambulances thirty or forty wounded men, for whom little had been done since the previous evening. It was impossible for these longer to follow the division. Dr. Phelps and the chaplain of the Eleventh were directed to place them in hospital as near as might be to the Junction. Half a mile distant to the east, was a small dwelling, occupied by two old persons, who strongly objected to having their house taken for a hospital. But it was the only building near, and we were compelled to disregard their protest. The sight of suffering, however, touched the heart of the old lady, and, woman like, she did willingly what she could to make the wounded easy and comfortable.

CHAPTER IV.

SECOND BATTLE OF BULL RUN.

During Friday afternoon Dr. Phelps was joined, at our improvised hospital, by two other surgeons of the brigade. Leaving the doctors in charge of the wounded, early Saturday morning we started in search of Ricketts's Division, going in the direction of Gainesville.

Four miles from the Junction, a squad of cavalry reported Gainesville in possession of the rebels, and that their picket line extended but a short distance up the road we were riding. Leaving a path so beset with danger, and taking the direction indicated by the cavalry, who pursued their way to Manassas, we came up with the troops north of the Warrenton pike, and in sight of the stone house. The division, diverted from its march to Gainesville by later orders, had passed the night near Bull Run.

Although there had been severe fighting most of the day of Friday by the several corps of the army, nothing decisive was gained. The rebel forces, since coming through Thoroughfare, had nearly completed a circle. Sweeping down over Manassas plains and along the hights of Centerville, capturing immense supplies of stores, and destroying a million of dollars' worth of property, all that day Jackson boldly manœuvred to rest his right flank on Gainesville.

At an early hour McDowell and Porter were ordered to move their respective corps to that point of the field, where Jackson might have been attacked on the flank and in the rear before reinforcements reached him. The troops in front listened anxiously for the signal of assault on the enemy's right. Repeated artillery discharges, coming from that direction in the afternoon, awakened the hope that Porter and McDowell were then both at work. But suddenly all was again quiet.

Some time later, General McDowell was announced through a courier as moving along the Sudley Springs road, to join the main army in front. Peremptory orders were then sent to General Porter, who commanded the largest corps in the army, and had undergone less fatigue, to move on to Gainesville, and at once attack the enemy. When a sufficient time had elapsed for Porter to get into position, a furious attack was made upon the rebel left, completely breaking the line, and throwing it back on the center; and if a like spirited attack had been made on the rebel right, the day would have been won to the Federal army. But the order of General Pope was disobeyed. Porter did not march to Gainesville, nor did he encounter the enemy.

The complexion of affairs throughout the entire field was materially changed on Saturday morning. Longstreet had united his corps with Jackson by way of Thoroughfare, and Lee's entire force was concentrated at Gainesville. The highest estimate of Pope's army, at that critical moment, was forty thousand men. He had given up all hope of any assistance from the army arrived at Washington and Alexandria from the Peninsula, and to delay the further advance of the enemy toward the capital, the Federal commander determined to renew the engagement.

The first movement was on the right, by Heintzelman and Reno, to whose support Ricketts's Division was at once sent. Colonel Stiles had been returned to his regiment, and Hartsuff's Brigade was under command of General Towers.

The order to move to the right reached the Eleventh as we sat around the mid-day meal of coffee and hard bread, spread out on the ground, with a gum poncho for a table cloth. Never will be forgotten that hurried dinner on the Bull Run battle-field. From the organization of the regiment, the headquarters' mess consisted of the three field officers and the chaplain. At that meal all were present, and with us, as invited guests, were the surgeon and the adjutant.

Soon after Heintzelman's attack on the right, the enemy made a furious assault along our whole line; but most severely was he felt on the extreme left. The left of the Federal line was south of the Warrenton turnpike, and terminated with Bald Hill, a low but commanding ridge rising above the road, and sloping down into broad open fields in front, that were bordered, half a mile away, by a thick forest of timber. McDowell's Corps was already on the left with its lines formed on Bald Hill, and recalled from the right, Ricketts's Division marched rapidly across the battle-field to rejoin it.

A score of batteries, posted on the top of the ridge, commanded every foot of the open fields; and though at each separate discharge whole lines of advancing rebels were swept down in death, still they came pouring forth from the dark woods beyond with daring impetuosity. Dreadful, too, was the carnage in the Union ranks on Bald Hill. Entire regiments seemed to melt away in an instant. One moment a strong line was seen advancing with steady step to the top of the ridge; the next moment it came rolling back in disordered and straggling masses. Other lines took the place of the broken columns only to meet a similar fate. The left was a maelstrom, that swallowed up everything coming within its fatal reach.

Conspicuous on that part of the ground was Towers's Brigade. "The conduct of the brigade, in plain view of all the forces on the left, was especially distinguished; and drew forth hearty and enthusiastic cheers. The example of the men was of great service, and infused new spirit into all the troops that witnessed their intrepid conduct." *

In the thickest of the engagement General Towers was seriously wounded and taken from the field. Colonel Stiles was absent on detached duty; Colonel Fletcher Webster, of the Twelfth Massachusetts, was among the early slain on the left, and the command of the brigade devolved upon Colonel Coulter, the next ranking officer.

"Do the best you can to hold the position, colonel," were the words of General Towers, as he passed to the rear.

The battle had gone seriously with the Eleventh. Colonel Martin was killed instantly. Major Frink was seen to fall, shot through the head. Lieutenant Dalby, of Co. E, and Lieutenant Hyndman, of Co. D, were killed at the same moment. Captain Cribbs, of Co. I, and Lieutenant McClintock, of Co. C, lay at the foot of the hill in a dying condition. Lieutenant Weaverling, of Co. A, Lieutenant Haines, of Co. B, Captain Bierer and Lieutenant Shawl, of Co. C, and Captain E. H. Rauch, of Co. H, were among the severely wounded. The command of the regiment devolved upon Adjutant Uncapher, and maintained its place, until of three hundred and forty-six

---

* Pope's official Report.

men, twenty-two were killed, and one hundred and fifty-four wounded and missing.

But no valor or heroic daring could withstand the numbers and fury of the rebels. Reinforcements were coming up slowly, and resistance was almost at an end, when a wild hurrah, and a murderous volley of artillery and musketry far to the left, told that the enemy had completely flanked our position, and the day was lost.

Singly and in squads of a dozen, but hardly in companies, the Army of Virginia retreated across Bull Run, resting at night on the hights of Centerville.

The miserable town presented a woeful appearance on that next Sabbath morning. Those of the wounded that could endure to walk had found their way hither from the battle-field, and could now be seen by scores stretched out in the yards, and along the side-walks, as well as crowded into the houses and out-sheds of the wretched place. There were wounds about the head that stained the face and matted the hair with blood. Others were carrying hands mangled and torn by bursting shells, while many were faint and dying from loss of blood and want of nourishment. Many hands, though the willing instruments of hearts full of sympathy, and actively engaged throughout all of that day, could do scarcely more than reach the most needy of the needful throng.

Fearful of those formidable Centerville hights, that his own men had rendered impregnable, General Lee did not venture to follow our retreat across Bull Run. But the whole country to the left was opened before him, and with scarcely an hour's halt in his movements, the first of September showed his troops on the Aldie pike, marching hard upon our right flank. The design of the enemy was too transparent to be disguised. It was a bold attempt to reach Fairfax Court House in our rear. Centerville was no longer tenable ground; and with its thousands of wounded and dying, was given up to the enemy.

If the persistent foe, elated by a second victory at Bull Run, expected to make short work of the jaded and worn-out Army of Virginia, by cutting off its only avenue of retreat, he made a sorry mistake. Within three miles of Fairfax his path was crossed by a triple line of brave and valorous hearts, that neither incessant marching, nor skirmishes, nor battles with thrice their number, could overwhelm or defeat.

The battle of Chantilly, where the gallant Kearney gave up his life, was a final check to all efforts on the part of the Confederate general to get in between Pope and the capital. But as the rebels continued to march by the left flank, and were disappearing from our front, Pope's entire army fell back within the fortifications of Washington. On the morning of September 2d, moving from the banks of Difficult Creek where it had been placed in position the evening before, holding the enemy in check in front, while Reno and Kearney attacked on the flank, Ricketts's Division encamped at night on Hall's Hill, in sight of the Potomac.

Pope's Virginia campaign was now at an end. Seldom has one army been asked to undergo what the men of the Army of Virginia performed. "For fifteen days, with scarcely half a day's intermission, it was either making forced marches, many times through the night, and many times without food, or else engaged in battle. These fatigues were most severe toward the last, when, on account of the movements of the enemy, we had separated from our supplies, and many generals, as well as private soldiers, had no food, or only such as could be picked up in the orchards or cornfields along the road. In all this the patience and endurance and good conduct of the men were admirable. To fight and retreat, and retreat and fight, in the face of a superior force, is a severe test of soldiership." *

But General McDowell omitted to say, that all the fatigues of that campaign were endured by the men, not only without that confidence in the leading generals, from which comes the enthusiasm of an army, but with a positive aversion

---

* McDowell's Report.

toward them. At the very outset, by the tone of his orders, and the self-superior style of his addresses, General Pope made an unfavorable impression upon the troops,—an impression that was never corrected.

With General McDowell the case was still worse. Besides an utter want of faith in his competency as a field commander, the wildest stories of complicity with the rebels were circulated and believed concerning him. During the excessive hot days of the campaign, the general wore a cool and becoming bambo hat, of peculiar shape. But the troops declared that it was especially designed as a distinguishing mark to the enemy. To such a hight did the feeling prevail, that when the rumor was circulated, on the last day of the Bull Run battle, that McDowell had been shot by Sigel for open acts of treason, there were few who cared to call the truth of the rumor in question.

New light has been thrown upon that unfortunate, though valorous campaign, chasing away the darkness of ignorant and unfounded prejudice, so damaging to the reputation of a gallant though unsuccessful officer. In that new light the country can also see how the second battle of Bull Run might have been a victory instead of a depressing defeat.

IV.

CHAPTER I.

REBEL INVASION OF MARYLAND.

THE broad Potomac rolled on toward the Atlantic, through the deep bed of its channel, as placidly as though no defeated army rested on its banks, and all unconscious of the sanguinary contest so soon to be decided near its upper waters.

The unusual quiet of the few nights passed at Hall's Hill, wherein there was neither booming of cannon, nor tramping of men, was a generous relief to soul and body. To sleep under the shelter of a tent, with our colored cook Strauthers, ever faithful and true, to see that the mess-chest was well supplied, were comforts we had not forgotten how to appreciate. But we sadly missed our genial mess-mates, Colonel Martin and Major Frink.

Colonel Martin fell at the post of duty, and at the moment when, with bitter curses and loud imprecations, the rebels were charging upon our lines on Bald Hill. It was a critical moment, and every man belonging to the Eleventh was needed in his place. With an unselfishness perfectly characteristic, the dying officer said to those who saw him fall, and had gone to his assistance:

"Never mind me, boys; never mind me. Go back to the regiment. You are wanted there."

The tide of battle soon swept us far beyond the spot where his companions left him to die. But the body was afterward buried by Dr. Woods, of the Ira Harris Cavalry,—an old Annapolis friend,—and the place of interment so carefully marked, that some weeks later the remains were recovered, and now rest in Monument Cemetery, Philadelphia.

Rarely have we met a person of such high social qualities, or one who combined so many elements of the true gentleman. No braver or more patriotic soldier fell on that field of Bull Run than Lieutenant-Colonel Thomas S. Martin.

Passing through the various hospitals in the City of Washington, looking after the wounded of the Eleventh, in the register of Armory Hospital, our eye fell upon this entry: "Bed 75— Major H. A. Frink, Eleventh Regiment Pennsylvania Volunteers." In the list of casualties, we had counted the major among the killed; and the frightful gash in the head, that the surgeon was dressing at the moment we entered, told how nearly that report had come of being correct.

The flag of truce party, sent out to gather up the wounded, overlooked him; and after days of suffering on the battle-field, without shelter and without food, and almost totally blind from the effects of the wound, Major Frink made his way first to Centerville, where the rebel authorities paroled him, and finally to Washington.

Among the losses in the brigade, outside of our own regiment, none was more keenly felt than the death of Colonel Fletcher Webster, of the Twelfth Massachusetts. Our first introduction at Falmouth, in the preceding month of May, had grown into an intimacy still remembered with pleasure. The colonel was a brave and chivalrous soldier; partaking largely of the warm impulses and noble nature of his illustrious father.

Four days of rest and quiet, short as was the time, told wonderfully upon the looks and spirits of officers and men. It must also be said that a new enthusiasm had taken hold upon the troops. As our depleted columns moved slowly back from Fairfax Court House, to an officer who rode up at our side, we said:

"This is sad work, captain. I am afraid the rebels mean to drive us across the river and capture Washington."

"No, sir," was the reply. "General McClellan is in command of the army. It will all be right now."

But not even four days of rest had been allowed to the Confederate army. A new thought was stirring the active brain of its daring commander. The seat of war was to be brought northward. Maryland was to be occupied, and such an uprising of the people to welcome him as their deliverer was anticipated by Lee, as to defy the power of the Federal Government longer to hold the State in the Union, or dislodge the Southern army from its firm foothold. The rebel general was already across the Potomac; and the day the Eleventh left Hall's Hill, Stuart's cavalry entered the City of Frederick.

It was midnight of September 6th, as we filed along the road leading to Georgetown bridge, across the Potomac, and through the streets of Washington. General Hartsuff was again at the head of the brigade, and General Hooker in command of McDowell's Corps. Hooker was moving with his corps toward Frederick, not directly, but over a route that covered the capital and defended Baltimore from a flank attack by the enemy.

Thursday evening we pitched our tents alongside the Baltimore and Frederick turnpike, twenty miles from the latter place. Whatever the rebel leaders may have thought of Maryland, it was quite evident to us that we were in the land of our friends.

At our second bivouac across the Potomac,

Captain John B. McGrew, of Co. G, and fifty men from Harrisburg, reported to the regiment. The first detachment, under Lieutenant Happer, had nearly disappeared in the battles of Thoroughfare Gap and Bull Run; and this arrival of the captain was a timely addition to Co. G. Here also, on the Frederick pike, we were joined by Dr. Phelps, direct from Manassas. Not two hours after we left the hospital, on the morning of August 30th, a force of rebel cavalry came in upon them, taking off nurses, drivers, ambulances, and horses. Even the horses of the surgeons were captured; but on application to Colonel Rosser, commanding the cavalry, these latter were restored.

The doctor soon learned of the defeat of the Union forces, and that all the intervening country between Manassas and Alexandria was in possession of the rebels. At the end of three or four days, the scanty stock of supplies with which the hospital opened, was entirely consumed, and how to subsist thirty or forty wounded men, in a country where there was nothing to buy, and nothing to forage, became a serious question. Riding out toward Centerville, in search of some one to whom he might apply for assistance, the doctor fortunately met the flag of truce party. Rations and ambulances were at once provided, and all the wounded left at Manassas were brought to Alexandria.

It was a Sabbath morning, clear and beautiful, when the Federal army marched through Frederick—an event always to be remembered. For one week the town had been under rebel rule, a time sufficiently long for even the most intense Southern sympathizer; and the sight of the Union ranks filled the people of the place with extravagant joy. Amid deafening cheers and flying banners and waving handkerchiefs we pressed our way through the crowded streets toward the South Mountain, that rose boldly in front to the hight of a thousand feet.

The route was along the National road. From the top of Fairview Hill could be seen the smoke of the enemy's batteries, and we knew that in posting himself in Turner's Gap (the main pass of the mountain), and on the hights on either side, by which he commanded every way of approach, General Lee had the advantage of position, and would hold the strong mountain defense to the last. The Corps of Hooker and Reno, forming the right wing of the army, were under command of General Burnside. To attack in front would have been the extreme of folly. The only hope was to get on the enemy's flank, and while Reno was manœuvring to the left of the National road, to secure such a result, Hooker's Corps moved to the right. A short distance from the Hagerstown pike we struck the old Braddock road, which crosses the mountain at a point not so high as that over which the main road passes, but of steep and difficult ascent. Two miles from the pike, we began our upward march. The Eleventh was on the extreme right of Ricketts's Division, and if it made rapid time in reaching the crest above, it was because we had learned at Thoroughfare Gap how to march and fight up the side of a mountain.

General Lee was too shrewd a commander to depend entirely upon that steep and rugged hillside to defend his left flank. Hid in the ravines washed out by the summer torrents, and sheltered behind breastworks leisurely constructed, the enemy awaited our advance. Half way up to the summit, the crest of the mountain suddenly gleamed with a sheet of flame. If some staggered and fell back, meeting those whistling bullets from above, it only nerved that advancing column with new determination.

The firing was severest on the left of the corps, held by the Pennsylvania Reserves; and when at last a prolonged cheer told that the left of the mountain top had been carried by Pennsylvania troops, the old Eleventh, fighting on the right, sent back the echo of victory from the same high level.

Many a brave heart met a soldier's fate, climbing up the South Mountain. But each foot of ground wrested from the enemy was securely held. Next morning, Hartsuff's Brigade moved cautiously along the Braddock road, over the deserted breastworks and rifle-pits of the enemy, until we struck the National pike at the Mountain House. Turner's Gap was now in the rear. The attack on the left—though the gallant Reno lost his life in making it—was as successful as that on the right; and the clouds of dust, rising from the plains below, told that Lee was in full retreat toward the Potomac, leaving his killed and wounded on the field.

If the South Mountain battle had not been followed so soon by that of Antietam, whose greater proportions now almost overshadow it, it would be considered, as indeed it was, a decided victory over General Lee. Its influence on the *morale* of our troops was of far greater advantage than the loss of men and material of war sustained by the enemy. It was a success when, of everything else, success was needed to restore the waning confidence of the rank and file. It was the silver lining to the dark cloud of reverses that had so long hung over the Potomac Army.

CHAPTER II.

M'CLELLAN AND LEE ON THE UPPER POTOMAC.

Every spot along the road in which a man could find room to lie down, out of danger of being trampled to death by the moving columns, was found occupied by the wounded. The church at Boonsborough, and many private residences, were converted into rebel hospitals, giving to the town the appearance of Centerville after the battle of Bull Run.

A Virginia chaplain remained behind to take care of the wounded of his regiment. Their loss was severe, numbering one or two hundred in killed and wounded. He was not disposed at first to be at all cordial, and our proposed good offices were politely refused. But afterward relenting, some assistance we were able to give was accepted with as much courtesy as it was before declined.

"Our recent successes over your army have made us too confident. We had no thought of being driven from South Mountain; and I fear that your rapid pursuit of General Lee will prevent him from crossing the Potomac without serious loss."

Turning off from the National pike at Boonsborough into the road leading to Sharpsburg, the army halted at Kedysville for several hours, waiting on cavalry operations in the front. Our advance came up with the enemy, stretched across the road over which we were marching, in strong force. When his position was fully known, it was too late to attack, and the Eleventh bivouacked for the night a short distance west of the village.

Tuesday morning revealed that the enemy had changed his position during the night, and was now posted along the line of Antietam Creek, his right near Sharpsburg and his left resting on Miller's farm. With his usual sagacity, the rebel general had selected a most advantageous position. His right flank was protected by a high ridge—a continuance of Maryland Hights, running northward,—and his left flank by the Potomac River, half a mile distant. Whether McClellan might determine to attack the rebel center, or on either flank, he was compelled to cross the Antietam, and move over ground swept by artillery planted on every available spot.

The Federal attack was to be similar to that made at South Mountain. Hooker's Corps, supported by those of Mansfield and Sumner, was sent to the right to fall on the enemy's left, while Burnside was to assault his right. Hooker's Corps consisted of the three divisions of Generals

Meade, Ricketts, and Doubleday. Three o'clock in the afternoon of Tuesday, leaving our bivouac near Kedysville, and marching in rear of the first division, Ricketts crossed Antietam Creek at the upper bridge and the fording at Pray's mill, and continued moving to the right as far up as Hoffman's farm.

The day was nearly spent when Hooker's Corps reached the position assigned it. There had been desultory firing during the afternoon in the direction in which we were marching, but for a time everything had remained in a state of quiet. Scarcely, however, did we come to a halt in a field of corn, before the enemy from a copse woods in front, opened on our ranks with infantry and artillery. The advance brigades came at once into action, and until ten o'clock the severe skirmish was continued.

Thus began, on the evening of September 16th, the battle of Antietam. Stonewall Jackson had formed his main battle line on Miller's farm, and the force so early encountered was a body of troops thrown out three-quarters of a mile in advance. If General McClellan had attacked Lee on Tuesday morning, he would have had thirty thousand less troops opposed to him. Jackson's whole corps was absent, and only by a forced march from Harper's Ferry did it reach the battle-field late on Tuesday morning. In the evening the troops were in position on our right, and the delay in the battle until Wednesday morning gave to Jackson and his soldiers a precious season of needed repose.

As the men rested on their arms during that clear, starlight night, no one could doubt what the morning would bring forth. Ever and anon, throughout its wakeful hours, the fierce firing of the pickets reminded us of the presence of a stubborn foe.

Just as the gray dawn of the morning of the 17th streaked the sky, a volley of musketry, out on the picket line, changed the whole appearance of those once quiet fields. Up from among the stalks of corn, sprung ranks of armed men; while from sheltered woods and every rising knoll, the artillery of friend and foe was sending forth shot and shell. Hooker had inaugurated the great conflict.

In front of General Hooker's position, with their backs resting against a skirt of timber, were the forces of Stonewall Jackson, consisting of the divisions of McLaws, Anderson, and A. P. Hill. They were the flower of the Confederate army, returned from their successful attack on Harper's Ferry, and placed opposite our right, because there were to be met the heaviest blows of the battle.

When Hooker said, "This is one of the world's great days," he must have felt what he expressed; for his own enthusiasm was imparted to his men. Nothing could withstand the impetuosity of that first attack on the right to carry the rebel position. The enemy's heavy line of skirmishers fell back almost without resistance, exposing his main lines to a determined fire of shell and canister, from batteries run out within the closest possible range. Over the plowed ground that intervened, through the fields of corn, and into the woods beyond, were driven the shattered lines of the rebels.

The fighting had now become general on the right, and heavy forces of reserves were brought forward to strengthen and hold the ground we had gained in our first assault. But in front of that woods into which the enemy was driven, our advance halted. Fresh rebel troops were coming to the rescue of their comrades. Volley after volley of musketry lighted up its dark bosom, as line upon line of Confederates issued from it.

The fortune of the day seemed suddenly to change. The rebels were now advancing; and our own gallant lines that but a moment before moved through the cornfield in such overwhelming force, came back broken and depleted. The watchful eye of Hooker took in the whole scene at a glance.

"Send me your best brigade," was his message to Ricketts.

In a moment, Hartsuff's Brigade, that had been in position on a slight elevation near the house of Joseph Poffenberger, came down the hill on a double-quick, through the open ground beyond, and into the cornfield; passing, as they went, the fragments of three brigades shattered by the rebel fire and now streaming to the rear.

"I think they will hold it," said Hooker, as he saw that splendid brigade of veteran troops moving on under a galling and destructive fire.

At the moment of entering the cornfield, a conspicuous mark to the enemy, the brave Hartsuff fell from his horse severely wounded.

"Forward, Third Brigade!" rung out the voice of Colonel Coulter, who succeeded to the command.

"Steadily, but not hurriedly, up the hill they go, forming on the crest. Not a man who was not in full view—not one who bent before the storm. Firing first in volleys, they fired then at will, with wonderful rapidity and effect. The whole line crowned the hill and stood out darkly against the sky; but lighted and shrouded ever in flame and smoke. There, for half an hour, they held the ridge, unyielding in purpose, exhaustless in courage. There were gaps in the line, but it nowhere bent. Their supports did not come, and they determined to win without them. They were there to win that field, and they won it. The rebel line for the second time fled through the corn and into the woods. I cannot tell how few of Hartsuff's Brigade were left when the work was done, but it was done. There was no more gallant, determined, heroic fighting in all this desperate day."*

The battle had reached a crisis on the right. Ricketts's Division exhausted itself in the vain endeavor to advance beyond the woods. Part of Mansfield's Corps was ordered in to their relief; but the general was mortally wounded, and the troops halted on the crest of the hill.

It was nine o'clock, and all the fighting had been done by the Corps of Hooker and Mansfield. Presently Sumner's Corps came on to the ground, forming to the left of Mansfield. Still later, French and Richardson arrived, and about noon the Corps of General Franklin. But though the troops had fought only in detachments,— Hooker in the morning, then Mansfield, then Sumner, then Franklin, and Burnside far on the left,—the enemy had been pushed back from many of his strongest positions, and when welcome night covered the ensanguined field, the vantage-ground belonged to the Federal army.

In the thoughts of the men, daylight would renew the battle, and each soldier stood in his place, waiting for the coming dawn. But the whole of Thursday passed without any demonstration from those lines,—still confronting each other,—that only on the yesterday were full of bitter hostility.

---

* Geo. N. Smalley, in *N. Y. Tribune.*

Again the shades of night covered Antietam. Ricketts's Division held the extreme right of the army; and the general was cautioned to take care of his flank. McClellan determined to renew the attack on Friday morning, with a vigor increased by one day of rest. But when Friday came, from every commanding ridge and hidden ravine,—from open fields and sheltered woods,— the enemy had disappeared, and the rapid Potomac rolled between the two opposing armies.

The Eleventh went into the battle on Wednesday morning, a mere handful compared with its former self,—nine commissioned officers, and two hundred and twenty-six men. The other regiments of the brigade were but little larger, for altogether it only numbered eleven hundred.

Hoffman's farm-house—a substantial stone building—was taken for a hospital; and every moment, from the firing of the first gun at break of day, until they were relieved by other troops, the wounded were coming in from Hartsuff''s Brigade. A wounded man naturally desires to be among his friends; and by keeping the brigade together, the surgeons were certain that all would receive like proper care and attention.

In what quick succession they seemed to come from that angry front. Scarcely eight o'clock, and seventy men of the Eleventh Regiment lay bleeding and groaning in the yard of that farmhouse. When the battle ceased, five officers out of the nine were disabled, and one hundred and twenty of the men killed and wounded. Of the eleven hundred of Hartsuff's Brigade that marched so steadily through that field of corn, only five hundred returned.

From the field of Waterloo, after the battle had spent its fury, and in the midst of its reeking carnage, the Duke of Wellington wrote to a friend: "I have escaped unhurt; *the finger of Providence was on me.*" And those brave men, as they looked over that field of Antietam, strewed with the harvest of death,—through which they had passed unhurt,—with a manliness of heart equal to that of the English duke, confessed that the finger of God was upon them.

The hospital is a place where one may look on the battle-field shorn of

"The pomp and circumstance of war."

To see those with whom you have been in daily intercourse,—with whom you have exchanged all the kind amenities of social life, and Christian fellowship,—to see these lacerated by gaping wounds, bleeding and dying, is a harrowing sight, from which you would gladly turn away.

Many of the young men of the Eleventh Regiment came from praying families, and during the gracious revivals of religion that preceded the rebellion, some had made a personal consecration of themselves to the service of God.

Not only at Annapolis, but through all the subsequent campaigns, however wearisome the marches or fatiguing the duties, there were a few who could always find the time and the place to pay their vows to the Most High.

Every foot of ground over which we marched and fought has a deep and abiding interest. But those secluded spots, just outside of camp limits, where the meeting for evening prayer was held, will live longest in the memory of all. Faithful to their Divine Master, they were also faithful to their country; and at Thoroughfare Gap, and Bull Run, and Antietam, the first to fall were from among these young men.

There was one thing belonging to the battle-field not to be seen in our hospital,—its foul spirit of hate. The term *foe* was there forgotten. All were now friends. A soldier from Maine and another from Georgia—the one having lost an arm, and the other a leg—occupied the same pallet of straw. A South Carolinian, slightly hurt in the head, was the cook for himself and two severely wounded New Yorkers. A volunteer from Pennsylvania and a conscript from Alabama, sheltered under the same tent, were as fraternal in their acts of kindness as though they had fought side by side, and not in opposing ranks.

With the earliest knowledge of Lee's retreat, a squad of surgeons and chaplains repaired to the battle-field. If any of the wounded that could not be reached during the first days' engagement had lived through Thursday, the object of our visit was to give them the speediest relief. But that field, furrowed by cannon shots and strewed in every direction with human forms, was a place of the dead. Cries of—water!—water!—uttered in tones of beseeching agony, fell upon our ears in the first hours of the battle. Now every tongue was still, and every heart had beat its last pulsation.

Death came to many with musket raised to the shoulder, in the very act of firing; and in falling forward, the dead soldier kept fast hold of his gun. Others, again, lay on the ground, with arms wide extended, and the last look of anguish fixed in the rigid features. In a single row, with scarcely two feet between them, were eighty-one of the enemy's dead. It was a battle-line moving forward, each man meeting death at the same instant. Such a volley, telling so fearfully on the front rank, was a complete check at that point; for there were no indications here of advance and retreat, as were seen on other parts of that ground, in the bodies of friend and foe falling together.

We had only to pass up through Miller's cornfield, and into the woods beyond, to find most of the slain belonging to the Eleventh. Writing the name of each man on a slip of paper, with the number of the regiment and the letter of his company, and fastening it to coat or shirt, the graves of our comrades were so plainly marked, that when friends came to remove sons and brothers, we could point with certainty to all that remained of brave and loving hearts.

CHAPTER III.

ARMY OF THE POTOMAC IN REPOSE.

Moving forward from the battle-field late Friday afternoon, Hartsuff's Brigade went into camp on a bluff overlooking the Potomac. The river was between us and the enemy; the firing heard at intervals during the day was away toward Harper's Ferry, and each soldier, wrapping up in blanket, promised himself a night of needed repose. But our slumbers were disturbed near midnight by a frightened courier, who reported a large body of Stuart's cavalry north of the Potomac.

The whole brigade was marched three miles up the river to guard the fording, and, if possible, intercept Stuart. The movement was sufficiently adventurous to arouse the most sluggish, as we passed over roads darkened by heavy forests, and every ear was strained to catch the faintest sound of tramping horsemen.

CAMP IN WALNUT GROVE. 135

The troops were disposed along the roads leading to the river to the best possible advantage, Colonel Coulter finding himself in the vicinity of his first explorations of the Potomac, under General Patterson. The watch was maintained until Saturday at sundown; but no foe showing himself to be near, the brigade was relieved and returned to camp.

Those were glorious autumn days that followed the battle of Antietam. The camp of our division was in a walnut grove, on the farm of James Rowe, with the Potomac in full view. It was not easy to realize that the narrow, rocky stream rolling below was the same Potomac, of such majestic proportions, that we had crossed at Washington. The course of the river was like that of an unpromising youth, disappointing all the ill prophecies drawn from a mean beginning, and developing at last a sturdy and magnificent manhood. They were also days of masterly inactivity. Company drill and battalion drill were observed as usual. But however interesting such exercises might be to the new recruit, to those veterans, who had made their evolutions to the music of charging columns and bursting shells, all ordinary drill was dull monotony.

There was business enough, however, at regimental headquarters. The numerous vacancies in the list of commissioned officers were to be filled, amounting almost to a reorganization of the regiment. Major Frink was promoted to the vacated place of Lieutenant-Colonel Martin. Captain J. B. Keenan, of Co. K, was made major. In Co. B Lieutenant Haines took the place of Captain Shanks, killed at Thoroughfare Gap; Second Lieutenant Tapp was made first lieutenant, and J. P. Straw second lieutenant. In Co. D Sergeant J. B. Overmyer was appointed captain in room of Captain Sees, honorably discharged; Jas. T. Chalfant, transferred from the Ninth Regiment Pennsylvania Reserve Corps, first lieutenant, in place of Lieutenant Saxton, killed at Thoroughfare, and Sergeant F. J. Cross second lieutenant, in place of E. T. Tiers, discharged to become captain in another Pennsylvania regiment. In Co. E, Second Lieutenant H. B. Piper took the place of Lieutenant G. R. Dalby, killed at Bull Run, and Sergeant Samuel J. Hamill was promoted to second lieutenant. In Co. F, Second Lieutenant E. H. Gay took the position of Captain D. M. Cook, honorably discharged; and Sergeant Robert Anderson, of Co. K, was appointed second lieutenant. In Co. H, Sergeant Daniel C. Tubbs was made second lieutenant in place of Lieutenant Hyndman, killed at Bull Run. In Co. I, Second Lieutenant Jacob N. Thomas took the place of Captain George A. Cribbs, who died of wounds received at Bull Run; and Sergeant A. Lobaugh was promoted to second lieutenant. Lieutenant Lobaugh died at Hagerstown, of wounds received at Antietam, before his commission from the Governor of Pennsylvania reached the regiment. In Co. K, First Lieutenant Walter J. Jones resigned; Second Lieutenant John Reed was appointed captain in place of Captain Keenan promoted, but died of wounds received at Antietam before his commission arrived. Corporal W. A. Kuhns was appointed second lieutenant; afterward promoted to first lieutenant, and Corporal Freeman C. Gay made second lieutenant.

Since the death of Colonel Martin, it had fallen to the chaplain to keep the mess—now increased to more than the original number by the addition of adjutant and surgeons—in rations. We were so nearly starved in Virginia, that in a land of plenty each one's appetite seemed determined on making amends for past compulsory fasting. "Sold out," was the reply to inquiries for any kind of provender, made of farmers living near the camp. Then we had to enlarge the circle of our operations, sometimes in one direction and again in another.

While the cook Strauthers, who always accompanied us on these foraging expeditions, rode off a short distance further to secure some articles for which he had bargained on a former visit, we remained at Bakersville, in conversation with an old woman with whom we had agreed for a supply of shanghais.

12*

"Them chickens were raised for my own use; but I am always ready to divide with a soldier, even to the last half a loaf of bread."

The old lady had no very flattering opinion of the Virginians, and was greatly delighted at the defeat of the rebel army.

"Them Virginians always thought they were a heap smarter than the Marylanders. But I told them they had better stay at home; that they would find out to their sorrow we had just as smart people here as they had over there. I always said this fight would come some day. But they said I was dumb, and didn't know anything. Well, I don't know much; but I know the good Book says the father shall rise against the son, and the son against the father; and aint that so, now? I knew it would come, but I was never afraid that the South would whip the North. It will all be right by-and-by, mind I tell you. I told my son John, the other day, that as I had seen the first of this war I should like to see the end of it; and John said, 'La, mother, do you expect to live that long?' Do you think the war will end soon?"

The arrival of Strauthers, and his violent demonstrations in the chicken yard, put an end to the harangue. It was four miles to camp, and night was coming on. We could not even guess how much longer the war would last; but sincerely hoping that all would be right in the end, we took our leave.

That old woman in Maryland was not the only one to entertain a mean opinion of her Virginia neighbors. A Louisiana captain said:

"There is nothing in Virginia to make any one fall in love with it. Her men are mean and her women ugly. I would trade off Virginia to-day for Maryland. I think there is more of the cunning Yankee and his cowardly disposition among the people of that State, notwithstanding their high pretensions to chivalry, than can be found among any other class of men in the Confederate service.

"There is General R. A. Pryor, whose political and dueling reputation got him a military position for which he is totally unqualified. He is not only a coward, but a knave. At one of the recent battles he lost his command, and offered some of the Louisiana boys a fifty-days' furlough if they would point it out to him. I have heard aids to our generals say that they would rather be dispatched with orders for any other officer on the ground in time of battle than Pryor, as he is always the most difficult person to find, and when found is usually posted as secretly as possible in some safe place."

SUNDAY, Sept. 20.—Another delightful day. The clouds that obscured the early rising of the sun, gradually floated away, and toward ten o'clock the morning was as bright as though no threatening rain clouds had marred its early beauty. Six o'clock in the evening we held our public religious services in connection with the dress parade. The sun had gone down behind the Virginia hills, as the regiment marched out upon the open green to the rear of headquarters. Almost every man in camp was present, each one manifesting by a becoming and quiet demeanor his interest in the duties of the hour. These words of Paul, addressed to the Ephesians, "My brethren, put on the whole armor," were read as a text.

It was remarked that they must all have observed the familiar as well as kindly manner in which the Scriptures address us. The Bible is a gift from God; but it came intermediately through men, men like ourselves, and therefore in its spirit it is like the address of one man to another. The Apostle calls us brethren, and as a brother he delivers his instructions. There is another thing that endears Paul to us. It is said that he was a soldier, and from the frequency with which he uses illustrations and phrases drawn from the soldier's life, this may be true. He talks about fighting a good fight; warring a good warfare; and of putting on the whole armor as though he knew all about it.

We are to understand Paul as teaching that everything that goes to make up the complete soldier is to be secured; no part of the armor must be neglected. The brave, valiant, and successful soldier is always fully equipped. You would not regard that comrade who should go into the battle with his cartridge box only, as fully armed; neither that one who, leaving his cartridge box behind, should take only his musket. In order to put on the whole armor he must have both gun and cartridge box, bayonet and scabbard.

A good cause, personal bravery, a spirit that will lead to death rather than turn the back to the foe, are essential parts of every soldier's armor. So far as these are concerned, you are fully armed. Your cause is the cause of humanity. It concerns all peoples. Are there anxious hearts here in our own nation awaiting the result of this contest? There are hearts as anxious in every nation under the sun. We have taught other nations that man is free; that God has made him capable of self-government. We have taught them new ideas; awakened in them new hopes. Through our teachings they have been aroused to action. If we succeed, a bright future opens to them. If we fail, a darker night, because of the already dawning day, closes around them. Our cause is good; it is our country's cause,—the country that God gave to us, and that bears the seal of our fathers' blood. As to your personal bravery, let the battle-fields of Cedar Mountain, Rappahannock Station, Thoroughfare Gap, Bull Run, Chantilly, South Mountain, Antietam, speak. That you are ready to die rather than forsake the cause in which you have engaged, or dim the glory of your flag, let our thinned ranks tell, let our three hundred killed and wounded declare.

This part of your armor is complete. But, according to Paul, my comrades, this is not the *whole* armor; and Paul knew whereof he affirmed. He was a soldier, and a courageous soldier. No craven fear entered his manly heart. He is, therefore, a proper person to teach, and his teachings ought to be regarded. We must ever remember that the circumscribed present is not the only field of action upon which the soldier who hears me to-day will be marshaled. The impudent foe, that threatens with insulting boasting, to demolish our fair fabric of State, is not the only one he is called upon to meet. We must remember that sacred as is our allegiance to country, laudable as is the ambition to deserve well at her hands, our allegiance to heaven is more sacred, and to be approved of God is an ambition higher than to be approved of man. Each one of us will soon overstep the boundaries of time, and enter upon the boundless eternity. Spiritual foes—whose name is legion—invest us on every side. The eye of the Almighty, looking through every covering, now beholds us.

It is for this higher service, for this more important field of action, and these more subtle enemies, that our brother Paul would prepare us.

And we may see in this kindly advice something of that regard which every soldier feels for his fellow-soldier. War may accustom one to scenes of carnage and bloodshed; but war also develops the most generous sentiments of our nature. Let a companion fall on the battle-field, and a score of hands are ready to raise him up. Let an enemy, wounded and bleeding, cast himself down before you, and he is treated like a brother. Paul knew the soldier's generosity, and with a generosity nearly akin to it, urges his brother soldiers to put on the *whole* armor, that having deserved well of his country, he might deserve and secure the more enduring honor of heaven.

How to secure this additional armor is an old story, my fellow-soldiers. The road to heaven's arsenal has ever been the way of the cross. Repentance toward God; an acceptance of Christ as our Saviour; a life of prayer, of trust, of obedience, of faith, puts us in possession of the *whole armor*, and equips the soldier entire. I must warn you against embracing that wide-spread fallacy, that the life of the Christian and the life of the soldier are so far apart as to make it utterly impossible for them to meet in the same person, and that the best soldier is the man who is least religious, or who has thrown off, to the greatest degree, all moral restraint.

Let me ask you what constitutes a good soldier? Certainly not brute force merely, nor an ignorant recklessness of life. Show me the man to whose courage and bravery is added a sense of his responsibility to God, one who believes that his motives and actions here are to give shape and coloring to his life in the other world, and I will show you the best soldier. If the path of duty leads him to the very mouth of the cannon, or upon the sharp points of the enemy's charging bayonets, will a preparation to die, and a sense of his acceptance with God, in the least degree interfere with the discharge of his duty? Rather has not such a one put on the whole armor; and who, more than he, is fit for such deeds of noble daring? A profession of religion hightens every joy of life. It does not blunt, but quickens every sensibility; and yet with every joy hightened, and every sensibility quickened, the Christian is brave to dare and bold to do whatever God or his country demands.

Let me ask you another question. If we neglect to put on the whole armor from those more subtle foes to which I have alluded, who shall defend us? Vice is always degrading. Every sin we commit detracts from our true manhood, and makes us mean and despicable in the eyes of the Almighty, in the eyes of good men, and in our own eyes. I am sorry that in this camp, and among our own brave men, so many vices prevail. Some of you are profane; some are intemperate; some are gamblers. How sad to see men who have nobly contended for so good a cause as ours, men who but yesterday were victors on this hard-fought field, to-day captives in the hands of these gross vices. Rouse ye, soldiers! In the name of Jesus, rouse ye! Put on the whole armor, and then you shall be able to meet every foe; those of your country, and those greater enemies of your souls as well.

There are loved ones at home who daily pray God to watch over and protect you. You cannot imagine with what intense interest everything from the battle-field is read by them. What heartfelt thanks went up to heaven that you had escaped where so many fell. But think you, comrades, they have no other concern than for your personal safety? Dearly as that wife or mother loves you, fondly as that sister thinks of you, she would rather you had died on the sanguinary field of Antietam, by the side of your brave companion, than to return to her arms a thing loathsome and degraded by vicious habits. Every interest conspires, brother soldiers, to make it our duty to put on the whole armor. Our duty to God, our duty to our country, our duty to self, our duty to friends, all require it. May you be thus equipped; and in every contest, whether with the enemies of our country or with the enemy that leads us into evil, be always conquerors.

CHAPTER IV.

TENT LIFE IN MARYLAND.

October 1.—The new month made its beginning with a genial shower of rain, which lasted long enough to lay the dust, and give to the trees a greener and fresher look. It is now night. The moon rides through a cloudless sky; while the hum of the myriads of insects that swarm this sylvan retreat, and the ceaseless murmur of the river, on its way to the sea, mingle their somnific music. In the tent, as joint occupants, are the two surgeons. They have already spread their blankets on the ground, and though present in body are absent in spirit in the land of visions.

The junior doctor is by himself. The senior and the chaplain are more social, and sleep on the same blankets. The junior has been spending some time at the Sharpsburg hospital, among the rebel wounded, and we have voted him out in a corner until he shall have completed his purification.

We could wish all things that crawl but to contaminate and annoy, might be kept in secessia where they belong by right of possession.

But even in this loyal State of Maryland, there are all sorts of creeping worms and flying bugs. They make of one's body, during the night season, a common highway. Just at that delicious moment of human existence, when the substantial world is fading into that out of which dreams come, did you ever have one of those long-legged spiders take the dimensions of your face? Or a black beetle persist in getting into your ear, while half a dozen over-large ants, mistaking your nose for an ant-hill, make a violent effort to stop up the channel through which you draw your ration of oxygen? Then you never made your bed on the ground, overlooking the Potomac, in the State of Maryland.

OCTOBER 6.—One o'clock this morning, General Porter, on the extreme left, sent word that the enemy was planting cannon on the hills opposite Ricketts's Division; and that forces were moving up the Potomac. The headquarter tents of the regiment, pitched near the outer edge of the grove, and that might serve as an admirable target from the other side of the river, were removed to a less conspicuous place.

OCTOBER 7.—All quiet along the Potomac. No enemy has shown himself on the opposite shore. The extensive laundry operations afforded by the river, somewhat curtailed through the rumors of yesterday, are again as active as ever. General Nelson Taylor, who has been assigned to the command of the brigade, arrived this afternoon. We have lost the title of Hartsuff's Brigade, of which we had reason to be proud. May we make a reputation as honorable under our new name of Taylor's Brigade.

During the last ten days our camp has been full of visitors. Some are here to see the battle-field; others come on the sadder errand of removing their dead to the quiet resting-place of the church-yard at home, or the family burying ground.

OCTOBER 11.—All *not* quiet on the Potomac. From Harper's Ferry to Cumberland there is confusion and alarm. If anything conceived by Lee could astonish one, the occupation of Chambersburg by the rebel cavalry would certainly do it. While we have been massing our army at Harper's Ferry, and sending reconnoitering parties as far south as Warrenton, the enemy steals northward around our pickets and invades Pennsylvania. When will we be able to cope with this wily, and, one might almost say, ubiquitous foe?

SUNDAY, October 12.—Last night the regiment was ordered out on picket, near where we did duty September 19th. It was merely precautionary, lest Stuart and his cavalry might feel disposed to recross into Virginia *via* Piper's Ford. Returned to camp late this afternoon, where orders were in waiting to cook two days' rations, preparatory to march.

October 14.—To cross the Potomac from Virginia into Maryland, at an unguarded ford, with one or two thousand cavalry, may not have been a great thing in a military point of view. But with that number of men, to make a detour from right to left of our army, through a densely populated country, compelling the surrender of a town of five thousand inhabitants, capturing hundreds of horses, and thousands of dollars' worth of property, and with all this booty, and without the loss of a man, to recross into Virginia, *is* something of a feat. If the enemy should be falling back on Richmond, as is reported, this raid will enable him to do so with better grace; while to a large degree it neutralizes the good effects of recent victories.

October 16.—The move for which preparations have been making for several days past, is likely to be retarded for some time longer. The rain is falling heavily on our tent-roof, threatening to sink the fordings of the Potomac too deep for crossing. But if the night is dark and cheerless without, we have anything but a cheerless party within. Two of the doctors are engrossed in a game of checkers, while two or three officers are discussing the battle of Antietam. Dr. Morris, the latest addition to the medical department, who weighs full two hundred pounds, in the vain attempt to adjust himself to an army bed, is loudly bemoaning the loss of home-sleeping comforts, only appreciated in their absence. Pushing aside the checker-board, Doctor Phelps inquired:

"Chaplain, did I ever tell you of that singular dream I had—if dream it was—after you left us in the hospital at Manassas?"

Not one of the company had heard it, and the doctor was urged to proceed.

"You remember that for more than a week I was on the sick list. The fight at Thoroughfare Gap, and the fatiguing march of next day to Manassas Junction made me so much the worse. Then came the tearing up of that old woman's house for a hospital. Scarcely through with that, the rebel cavalry made a dash on Manassas, capturing ambulances, drivers, doctors, and all. The horses and ambulances were appropriated to their own use; the drivers and nurses taken prisoners; the wounded paroled, and the doctors marched off to Colonel Rosser's headquarters. The colonel generously dismissed the surgeons, and sent them back to take care of the sick. I returned to the hospital completely prostrated; and for once you might have seen the strange sight of a doctor taking his own physic. The medicine quieted my nerves and produced a feeling of drowsiness. Lying on the bed, and conscious of everything around me, the two armies were seen confronting each other in line of battle. At the head of the rebel troops was a figure of giant size, that seemed to walk through our ranks with the utmost impunity, the whole Southern army following close behind. The Eleventh Regiment lay directly in his track, and the men were falling to the right and left like mown wheat. The exclamations of horror uttered at such a sight attracted the attention of some one in the room, who came to the bedside to inquire what was the matter. What is the matter! Why, the rebels are whipping us. Pope's army is giving way at all points, in rout and defeat. You all know that the result of the Bull Run battle was nearly to the letter as seen in my dream."

A long discussion followed on the philosophy of dreams and visions. It was certainly very ungenerous in one of the company to speak in that particular connection of Goethe's story of Dr. Faust, leaving us not only to infer that the huge figure at the head of the rebel army was the same well-known Mephistopheles, who formed such a close alliance with that ancient physician, but that the propensity to form similar alliances still belonged to the profession! Perhaps it was the pelting storm without, that in angry blasts drove the rain against our tent, and went howling dismally through the trees,—a real night for the witches of Brocken to be astir,— that suggested the thought.

V.

CHAPTER I.

M'CLELLAN SUPERSEDED BY BURNSIDE.

Four days from the close of October, Ricketts's Division bade good-by to Walnut Grove, and marched to Berlin. The delightful autumn weather was at an end, and with the beginning of winter, General McClellan commenced a new campaign against Richmond.

Never was there a more cheerless march; and though continued from three o'clock in the afternoon until midnight, so dark was the night, and so incessant the rain, and so slow the progress, that when we halted, the brigade had only made six miles,—not half the intended distance. Berlin, the destination of the first day's march, was not reached until the 28th. It was an inauspicious beginning, and proved prophetic of the whole movement. Two days later, the army crossed the Potomac into Virginia. Passing through Lovettsville, Bloomfield, and Salem, Ricketts's Division bivouacked at Warrenton on the 6th of November.

FEELING AMONG THE TROOPS. 153

The ground was covered with snow, and a frosty chilliness dwelt in the air. But it was not the winter storm, with its moaning winds, and sleet and snow, that so depressed the spirits of the troops. It was the order, read to the several corps, dismissing General McClellan from the chief command of the Army of the Potomac that filled all hearts with sorrow.

Long after the patience of the country was exhausted by his hesitancy and want of decision, the army still confided in their favorite general. The rank and file beheld McClellan only in the favorable light in which he first appeared among them,—as the organizer of the volunteer masses of the nation into splendid corps and divisions of well-trained soldiers. And when the ranks of that army were broken, and almost ruined by defeat and disaster, they remembered him as gathering up the fragments, reorganizing them, and marching through the victories of South Mountain and Antietam.

It would be to insult the common sense of our citizen soldiers, to say they did not see that some one was to blame for delays and defeats. Why the Peninsular campaign was such a fearful failure; why the battle of Antietam was not renewed on Thursday; why days and weeks, so favorable for military operations, were not afterward improved, were questions fully discussed. But with wonderful unanimity, all agreed in placing the blame anywhere else than on the chief commander. The authorities at Washington were charged with interfering with his plans and purposes; with withholding reinforcements and supplies; and when delays ensued, or defeat came, the whole blame was thrown upon the shoulders of others.

In a record of the lights and shadows of army life, the removal of McClellan must be set down as one of the shadows. The appointment of his successor was a wise though unintentional stroke of policy. Next to McClellan, General Burnside had the confidence and affection of the troops; and for the peace of the army there was more than happy chance in that selection.

The Confederate army was concentrated at Culpeper, with a strong rear-guard in the Shenandoah Valley. Abandoning the plans of his predecessor, who intended to march to Gordonsville, General Burnside proposed, by a sudden move, to throw his whole army on Falmouth, then cross the Rappahannock, take possession of the hights of Fredericksburg, and compel Lee either to attack him in that strong position, or fall back toward Richmond.

The plans of the new commander were inaugurated on the morning of November 8th by detaching Taylor's Brigade from the rest of the division, and sending it as a support to Bayard's cavalry, doing picket duty on the Rappahannock from Beverly ford to Kelly's mills. Regimental headquarters were established near Rappahannock Station. Across the narrow stream was Hartsuff's knoll.

If the boys of the Eleventh had an earnest desire to cross over and drive away the rebel pickets by which the knoll was guarded,—a desire they executed in gallant style one clear, frosty morning, capturing the entire camp equipments and the half-cooked breakfast of the absconding enemy,—it was because the scene of one of their early contests stirred anew the courage that held it, on the 21st of August, against such unequal numbers.

While the Eleventh was thus employed, taking care of the bridge and river fordings, the main army was moving on to Falmouth. Pleasanton's cavalry relieved the infantry on the evening of the 18th, and setting fire to the railroad bridge,—rebuilt by the rebels since its destruction in August,—we rejoined the division at Stafford Court House.

Before the army left Warrenton, General Halleck and General Meigs were in consultation with Burnside. The Orange and Alexandria Railroad was to be given up, and the troops supplied by way of the Potomac; the Aquia Creek landing was to be repaired, and pontoon bridges, on which to cross the river at Fredericksburg, at once sent forward. These were essential parts of Burnside's plans; and to facilitate these movements, a picked force of cavalry under the gallant Captain Dahlgren, cleared the railroad from Aquia Creek to the Rappahannock of all the enemy's pickets.

But when the army reached Falmouth neither was the wharf at Aquia repaired, nor were the pontoons where Burnside expected to find them. The Rappahannock was too high to be forded, and for want of the bridges, the occupation of Fredericksburg was defeated. One day later, the enemy left at Culpeper was seen covering the opposite hights, and confronting us with bayonet and cannon on the south bank of the river.

Burnside's force was composed of three Grand Divisions, commanded respectively by Sumner on the right, Hooker in the center, and Franklin on the left. It was the 9th of December before the several Grand Divisions moved forward into position along the Rappahannock. The purpose of the Federal commander to attempt a crossing of the river was surmised by the enemy, and those Fredericksburg hights, formidable enough in themselves, were terraced from bottom to top with rifle pits, and crowned with bastions. A feint was made, as though the crossing would be effected at Port Conway, twenty miles below, and a large force of the rebels had marched in that direction. The object of Burnside was now to cross immediately in front, and throw his whole united army against the divided army of the enemy.

General Ricketts had retired from the command of the division, and was succeeded by General Gibbons. Gibbons's Division was attached to Reynolds's Corps of Franklin's Grand Division, the other divisions of corps being those of General Meade and General Doubleday. In the order of the battle, Franklin's Grand Division was to cross four miles below the city, and that of Sumner directly opposite Fredericksburg, while the center division of General Hooker remained in reserve.

Five o'clock on the morning of December 11th, leaving our camp near White Oak Chapel, the Eleventh Regiment marched toward the river. The moon was high in the heavens, casting a calm, clear light on all beneath, while the air of the early morning was just cool enough to make the brisk walk at which the men started off impart a gentle warmth to the blood.

Passing through the several regiments formed in line, and waiting to fall in behind us, a group of officers were gathered around their colonel, who was addressing his men:

"Keep your eye on the flag. If the shot and shell of the enemy break your ranks, let that be the rallying point. Don't crowd together. Give room for the balls to pass between you; but always rally on the flag. There will be hard fighting to-day, and every man must do his duty. Do your duty, and a grateful country will never forget you."

The hour,—the foreshadowings of the day,—the full tones of the orator, were all impressive; and the good, round cheers that followed told that the speaker had an appreciative audience.

At daylight the troops rested on the hills above the river. The bridges on which the Left Grand Division was to cross were laid at the mouth of Pollock's Creek, and with little opposition. But Franklin was not to pass over until Sumner's bridges were completed. The opposition to Sumner was fierce and decided. Sharp-shooters, concealed in the houses along the river, picked off the bridge-builders with deadly certainty. Several of our batteries fired occasional shots into the city, but with what effect could not be told for the dense fog that enveloped it. We knew that the sharp-shooters had not been driven from their hiding-places, for every attempt to complete the pontoons drew forth a vigorous and fatal fire.

The plain on which Fredericksburg stands is completely commanded by the hills of Stafford. Toward noon, the fog having rolled away, and the bridges still remaining unfinished, the order was given to concentrate the fire of all our batteries on the city. Riding a short distance through the woods from where the regiment rested, we were at a point affording a full view of Fredericksburg, and the position of many of our guns. Already the town was on fire in several places, and the flames of the burning buildings mingled with the white smoke of the bursting shells.

One could not look upon an exhibition of war so sublime in its terrors without conflicting emotions. When all the time-honored associations belonging to Fredericksburg were remembered,— that a large part of the youth of WASHINGTON was spent there,—that for years it was the home of his mother, and her last earthly resting-place,—we could wish such a fate had not overtaken the old town. But when we reflected that sacred memories and associations were no longer regarded by those who lived among them, and that the glorious past was forgotten in the bitterness of the present, there was a subdued feeling of satisfaction as the angry flames, approaching from different directions, threatened to leave the doomed city a mass of ruins.

One of our batteries on the left had thrown several shot at a large house standing near the river, and from which could be seen issuing the smoke of the rebel picket, as in his concealment he fired upon our unprotected men. The chimneys were knocked away, and a solid shot had broken through the roof. But every few minutes a wreath of white smoke, curling up from door or windows, indicated the presence of the persistent Southerner. The four guns of the battery were depressed to range with the windows in the lower story of the building. When the smoke of that last discharge cleared away, the front wall had fallen out, and carrying down the roof with it, crushed to death every living thing within.

In the midst of this furious bombardment, attempts were made to complete the bridges. But each effort was ineffectual. Despite all the artillery firing, the enemy lay concealed on the opposite shore. Impatient at the delay, and aroused to deeds of daring by the daring of the enemy, the Seventh Michigan, under command of Lieutenant-Colonel Baxter, volunteered to cross in boats, and drive away the sharp-shooters. It was an act nobly done. Rushing down the river bank, and filling the pontoons, the brave fellows pushed out into the river. More rapid than ever came the whistling bullets from the south shore; more vigorous than ever they pulled at the oars. As the boats touched the beach the men leaped forward with a shout, and forth from their hiding-places started the lurking foe. But swift of foot though they were, swifter were the musket balls of those sons of Michigan that struck a score and more of them to the earth, dead or dying.

Ten thousand spectators beheld the valiant feat; and as boat after boat landed its crew, wild huzzahs filled the air. Half an hour later Sumner's bridges were completed; and from right to left the army was preparing to cross the Rappahannock.

CHAPTER II.

BATTLE OF FREDERICKSBURG.

A few troops on the left crossed the river Thursday evening, but not until the morning of the 12th did the entire force move to the south side. A dense fog covered hill and plain. The same ominous silence observed by the rebels during the bombardment of Fredericksburg was maintained. Their pickets slowly retired before our advance, and Franklin's Division crossed the bridges without drawing from the enemy more than a single shot.

There was no longer any break in the rebel line. The troops that marched to Port Conway, in anticipation that the Federal army would there cross, at the discharge of the first gun on Thursday morning, hastened back; and now from Marye's Hights, at Fredericksburg, to Massaponax Creek below, the Corps of Longstreet and Jackson were in well-chosen positions.

Running through the plain on which Franklin's troops formed their ranks, and in a line parallel with the river, is the Fredericksburg and Richmond Railroad. The railroad crossing of the Massaponax was the extreme right of the rebel line, held by Stuart's cavalry and a battery of three or four guns. Next came the Divisions of A. P. Hill and General Early, with D. H. Hill's Division in reserve, forming Jackson's Corps. These troops occupied the low hills in our immediate front, and were joined on the left by Hood's Division of Longstreet's Corps.

Reynolds's Corps, occupying the extreme left of the Union line, was formed with Meade's Division on the left, Gibbons's on the right, and Doubleday in reserve. Gibbons's Division was in three lines of battle—Taylor's Brigade in the first line, Colonel Lyle in the second, and Colonel Root in the third line.

Thursday was spent in laying the bridges, and Friday in crossing the troops and placing them in position. If that marching and countermarching of brigades and divisions had been preparations for a grand review, the enemy could not have observed it with less apparent concern. When the day closed, the pickets of Taylor's Brigade were across the Bowling Green road. Excepting here and there a solitary sentinel, scarcely a Southern soldier was to be seen; but throughout the night could be heard the hum of voices, and the falling of trees, and the dull rumbling of moving artillery. A few indulged the hope that the enemy would quietly slip away, leaving us in possession of the coveted hights, while others, again, argued little good of his sullen reticence.

They were veteran troops that composed the Left Grand Division, and in view of the coming morrow, each man, hugging close his musket, was soon seeking rest for the present and endurance for the future in such sleep as only comes to the tired soldier.

The Eleventh had not greatly filled up its ranks since the battle of Antietam. A few of the wounded had returned to duty; but altogether we only numbered on hundred and eighty officers and men. Colonel Frink and Major Keenan were in hospital. Adjutant Uncapher had lately resigned. Doctor Jackson was absent on detached service. Doctor Anawalt had been promoted to surgeon, and was transferred to the 132d Regiment Pennsylvania Volunteers. Doctors Phelps and Morris were at the hospital on the opposite side of the river; leaving the chaplain the sole representative of the colonel's staff present that night before the battle.

Saturday morning, December 13th, was like the several mornings that had preceded it. A thick haze enveloped the entire plain, and hung before the army like an impenetrable veil. Even our own pickets, though only a few yards in advance of the battle-line, were hid from view by the fog. Toward ten o'clock, the rays of the sun beginning to part the heavy curtains, the lines of Reynolds's Corps, from right to left, were ordered to move forward. Scarcely quarter of an hour later, there was an irregular and scattering exchange of picket shots. Then came a volley of musketry, sharp and compact, and the battle had begun in fearful earnest.

Those quiet hills, no longer concealed by the fog, were seen to be filled with cannon, enfilading every foot of the plain; while from behind the railroad embankment, and from the woods beyond, the double lines of rebel infantry discharged their rifles in the face of our advancing columns. The enemy had now revealed himself, and firing over the heads of our own men, who were ordered to lay close to the ground, a hundred cannon from Stafford hights were turned upon those woods and hills.

An hour of such work as made the very earth to shake, and filled the air with fiendish sounds, was followed by a moment of quiet. It was the signal for a renewal of the advance. The plain was again a sheet of flame, as if ten thousand muskets had been discharged by a single touch. Again those reticent woods were sending forth sounds of death. But the Third Brigade moved steadily forward, followed by the Second and the First, within a few yards of the railroad.

The Eleventh was on the extreme left of the

first line, and moving obliquely toward the railroad, encountered the concentrated fire of the enemy. Three times had the flag been shot down, carrying with it at each prostration the brave heart that bore it aloft. But only for a moment was it suffered to trail in the dust. Others were there to venture limb and life in maintaining it erect in sight of the foe. Before the railroad was reached eight of the regiment killed and seventy-three wounded, including the colonel and five other officers, marked the ground over which we had passed.

Through the ranks of the Third Brigade came Colonel Lyle, at the head of the Second Brigade, charging against the weakened line of the enemy across the railroad, and into the woods in front; while the First Brigade, further to the right, making a similar move, penetrated the enemy's line, capturing two hundred prisoners. The Pennsylvania Reserves, on the left of Gibbons's Division, were equally successful in breaking through the lines of A. P. Hill, and throwing them back on those of Early. Reinforcements were needed to hold the advantage we had gained, and to press the yielding rebels still more furiously. But reinforcements did not come. The enemy was quick to see the delay; and massing his forces at the threatened point, compelled us to abandon the ground so dearly bought, and that we ought to have held secure.

It was late in the afternoon; and falling back across the Bowling Green road, the Eleventh took a position near the bivouac of the previous evening. Darkness ended the strife, and hill and plain, so recently thundering with artillery, and rattling with the sound of exploding muskets, were wrapt in the silence of night.

On the north side of the river, occupying Pollock's mansion, was the hospital of Gibbons's Division. The large tents that were pitched on the lawn in rear of the house, and reserved for serious cases, were soon crowded. But a kind Providence cared for all. Thick matted grass covered the ground, and the mildness of summer was breathed into the air of December.

At no previous battle had there been such perfect system introduced into the hospital. A part of the surgeons were detailed for the operating rooms, while to the others were given the care of the wounded in the tents and out on the lawn. All kinds of supplies of medicines and rations were in desired abundance; and if the percentage of deaths among the wounded of the division was smaller than it had ever been, the reason was to be found in the character of the treatment they received.

To the chaplain of the Eleventh was assigned the duty of keeping a general record of the deaths, and burying the dead. A spot of ground near the house was made sacred as the cemetery of our companions; and with all the care and skill displayed by the surgeons, the performance of our solemn duty was painfully frequent.

"Dig deep, boys," said the corporal in charge of the grave diggers. "The old man that owns this ground won't have much respect for these graves after we leave. He may level them down, but we'll show him that he can't reach the bodies."

If daylight of Sunday morning seemed to come too soon, it was because each one anticipated a renewal of the desperate work of Saturday. During the night, Gibbons's Division moved a mile further to the left, forming in the rear of General Doubleday. The same hazy cloud of yesterday hung over the plain, limiting the view to a few yards on either side. As the morning advanced, the boundaries of vision enlarged, until hill and plain were again in full sight. No change was to be seen, except here and there a tree, denuded of its top branches, or shivered in trunk and limb as if struck by a thunder-bolt, caught the eye. The enemy had relapsed into his former silence; and though once or twice during the day the lines were formed for an advance, none was made.

Rumors began to reach us of a disastrous repulse on the right. Sumner's Corps, that was only to hold the enemy in check, while Franklin, supported by Hooker, endeavored to turn his right, had attempted to carry Marye's Hights, and utterly failed.

The quiet of Sunday was continued throughout Monday. The Eleventh, under command of Captain Kuhn, was detailed for picket duty on the extreme left of the line. Three o'clock Tuesday morning the order was given to retire toward the pontoon bridges; and by daylight of the 16th all the troops had crossed to the north bank of the river.

CHAPTER III.

AFTER THE BATTLE OF FREDERICKSBURG.

"HOSPITAL OF SECOND DIVISION,
"*Pollock's House, Dec.* 18, 1862.

"CHAPLAIN WILLIAM H. LOCKE, of the Eleventh Pennsylvania Regiment, is hereby detailed to proceed to Washington with the wounded of Gibbons's Division, Reynolds's Corps, Franklin's Left Grand Division.

"CHAS. J. NORDQUIST, *Surgeon-in-Chief.*"

Winding round the base of Stafford hights, the long line of ambulances at last drew up at the railroad station. A train of cars was in waiting to convey us to Aquia Creek landing. From thence to Washington the transportation was by boat; and as our coming was expected, the cabin floors of the steamer had been covered with beds for the reception of the wounded. In many cases the bed was only a truss of hay; but it was a softer couch than usually invited the wounded soldier to repose. The transfer of six hundred men from the cars to the boat occupied us until after midnight, and delayed our arrival in Washington until the next day. Surgeon-General Hammond, and a corps of assistants, were at the wharf, to whom we turned over our responsible charge.

The War Department had refused passes to civilians to visit the front since the battle; and the arrival of the steamer was awaited by many anxious friends. How each stretcher that passed over the gangway, bearing a bruised and mutilated form, was closely scanned! Again and again the earnest glance turned away in disappointment. But the looking was not all in vain. In one case the recognition between a gray-haired father and the son who had left his arm in front of Fredericksburg, was so full of affection as to impart a joy to every beholder.

Washington was in a state of intense excitement. Every one demanded to know who was responsible for the move across the Rappahannock; and, as usual, every one placed the blame on the Commander-in-Chief or the Secretary of War. Said a prominent official:

"The nation is tired of the rule of these ignorant pretenders; men who have never seen a battle, and yet undertake to lead an army sixty miles distant, by the click of the telegraph."

Returning to camp a day later, the same spirit of discontent manifested itself. Ten thousand men had been killed and wounded, and yet nothing was accomplished, not even a cannon or a battle-flag taken from the enemy.

With characteristic magnanimity, General Burnside assumed the entire responsibility of the attack on Fredericksburg. But every drummer-boy connected with the army knew of the disappointments to which the general had been subjected, and of the criminal neglect of those to whom important parts of the undertaking had been intrusted. It was also painfully apparent that there was great want of hearty co-operation on the part of leading generals, amounting to positive disobedience of plain and explicit orders.

Franklin was to attack on the left, as that was the salient point, with his largest corps, and then to follow up with prompt and heavy supports. Sumner was to *threaten* Longstreet on the right, and thus prevent him from reinforcing Jackson. If the orders had been reversed, they would have been carried out to the letter. It was Sumner that made the vigorous assault, throwing his whole Grand Division against those unyielding hights, and filling the streets of Fredericksburg with his dead; while Franklin, attacking with his smallest corps, left it to accomplish its wonders of valor without reinforcements, and without proper supports.

Moving back from the river, the line of defense occupied by the Federal army extended from Hartwood church on the right, to King George County on the left. On the Northern Neck, midway between Potomac Creek and the Rappahannock, lay Reynolds's Corps. The camp of the Eleventh was near Fletcher chapel, an unpretending frame building, thirty feet long and forty wide. The disproportion in its width was owing to an addition to one side of the main edifice, an afterthought, we were told, for the accommodation of the colored people, as the church was without the gallery usually appropriated to their use.

The contour of this section of the Northern Neck is peculiar,—a succession of sharply defined ridges and deep ravines. Getting to the leeward of one of these ridges, the quarters of the men were constructed along the sloping side, while the top of the ridge was crowned with the several tents that made up headquarters. There was no formal announcement that the army would go into winter quarters, but taking it for granted that active movements were at an end, the men made themselves comfortable to the extent of their ability. Excavating some eight or ten feet in length and breadth by three feet deep, the dirt was thrown up at the sides, on which a frame work of logs was placed. Using the shelter tents for a roof, an apartment was thus constructed large enough for five or six persons to live in. A fire-place, made through one of the sides, with an old barrel for a chimney, completed the heating apparatus, in perfect keeping with the primitive style of the domicile.

DECEMBER 31.—In two hours the year 1862 will be dead. Personally, we must speak well of the dying. His daily visits have been full of blessings. In camp, on the march, and on the field, a kindly hand has been over us. Nationally, the old year has been one of disappointment. The rebellion, dark and terrible, that 1861 brought upon the country, we were led to hope 1862 would surely end. But it still rages. The hungry spirit of war, though devouring tens of thousands, cries for more. After twenty months of varied fortunes, the enemy is proud and defiant as ever.

JANUARY 1, 1863.—The winds that went moaning wildly through the live-long night the requiem of the dying year, have gone to sleep. Not a cloud is in the sky, while the warm sun, now shining out brightly on camp and field, drives away the frosty breath of winter. Auspicious beginning of the New Year. May it foreshadow to the Nation the coming of its glorious summer! Lieutenant-Colonel Frink, who has been absent since the Bull Run battle, arrived in camp to-day and took command of the regiment.

JANUARY 3.—Reveille at 6 o'clock A.M.; breakfast at 7; dinner at 12; supper at 5 P.M.; tattoo at 9, with drills, guard duty, and dress parade, make up the routine of camp life, day after day. But this dull monotony does not extend to the world without. The President has issued his Emancipation Proclamation, and the slaves in all the States and parts of the States now in rebellion are declared forever free. "Events, not hours, are the measure of progress."

JANUARY 7.—The breaking out afresh of the old wound has compelled Colonel Frink to return home. Lieutenant-Colonel Batchelder, of the Thirteenth Massachusetts, is assigned by General Taylor to the command of the Eleventh.

JANUARY 10.—There was a wedding at Belle Plain Landing this afternoon. Too late to witness the ceremony, we spent the time that the boat was getting ready to leave for Washington in a familiar chat with the bride and groom. It was the same old story over again. They were both natives of Stafford County. The groom had enlisted at an early stage of the war in one of the Virginia regiments. He was with Johnson in the Shenandoah Valley, and at the first battle of Bull Run, and latterly in North Carolina. But a pair of handsome eyes were ever in his memory, haunting him in camp, or bivouac, or battle. One dark night, while doing picket duty on the Edisto, so deep a yearning came over him, that deserting the picket post, and braving the dangers of many long and wearisome miles, he started for Virginia. After various fortunes and hair-breadth escapes by land and by flood, the deserter arrived in Stafford County just at the moment the Federal army occupied Falmouth, glad to find himself secure within the Union lines. Those handsome eyes were now by his side, all his own. One of our chaplains had married him and them, and with a pass to Washington, signed by General Hooker, he and his wife, without a friend, or even an acquaintance, but with implicit faith in each other, were to try their fortunes in the free and glorious North.

JANUARY 12.—Except a small camp-guard, the whole regiment is out on picket. Since Stuart's cavalry passed around the right of the army as far north as Dumfries, picket duty on the left has been something more than mere name. Three lines extend from the Potomac to the Rappahannock, two of cavalry and one of infantry. The last line is within a mile of our quarters. The rebels make nightly visits to King George Court

House, and there is a lurking suspicion that they contemplate the larger game of falling upon our camp or of attacking Belle Plain Landing, from whence the Left Grand Division draws its supplies.

On our way back from the outer picket line, whither we had gone in company with the division officer of the day, we came up with a citizen of the Old Dominion, clothed in regular homespun of the most approved butter-nut color. We found him ready to converse, and so, by our questions, led the way. We talked about his farm, whose boundaries were pointed out as marked by a "wattle fence," inclosing three acres, strict measure. Corn and potatoes were named as its principal productions. Two cows supplied the family with milk and butter—when there were no soldiers about; for the citizen declared that every Yankee could milk a cow as good as a woman, and that since the picket line came so near him, his wife was saved that trouble.

The house was a frame building, of single story and a single room, with door and window in one. And yet so insidious is pride, and withal so exacting, that even there, in that humble dwelling, it demanded a place, and the good man complained of it.

"Times aren't now as they were when I was a boy. Then we spun our own cloth, and made our own clothes. But people have got too proud, sir; they won't have looms in their houses any more."

The result was, that all the chickens they could raise, and the geese, and turkeys, and ducks, were sold in Fredericksburg to buy clothes, which, but for the pride of this later generation, might have been made at home. After he had finished enumerating the sources of his income, the Virginian must have detected the thought in our mind,—certainly it did not find expression,— that, putting all together, the chances for a living were still exceedingly slim; for he added that he *farmed* only in a small way. *He* was a school teacher, and had been such for thirteen years. Here then was a real pedagogue. We were misinformed. They did have that useful person in Virginia, and we stood in his presence. In deference to the memory of other days, we made a low bow, and expressed ourselves as happy at such an unexpected meeting. The pedagogue went on to say that his stock of corn and potatoes, of poultry and pork was considerably increased by the useful occupation of school teaching, as in one or the other of these articles his pupils always paid their tuition fee. It was as good to him as money, he said, besides making it much easier for people who want to "school" their children to bear the expense,—an out-cropping of the same spirit of forgetfulness of self for the good of others, that everywhere animates the brotherhood of teachers.

If we rode on toward our quarters, thinking how many pounds of bacon, or how many pairs of chickens, or bushels of potatoes were concerned in the education of the Southern chivalry, it must have been because their camp-fires, on the opposite side of the river, beginning to show in the darkening twilight, called our thoughts in that direction.

THURSDAY, January 15.—Private Charles W. Adams, of Co. B, died in hospital yesterday morning of intermittent fever. The funeral was attended this afternoon by the entire regiment. We buried him near Fletcher chapel, in a pine grove, secure from the foot of the heedless intruder. Almost every part of Virginia has become sacred to us as the burial place of our companions; and each new grave is as an another reason why the Old Dominion must not be given up. Not only her battle-fields, but her grave-yards and highways belong to the North as the endeared depositories of its noblest and bravest sons.

CHAPTER IV.

BURNSIDE TO CROSS THE RAPPAHANNOCK.

For two weeks Burnside had been making preparations for a second crossing of the Rappahannock. Where the attempt should be made was difficult to decide, and required a careful survey of a large stretch of river shore. The lines of the enemy extended twenty miles above Fredericksburg, and an equal distance below, while every fording of the Rappahannock was defended on the south side by earth-works and rifle-pits.

A point below the city was thought to offer superior advantages for such a move; and fatigue parties were kept at work day and night constructing roads and bridging water-courses and ravines. But as far down as Port Royal, the opposite shore differed little in formation from that in our immediate front. There was the same terrace of hills, and the same broad plain over which we must march, promising, in case of attack, no more favorable results than the 13th of December.

Above the city, both sides of the river were alike, the bluffs running down to the water's edge, and forming a deep gorge for the bed of the stream. The south bank was within easy cannon range, and a crossing once effected, the carrying of the hights could be made by assault, where the advantage of attack or defense was much more nearly equal. United States Ford, ten miles above Fredericksburg, offered the best facilities for laying pontoon bridges, and was the place selected for this new adventure. Great secrecy was observed in all the movements; and on the 20th of January the Divisions of Franklin and Hooker, keeping behind the Stafford hills to evade the rebel look-outs, were marching to the designated point.

The success of the present advance depended entirely upon the celerity with which the several departments of the army carried out the duties assigned them. Five bridges were to be laid, and the pontoons must not be a moment behind the appointed hour. A large force of the enemy was at Port Royal, and the crossing must be made before Lee could have time to draw in his extended lines. Nothing had been forgotten by the commanding general. The road over which each division was to march, where it would bivouac, and where park its wagon trains, were all marked out.

For two or three weeks the weather had been charming, leaving the roads in excellent condition for the movement of troops. But the men had lost all their wonted enthusiasm. A mile from camp, the order of General Burnside, announcing that the Army of the Potomac was again to meet the enemy was read to each regiment. The spirited words of the address did not awaken a single response. A moody silence closed the mouths of officers and men.

Those were dark days in the Army of the Potomac. It had lost confidence in itself, and in its commander, and confidence in the Cause for which it had endured so much. Not only private soldiers, but general officers, maligned every act of the government, and talked of compromise with the South on the best terms that could be made. Men that had stood in their places on every battle-field of the Peninsula, and at Bull Run and Antietam,—many of them bearing the marks of honorable wounds,—were now deserting by scores. Private letters, received from different parts of the North, increased the feeling of depression by their desponding tone, or encouraged desertions by their defiant language.

From Western Pennsylvania one wrote: "Deserters are coming home rapidly, and meet with such countenance and encouragement, that it would be useless to try to arrest them. Any severe punishment there [with the regiment] would raise a storm of excitement and indignation. The war seems to be more unpopular than ever. There is a growing disposition to fight for white men's rights, and to crush the despotic power now so intent on making these subservient to those of the negro. A revolution, peaceable or forcible, is pending in the North."

Whether the successful crossing of the Rappahannock and a sight of the old foe would have aroused the flagging courage of the Federal army, is a question that cannot be answered. But in view of the vast interests at stake, it is well, perhaps, that an experiment so full of peril was not pushed to the issue.

Long before the Eleventh had reached its place of bivouac, the clouds that overcast the noonday sky were pouring forth a drenching rain accompanied by a tempest of wind. On an open field, without even the protection of a forest, the men pitched their shelter tents. Cold and stormy was the night that now set in, whose wearisome and comfortless hours seemed to stretch themselves to interminable lengths. But above the beating of the rain, and the whistling of the wind could be heard the terrible oaths of the cannoneers and the bridge builders, urging forward their jaded teams drawing pontoons and artillery.

Daylight of the 21st came through murky clouds and a drizzling rain. The march was continued within a short distance of the river. What a change in twelve hours! The hard roads of yesterday had sunk two feet below, and the army waded through a sea of mud. Pedestrians and horsemen, by slow plodding, and tedious windings, could barely navigate; but everything on wheels was hopelessly bemired. Thirty-four pounders and twelve pounders; commissary wagons and caissons; pontoon trains and ambulances, were at a dead lock, hub-deep in the mud.

According to orders, the bridges were to be laid at earliest dawn of this day. One hundred boats were needed, but only fifteen had reached the ford—not enough for a single spanning of the river. A hundred and fifty cannon were to be posted along the overlooking hights—not a third of that number was up with the troops.

The watchful foe on the opposite shore was now awake to our intentions. Still Burnside was many hours in advance of any concentration of forces that General Lee might attempt; and throughout Wednesday earnest efforts were made to bring up the artillery and the rest of the bridges. Double teams and triple teams were put to a single gun. Regiments of men pried at the wheels and pulled at the ropes, but the deceptive soil, so easy to penetrate, with its surface of sand, held fast in its under-stratum of clay by a grip impossible to escape.

Thursday morning, new earth-works began to be seen on the other side of the Rappahannock, and by railroad from the right, and plank road from the left, the Southern legions were drawing near the threatened point of United States Ford. There was scarcely any abatement in the storm, and no improvement in the roads. The elements were against us. The time for striking a decisive blow had passed.

FRIDAY, January 23.—Again in camp near Fletcher chapel. Last night we were bivouacked in the woods, half a mile from the river, expecting every moment to be ordered across. To-night, knowing that the winter campaign is ended, the troops of the division are enjoying the log-cabins and clay huts erected weeks ago. So little confidence was there felt in the success of the last move, that the men did not destroy their quarters. There was nothing to do, on our return, but to put on the canvas roofs to make them as good as ever, except considerably dampened by the heavy rain. The order to move back from United States Ford came at daylight this morning. We reached camp about five o'clock this afternoon, having marched twelve or fourteen miles over roads whose like for mud we never wish again to see. One must be here, and tramp through it, to know the effects of a few hours' rain upon the half sand and half clay soil of Virginia. The rebels are in high glee at our failure to cross the Rappahannock, and are giving expression to their joy in shouts and cheers that we can distinctly hear. Perhaps if they knew how many on this side of the stream regard that failure as the salvation of the Union army, they would be less exultant.

VI.

CHAPTER I.

BURNSIDE GIVES PLACE TO HOOKER.

THREE days later in the month of January, General Burnside was relieved of the command of the Potomac Army, and General Joseph H. Hooker appointed his successor. Franklin, of the Left Grand Division, and Sumner, of the Right Grand Division, were also relieved of their respective commands.

The announcement of these several changes was received by the troops with manifest unconcern. Who commanded outside of their own regiment—certainly outside of their own brigade—had come to be regarded as a matter of perfect indifference. There was, therefore, neither regret for the departure of Burnside, nor enthusiasm over the promotion of Hooker.

Desertions were still frightfully frequent—counting up two hundred a day. Those who were successful in evading the pickets, wrote back to camp, for the benefit of others that might wish to leave, minute directions how to proceed — what route to take, where the line was weakest, and where to inquire for help.

The route through Maryland was discovered to offer fewer risks of detection to the runaway, and therefore the most popular. Crossing the Potomac in small boats that could easily conceal themselves in the numerous coves along the shore, once in any of the lower counties of the State, the deserter found himself among friends, where he might change his attire of blue for that of the citizen. When the picket boats were more than usually watchful, and the sort of craft in which the deserter took passage could not come from the Maryland side, the crossing would be attempted on the frailest kind of improvised floats. Many of these rafts, in the darkness of the night — the time always selected for such an adventure — are known to have been run down by steamers; and among the "missing" on the army rolls, whose mysterious fate is still the wonder of the household, are those who thus ingloriously found a watery sepulture.

Besides its bad effects on the men that remained, to lose by desertion at the rate of a regiment a week was no small drain on the material strength of the army. To stop this leak was the first concern of the new commander. A squadron of cavalry was sent across into St. Mary's County, Maryland, with orders to guard well all the roads running north. The picket lines in Virginia were also re-established and extended; but with little perceptible improvement. There was evident collusion between the vedette and the deserter. Even those that were apprehended and brought back, though in several instances severely dealt with, failed to prove wholesome examples to others. The true spirit of the soldier was gone. Politics had supplanted patriotism; and a discontent, as broadcast as it was craven, wasted the efficiency of officers and men.

At last the new feature of a complete system of furloughs was introduced. Two commissioned officers in a regiment, and two privates out of every one hundred men, were granted ten days' leave of absence at a time. Cleanliness in appearance, and proficiency in the manual of arms, were also rewarded by furloughs. The publication of this order was the first successful check to desertion. Every man had now a hope of visiting home, and for the sake of an honorable visit, could well afford to bide his time.

The door once opened, numerous letters were received by the commanding general from the wives of soldiers, asking a short leave of absence for their husbands. In all such cases the letters were sent to the several regiments, so indorsed by General Hooker as to secure a furlough to the happy husband of the interceding wife. It will be no violation of confidence at this late day, nor any detriment to the service, to mention by way of passing, that many of those wives were the veriest myths, with but an imaginary existence, or at best only wives prospectively!

Another measure of General Hooker, not less magical than the furlough system in its good effects on the *morale* of the troops, and his own popularity as a commander, was the generous reinforcement of the commissary department. The blood of the men had become degenerated. They had lived too long on the low diet of hard tack, salt pork, and coffee. Now to Uncle Sam's bill of fare was added potatoes, onions, rice, and molasses—all unknown luxuries;—and the commissary sergeants gave out that in the opening of spring, butter and eggs, and chickens already roasted, would be issued as regular rations! Ovens were ordered to be built in every brigade, and soft bread, of an excellent quality, was given to the men instead of the inevitable hard cracker.

With the Potomac River as the line of communication with Washington—a line perfectly secure from the interruption of guerrilla attacks—and a fleet of steamers, larger than that guarding the North Carolina coast, to convey supplies, the rations were as abundant in quantity as they were good in kind and agreeable in variety. The allowance to ten men for a period of thirty days, as compared with the actual consumption of a family of equal number in civil life, will show that the charge of starvation could not be successfully maintained against the military authorities of that winter.

To ten men in camp were issued in the course of thirty days three hundred pounds of meat; four hundred and thirteen pounds of bread—over two barrels of flour; thirty pounds of rice; ninety pounds of onions; forty-five pounds of sugar; twenty four pounds of ground coffee; ninety pounds of potatoes; four pounds of candles; twelve pounds of soap; one pound of pepper; six quarts of salt; three quarts of molasses; three gallons of vinegar.

A regiment of one thousand men consumed weekly within a fraction of twenty-four thousand pounds of rations. Every man weighing not more than one hundred and forty-five pounds, during the four months of our stay at Fletcher chapel camp, consumed nearly three times his weight in coffee and sugar, bread, meat, onions, and potatoes.

The winter passed through all the variations of climate peculiar to that region of Virginia; one day mild and spring-like, and the next day cold as the latitude of the Alleghany Mountains. But an improved condition of affairs soon manifested itself among the troops. There was a more cheerful submission to discipline, a more hearty discharge of duty; and as each man began to think better of himself, he thought better of the Cause for which he was contending. Well clothed and well fed, the old enthusiasm that carried the army through the campaigns of the former year was seen to return.

Though there were no battles to be fought, there was work enough on picket, and in the details for fatigue duty, to keep all employed, thus driving away the evils ever attendant upon a stationary army. Thousands of men were engaged every hour of the day at the several landings where supplies were received, in unloading steamers and loading up wagons. Miles of corduroy road were constructed, leading from the numerous camps to Belle Plain, Falmouth, and Aquia Creek. Ancient highways and landmarks were utterly ignored in the construction of these roads, and the landowner will find the evidences of Yankee industry where he least expects them, and where he least desires them—sometimes running across the meadow, and over the lawn, and through the barn-yard. For generations to come those old corduroy roads, so different from anything natural to Virginia in their vast expenditure of labor and skill, will be interesting remains of the great conflict.

But with all this work to do, there were many leisure hours; and the chaplain could see the improved spirits of the men in the manner in which they employed their leisure. No church choir, with its accompaniment of splendid organ, ever sent forth grander sounds of music than the evening breezes then wafted from the group of men that used to meet in the clear, open moonlight, for praise and prayer. There was also a closer intercommunion, through letter writing, with the better associations of home, prompted doubtless by the excellent mail arrangements of the army.

Even the recreations of the camp took a different turn, and wore a changed complexion. With many of the men it was an impossible undertaking to convince them that there was any harm in a simple game at cards, only engaged in to pass the time, and where nothing was lost or won. But the game did not always maintain this assumed innocency of character. The morbid state of mind, growing out of the wide-spread discontent, found a momentary relief in desperate venture, in which officers and men alike indulged, and where the only support of dependent ones at home was oftentimes wickedly squandered.

It was the sign of a healthier state of morals, as well as of physics, when the men began to seek recreation in the open air, in trials of physical strength, and in the dextrous pitch of the quoit, or toss of the ball. And when, in the exuberance of their spirits, a delinquent mess-mate was placed on a blanket made taut by the grip of a score of hands, and bounded ten feet into the air, to come down again in the midst of the merry group, only to make a second and a third such involuntary upward flight,—it was always more pleasant to hear the hearty laugh, over these rough out-door camp sports, than to reflect that, for want of the spirit to engage in more manly recreation, many were dissipating body and soul around the card-table or the dice-board.

Not content with its own proper allotment of time, the winter made heavy draughts upon the spring months of March and April. Through much of the former month we were disposed to think that there had been an upheaving in other affairs than those of the nation, and that somehow March had jostled itself into the place of February. Such blustering and biting winds as swept over that northern neck of Virginia are scarcely more pleasant to think of than they were to endure.

One particular night the winds made the camp of the Eleventh the point of their fiercest assaults. Away down the ravines, and over the hills, we could tell by the deep and sullen roar that there was a gathering of those ariel troopers. Waken when we would, they were howling round the tent, straining at the ropes, and striking such angry blows against its sides and roof as to make one wonder whether the next minute would not leave him houseless in the unpitying storm.

At last there was a momentary lull. Morning

was nearly ready to dawn, and we thought the disturbers of our dreams had fled to their secret hiding-places. It was a fond thought! Gathering all their forces for a mighty effort, before the sun should see them at their furious work, a thundering blast struck our tent. The long-strained ropes parted in every strand. The sides, first collapsing, were thrown madly back upon the roof, while unseen arms, catching up the ruined tent, hurled it to the ground fifty feet distant.

The same rude blast that carried away our house stripped the bed whereon we lay of all its covering, and but for the timely assistance of the thoughtful quartermaster, we should have been left to meet the keen morning weather with far less covering than that required by army regulations.

But the March winds, hardening the mud, put a new bottom in the worn-out Virginia roads, and early in April, throughout every department of the troops, there was the usual hurry attendant on an important movement. Discarding the Right, Left, and Center Grand Divisions, Hooker had reorganized his army into corps. The First Corps, under command of General John F. Reynolds, included the Divisions of Wadsworth, Doubleday, and Robinson, to the latter of which belonged the Eleventh.

The roll of the drum and the sound of the bugle called forth from the log cabins and clay huts, in which they had passed a third of the year, one hundred thousand men. It was the opening of the spring campaign, and Hooker was to repeat the undertaking in which Burnside had twice signally failed.

CHAPTER II.

THE CHANCELLORVILLE CAMPAIGN.

Every possible crossing of the Rappahannock had been rendered doubly secure by the industrious enemy, and the game of strategy commenced now was more desperate than ever. Stoneman's cavalry had already started on its perilous journey to the rear of the rebel army, designed to sever all communication with Richmond. Doubleday's Division of the First Corps was sent to Port Conway, and kindling fires along the route gave out the impression of a large force preparing to cross there. Following after Stoneman were the three corps of Slocum, Howard, and Meade. Marching far to the right, and crossing first the Rappahannock and then the Rapidan, these corps were concentrated in the

Wilderness, near Chancellorville, before the foiled and baffled enemy knew where the Federal commander intended to strike his first blow.

Longstreet's Corps was absent from our front, operating in the neighborhood of Suffolk. A part of Lee's forces had been drawn off in the direction of Port Conway, and further to divert attention from the right, on the afternoon of April 28th the First Corps moved directly toward the Rappahannock. There was now no lurking suspicion that the Eleventh would ever again occupy the old camp. Quarters that had been built with great care, and at an outlay of much muscle—in keeping with true soldier policy to destroy what cannot be used—were either leveled to the ground or given to the flames.

A short march of two or three miles, and we bivouacked in the woods until three o'clock next morning. Then continuing the advance, by daylight of the 29th the corps was massed along the river, in front of the Fitzhugh house. Over against us, clothed in the bright green of spring, were those murderous hights and that fatal plain of the last December. But neither the recollection of former defeat, nor the threatening line of rifle-pits occupied by the enemy, abated the ardor of the men. The pontoons were quickly laid, and Wadsworth's Division crossed to the south side, losing in the transit nine men killed and forty or fifty wounded, but clearing out the rifle-pits with a loss to the enemy of twenty-three killed and one hundred prisoners.

Fitzhugh mansion was the residence of Major Norman Fitzhugh, of the Confederate army. The estate contained a thousand acres, and from the broad veranda in front of the dwelling was presented a scene of rare landscape loveliness. The parlor carpets had been taken up and sent to the Richmond hospitals, to be used as substitutes for blankets, but there still remained costly tables and sideboards, elegant chairs and sofas, and rich adornings of damask curtains, and choice paintings. These parlors were converted into a hospital, and amid such surroundings we attended our wounded, while the surgeons spread their amputating tables in the spacious hall.

"When was your master home, uncle?" we inquired of an old servant.

"Only 'tother day, sah. He is in de camp jist across de riber, dah. He can see now all dat's gwine on ober here."

Early on the morning of the 30th, the enemy was seen moving up the river in considerable force, and filing off behind the Fredericksburg hights. Turning our guns upon the column, that came within easy range at the fording of Massaponax Creek, we attracted the fire of several rebel batteries, that for an hour devoted themselves to the destruction of our pontoon bridges. One shell, exploding in the Thirteenth Massachusetts, that lay to our right, killed Captain Bush and five men, and severely wounded ten others.

Occasionally, through the night of the 29th, as the First Corps still maintained its position on the left, a cannon discharge was heard high up the river, indicating important movements in other parts of the field. With morning came a dispatch from General Hooker, announcing that the operations on the right had been so successful that the enemy would be compelled to come out from behind his intrenchments, and fight on open ground, or give up his strongly fortified position. The Union army had an abiding faith that on an open field it must be victorious, and the announcement was received with shouts so loud and long that the rebel column halted in its march, startled by the awakened echoes.

Saturday, May 2d, Fitzhugh hospital was given up to those wounded on Wednesday and Thursday, and the First Corps marched to Chancellorville. Besides sixty rounds of ammunition, the men carried in their haversacks eight days' rations. Thus equipped, those twenty miles were a fatiguing march; but every belching cannon seemed to tell that our presence was needful to success, and the men toiled bravely on. It was midnight when the Eleventh, at the head of the Third Division, reached the banks of the Rappahannock. Filing down the narrow and tortuous road to the river, and crossing at United States Ford, on the opposite side we entered the Wilderness.

Never was a dreary and desolate belt of country more properly named. It is a region of dense woods, not of large trees, but of gnarled and illshapen oak, so thickly studding the ground, which in many places is broken and marshy, that a man could hardly march through it without trailing his musket. But the Wilderness on that night was a scene of appalling grandeur. The bursting shells had ignited the dry leaves, and the red flames, running up the tree trunks and enveloping the highest branches, made the whole country like an ocean of fire.

Up to Saturday afternoon, all had gone well at Chancellorville. Considering the nature of the ground, the troops were in admirable position for attack or defense, patiently awaiting the development of General Hooker's plans. Toward four o'clock a suspicious movement was observed on the part of the enemy. Stonewall Jackson, with a force of forty thousand men, was coming around on our right flank. Whether it was a retreat, or a contemplated attack upon some point of the line, did not at once appear. The column was a mile distant, marching along the plank road leading from Fredericksburg to Gordonsville; and to ascertain its destination, a division of the Third Corps was pushed out on a reconnoissance. It was soon found that whatever else the movement meant, it did not mean a retreat, and another division of the same corps, with a part of Pleasanton's cavalry, was also sent forward.

It was now dark, and falling upon the flank of Jackson, the advance of the Third Corps promised to be a brilliant success. But meanwhile the enemy, acting out the peculiar strategy of Jackson, massed a heavy force in front of the Eleventh Corps holding the Federal right; and without throwing forward so much as a skirmisher, hurled his whole force against that one point of our line. Unable to resist the impetuous assault, and stricken with panic, the entire corps gave way. Scarcely a shot was fired in their desperate haste, and the mass of fugitives throwing away guns and haversacks, and stampeding artillery and ambulances, well-nigh confounded the whole field.

While these terrified troops were thus streaming to the rear by hundreds, others, throwing themselves into the deserted place, were performing deeds of heroic valor. General Pleasanton, coming to the right with two regiments of cavalry, took in at one glance the whole measure of the catastrophe. The rebels were already in rear of our troops, and still pressing onward. "I saw," said the general, "that it was a critical moment. Calling Major Keenan, of the Eighth

Pennsylvania Cavalry, I said to him, 'Major, you must charge into the woods with your regiment, and hold the rebels until I can get some of these abandoned guns into position. You must do it at all cost.' I gave this order to the major because I knew his character so well; that he was the man for the occasion. He replied to me with a smile on his face, though it was almost certain death:

"'General, I will do it.'

"He then started in with his whole regiment of about four hundred men. It was one of the most gallant charges of the war. The major was killed at the head of his troops, but he alarmed the enemy so much that I gained about ten minutes of precious time. I immediately run up my horse battery at a gallop, put it into position, ordered it unlimbered and double-shotted with canister, and directed the men to aim at the ground line of the parapet that the Eleventh Corps had thrown up, about two hundred yards off. I then set to work with two squadrons of the remaining regiment to clear this field of fugitives, and to stop what cannon and ammunition that we could and put them in position. I managed to get twenty-two guns loaded, double-shotted, and aiming on this space in front of us The whole woods now appeared to be alive with men. I had ordered the pieces not to fire unless I gave the word, because I wanted the effect of an immense shock. Presently the rebels commenced leaping over the parapet, and as they did so, I saw eight or ten battle-flags run up the line. I immediately gave the order—*fire!*—and the fire actually swept the men away; it seemed to blow those men in front clean over the parapet."

Sunday morning the battle was renewed on this disputed part of the field. But though the rebels came to the work with great spirit, their attacks showed the absence of the intrepid Stonewall Jackson. In the assault of the night before, either by the shots of his own men or the murderous fire of Pleasanton, Jackson had been mortally wounded, and the hero of so many battles was now far to the rear, in a dying condition.

The same volley that struck Jackson to the ground, killed, wounded, or dismounted his entire escort, except one aid-de-camp and a signal officer. In removing the dying general to the rear, one of the men carrying the stretcher on which he lay was shot through both arms, and dropped his burden. His companion did likewise, hastily flying from the dangerous locality, and but for one of the officers present, who caught the handle of the litter, it would have fallen to the ground.

"Under these circumstances the litter was lowered into the road, and the officers lay down by it to protect themselves in some degree from the merciless hurricane of grape and canister which whistled through the air. They lay in this manner without moving, and in the midst of the most terrific confusion. A few minutes before, the road had been crowded, and now no man or beast was visible except those writhing in the agonies of death. The wounded soldier and his companions were the sole living human beings upon the gloomy scene."*

The rout of the Eleventh Corps lost to Hooker the key of the position at Chancellorville. But the original line was maintained throughout the night, though at great disadvantage, for the purpose of co-operating with the movement of General Sedgwick on the left. The First Corps took position on the right of the army, with Robinson's Division as the extreme right of the corps. Occupying the center of the division, Taylor's Brigade was thrown across the road leading to Ely's Ford on the Rapidan. Excepting the narrow road in front, and here and there a bare place of several yards in extent, this part of the line was a dense woods. Into the deep underbrush, the Ninth New York was deployed as pickets, while the rest of the brigade strengthened the position by throwing up intrenchments. Thompson's Pennsylvania Battery was also added to the force, which completed the preparations for a stubborn resistance, should the enemy again attempt to break through the right.

---

* Cooke's Life of Jackson.

Though the attack of Sunday morning did not reach our immediate front, many of the enemy's wounded, lost in that entangled wilderness, came within our lines and were captured. A half-famished rebel picket, leaving his musket in charge of a companion, crawled a few feet through the brush, where the ground seemed to slope a little, to a marshy spot that promised a canteen full of water. So near were the opposing lines, and yet so completely hidden from each other, that those few feet brought the Georgia ranger within reach of our own watchful picket, keeping guard on the counter slope of the same shallow ravine.

Monday morning was ushered in by a daring attempt, some distance to the left, near the Rappahannock. Discovering a wide gap in the Federal lines, the enemy boldly pushed forward four guns to the brow of the river hill, and discharged their contents into our wagon train, parked on the north side. It was the last fire of that battery against us. Closing up the gap, and before they had time to reload, gunners and guns were added to the list of captives.

General Sedgwick had taken the hights of Fredericksburg, and was reported as marching up in rear of the rebels. As we sat behind our intrenchments, listening to the heavy sound of exploding cannon, we tried to imagine that each distinct report was coming nearer. Later in the day, attention was diverted from the left to the front. So fierce was the fire of musketry and artillery, that for a moment it was believed that Sedgwick had driven the entire rebel army upon us; and that they were determined to make up on the right what they were certainly losing on the left.

When comparative quiet was restored, the Ninety-seventh New York, that had relieved the Ninth New York of picket duty, was in turn relieved by the Eleventh. There was evident uneasiness all along the rebel front; but the frequent alarms throughout the night, when the discharge of a single gun drew forth the fire of the whole picket line, made another attack like that of Saturday night impossible.

Tuesday morning, May 5th, General Hooker's plans had entirely miscarried. Compelled to retire from his first line at Chancellorville by the breaking of the Eleventh Corps, there was an equally disastrous failure on the part of General Sedgwick to carry out the operations assigned to him. Instead of uniting his forces with those on the right, the advantage of the capture of Fredericksburg hights was all lost; and to save his command from destruction or capture, Sedgwick was compelled to retire by way of Bank's Ford to the north side of the Rappahannock.

Hooker now determined to withdraw from

Chancellorville. The movement was to commence on Monday night. But a heavy rainstorm, swelling the river to flood-hight, and making it necessary to take up one of the pontoon bridges to lengthen the remaining two, delayed the crossing until Tuesday. The retrograde march was from left of the line to right. Early Wednesday morning Colonel Coulter was ordered to call in the Eleventh, still on picket, as quietly as possible. An hour later, the regiment was concentrated in the intrenchments, now abandoned by all but the One-hundred-and-seventh Pennsylvania. We were the rear-guard of the army.

Moving quickly back toward the river, with flanks and rear protected by a strong line of skirmishers, of all the thousands of men who had marched over that ground, and the hundreds of wagons and artillery that were going and coming night and day for a week past, nothing was to be seen. The fire that blazed so furiously in the midnight of Saturday, had burned far into the woods, leaving the road-side lined with charred and smouldering tree trunks, while here and there a noble oak, growing among its meaner kind, and more tenacious of life than they, presented in that early morning a heart still glowing with fire.

Not a foe followed our retreat; and by eight o'clock of the 6th of May, the army of General

Hooker, excepting the brave men that lay dead or wounded on the field, had recrossed the Rappahannock.

CHAPTER III.

AFTER THE BATTLE OF CHANCELLORVILLE.

The heavy rain that threatened to carry down the pontoon bridges, and leave Hooker without a way of retreat from the Wilderness, had a damaging effect upon the fine smooth roads over which, but a few days before, the army had marched to Chancellorville. In the depth of the mud, now worked up to the consistency of thin mortar by the troops that preceded us, the rearguard had much to remind it of the muddy march of the last January. But unincumbered by either wagons or artillery, the men picked their way, as best they could, first on one side of the road, then on the other, bivouacking at night two miles above Falmouth.

A depot of rations, found not far from the ford, without commissary sergeant or guard, was seized as public property, from which the men replenished their empty haversacks. Thus provided for an ample feast, after the hurried eating on the battle-field, which is never scarcely better than a semi-fast, the hour of bivouac was heartily welcomed.

Hooker's new line of defense was nearer the Rappahannock than that maintained during the winter, throwing the First Corps still further down the Northern Neck, and bringing the camps of the Third Division some distance below the mouth of Mattaponax Creek. One day later than the rest of the troops, the Eleventh joined the division, once more taking position on the extreme left, and again near the outer line of pickets.

There was no longer any need of winter quarters; but the warm sun, every day growing warmer, suggested a protection from its exhausting heat, which was dignified with the home-sounding title of summer-house. A frame work of saplings, so constructed as to cover the top of the tent and extend some distance in front of it, was overlaid with branches of spruce and hemlock, making a roof that at once screened us from the rays of the sun, and threw an agreeable shade around our canvas dwellings.

Within the shadow of these bowers was discussed the successes and failures of the last battle. In the Union army, where every man had access to newspapers containing such admirable correspondence from every part of the field, all the different points of a campaign came very soon to be well understood and freely canvassed.

It cannot be said that the failure of Chancellorville had any bad effect on the troops other than that it was a disappointment. There had not been enough of hard marching or unsuccessful fighting to dishearten them. A comparatively small part of the army was actually engaged with the enemy, and the larger part that remained idle in the hearing of guns and in the sight of battle-lines, felt disappointed that the whole of General Hooker's splendid army had not been brought against Lee; as in that event victory would have been certain.

The men of the army always spoke of their commander as "Fighting Joe." Playing upon that familiar mode of expression, the rebels now called him "Fallen Joe." But though Hooker had failed of positive success in the Wilderness, he had crossed the Rappahannock; surprised the enemy in his intrenchments; captured five thousand prisoners, and disabled eighteen thousand of his chosen troops. The battle of Chancellorville was accepted rather as an earnest of what Hooker *could do*, than a proof of what he *had not* done.

Not far from the camp of the Eleventh was another of those Virginia mansions, resembling in its generous dimensions, as in its internal finish and outward beauty of grounds, the residence of Major Fitzhugh. The proprietor was in the South, and for two years the fields had been uncultivated, and the garden and lawn suffered to grow wild with weeds, save the little attention given to them by a family of miserably poor white retainers living on a part of the estate.

In two days after our arrival, if one had made a tour through the encampments of the First Corps lying nearest this mansion, he might have found distributed here and there, as additions either ornamental or useful, almost everything that could be carried from the forsaken house. The heavy panneled doors were transformed into camp bedsteads of the most approved style, or made to serve the meaner purpose of a tent floor. In one of our company streets, cool and airy quarters were constructed of its venetian shutters; and though all the glass had been broken from the windows, members of another company, not to be outdone by the inventive genius of their neighbors, carried away the empty sash, of which they built quarters still more cool and airy.

Scattered over the floors, and mingled with broken china and mahogany, were papers and letters doubtless of great value to the family, because of the many years through which they had been preserved. An old ledger told that in the beginning of the present century, the elder proprietor was a merchant, living in Port Royal, on the Rappahannock. The Fitzhughs, and the Lewises, and the Slaughters, and Hedgman, and

Taliferio, were among his customers; in many instances buying at a single purchase of shoes, cotton goods, and calico (supplies for their slaves) to the value of £50.

A soldier, with nothing else to employ his leisure time, gathered a bundle of these scattered papers and brought them into camp. It was a strange coincidence, that two of the letters thus preserved should present the old Virginia merchant in such different phases of character. One letter was from a clergyman, thanking him for his "thoughtful gift" of twenty pounds. The other was from a lady, appealing to him, as the executor of her deceased husband, to deal justly with herself and dependent children.

Our field glasses revealed a state of things on the south bank of the Rappahannock very like to that existing on its north side. There, too, summer bowers could be seen, mingling their dark green with tents bleached to pure whiteness by the spring rains and the summer sun. The pickets were in easy speaking distance of each other, and for a time neither army seemed disposed to do more than lazily patrol the opposite shores of the river.

Then came alarms from the rebel side. There were movements of artillery, and marchings of infantry, that awakened suspicion, and led to the belief that the enemy contemplated a crossing somewhere on the left. Between corps headquarters and the pickets, a line of couriers was established, and the old spirit of vigilance, suffered to sleep awhile after the battle of Chancellorville, was fully aroused.

Toward the latter part of May, the camp was astir at midnight by a report that the enemy was crossing the river in large force. Wagons were packed and moved out to the road, and the troops got in readiness to form in line at a moment's notice. But it turned out to be a false alarm, thus accounted for by one from the south side: "Night before last an incident occurred which exhibited their [our] nervousness. A party of Mississippians undertook to draw a sein in the river near Knox's mills. The Yankees concluded that the Rappahannock was being crossed by the Confederate army, and at once the heavens were illuminated with their rockets—the picket lines were doubled, and their whole camp gave every indication of fearful apprehension. Fallen Joe, however, was permitted to pass the night unmolested by the sein-haulers."

These alarms, far down on the left, were a part of General Lee's plans. With their resources well-nigh exhausted, and hard pressed to subsist the army in the impoverished country where it had passed the winter, the authorities at Richmond again and again demanded of Lee to assume the offensive. Hooker's failure was accepted as the dawning of the propitious hour for such an undertaking, and behind the hills, across the narrow channel, the Southern leader was marshaling his legions for the invasion of the North.

The strength of the First Corps was greatly reduced by the discharge of troops whose term of enlistment had expired, compelling a reorganization of its divisions and several of its brigades. After the battle of Fredericksburg, General Taylor resigned the command of the Third Brigade, and retired from the service. During the Chancellorville campaign, it was under command of Colonel Leonard, of the Thirteenth Massachusetts. In the reorganizing of Robinson's Division, the three brigades that formerly composed it were consolidated into two brigades. The Thirteenth Massachusetts, One-hundred-and-fourth New York, One-hundred-and-seventh Pennsylvania, and Sixteenth Maine, formed the First Brigade, under command of General Paul. The Eleventh, Eighty-eighth, and Ninetieth Pennsylvania Regiments, and the Ninth and Ninety-seventh New York Regiments, formed the Second Brigade, under command of Gen. Henry Baxter.

General Baxter was at the head of the Seventh Michigan Regiment in its charge across the Rappahannock in pontoon boats, on the 12th of December, driving away the rebel sharp-shooters, that for half a day retarded the laying of Sumner's bridges. The gallant feat won for him a brigadier's star. Baxter's fame had preceded him, and when he took charge of the brigade, the men were as proud of their new general as the general himself was proud of his new command. The Eleventh began its march northward with two hundred and eighty-eight men, scarcely a third of the number with which it had marched southward a year before. Some of its numerous wounded had recovered and were again in their places; while many others, including the two subordinate field officers, were still absent.

The vacancies occasioned among the line officers, by death or resignation, were mostly filled. Sergeant-major Arthur F. Small was promoted to adjutant; and Commissary-sergeant Allen S. Jacobs to be quartermaster. Doctor W. F. Osborne, of Westmoreland County, Pennsylvania, had been assigned to the regiment as second assistant surgeon, vice Doctor Morris resigned, before we left Fletcher chapel. The time of service of the 132d Pennsylvania Regiment having expired, Doctor Anawalt was returned to the Eleventh as surgeon.

FRIDAY, June 12.—Between five and six o'clock this morning, the Second Brigade of the First Corps moved out of camp. Three hearty cheers were given for General Hooker as we passed army headquarters. We are now bivouacked at Deep Run mill, on the road leading to Warrenton, twenty-two miles from the point of starting.

The heat of the day was oppressive; and what with their knapsacks on their backs, and the dust settled in hair and eyebrows, the men looked like a regiment of octogenarians, instead of the stalwart Western boys that they are. That part of the road lying between Falmouth and Hartwood church was passed over last spring in our march from Manassas to Fredericksburg. Deep Run mill is a large stone building half a century old. The flood-gates are torn away, and the burrs removed, to prevent its use by the Yankees.

SATURDAY, June 13.—It was nearly seven o'clock this morning before the column got fairly started; and although the rests were frequent, the march was full of weariness. We are halted for the night in a thick woods between the Rappahannock and Bealton Station, on the Orange and Alexandria Railroad. A large rebel force is reported to be concentrating on the opposite side of the river, and the troops are going into bivouac in line of battle. During last August, while the Eleventh was engaged at the bridge just below, holding the rebel advance in check, Jackson's forces passed to the right, and made their appearance on the plains of Manassas. Many express themselves to-night that the same programme is to be enacted; and that the annual battle of Bull Run will be fought some weeks earlier.

MONDAY MORNING, June 15.—Three days ago

we were eight miles below Fredericksburg, on the Rappahannock; this morning the First Corps is encamped at Manassas. General Halleck once said that the great want of the Army of the Potomac was legs. He will be glad to learn that we have come into possession of those valuable appendages, and know how to use them. The march of yesterday, if not the longest in miles, was the longest in hours we have ever made. Leaving the woods near Bealton at nine o'clock A. M., Sabbath, the regiment halted this morning at four o'clock, marching nineteen hours, with only one hour's rest at Broad Run. From Bealton to Bristow the route was new to the Eleventh, and made up the broken link in the chain of marches through this part of Virginia We have now traversed almost every foot of its territory from the Potomac to the Shenandoah, east and west, and from Alexandria to the Rapidan, north and south.

MONDAY EVENING.—Shortly after eight o'clock this morning the march was resumed across Manassas plains toward Centerville. Every spot was familiar, for no less than six different times have we encamped on this ground. Manassas never looked so beautiful as now, clothed in the rich verdure of early summer. But although the green grass covers up many a foul spot, and hides from view the graves, and in some instances the unburied bones of our companions, nothing can wipe out the memory of the terrible conflicts that will always be associated with this sanguinary battle-field. To-night we are encamped on the hights of Centerville.

CHAPTER IV.

THE STRATEGY OF HOOKER AND LEE.

"The service required of the First Corps will be of such a nature that all unnecessary baggage must be left behind," read the order of General Hooker the day before the corps left the Rappahannock.

When General Lee commenced moving it was uncertain whether he was making for the Shenandoah Valley or the Orange and Alexandria Railroad, by way of Thoroughfare Gap. In either event, the possession of Manassas and the hights of Centerville was of vast moment to the Federal commander, and hence the rapid marching of the First Corps to those points. At the same time of our bivouac at Centerville, the head of the rebel column reached the vicinity of Winchester, and from all the signal stations came the same report—that Lee was concentrating a large army in the Valley. Still, the real object of the

Confederate commander did not clearly appear, and then commenced that series of strategic operations between Lee and Hooker that reflected such credit upon the latter.

In less than one week all the corps of the Potomac Army were massed in the region of Fairfax Court House. The Blue Ridge rose between the two opposing generals, hiding from each the movements of the other. The wily Lee, who marched so rapidly at the first, halted his main column under cover of the mountain, sending only a part of his forces to ravage the shores of the Potomac. He had expected to see General Hooker, in his eagerness to protect the threatened border, cross his forces into Maryland, and leave open all the easy approaches to the national capital. But the brave Pleasanton, with his fearless troopers, penetrated the gaps of the Blue Ridge, and revealed the designs of the enemy.

While the First Corps was halted at Guilford Station, on the Loudon and Hampshire Railroad, Pleasanton's cavalry was approaching Aldie Gap. The outline of the country stretching away toward the Blue Ridge was such that, occupied by the enemy, he could hang upon our flank and rear, observe all our movements, and harass us at every step. General Stuart made a march of forty miles in one day to get into this territory, and on the morning of June 21st, in the very act of passing through Aldie, encountered Pleasanton. The fight was long and severe; but the rebels were finally driven back, and retreated through Middleburg. Lee's strategy was now at an end; and following in the wake of Ewell's Corps, his whole army invaded Maryland and Pennsylvania.

On the march from Centerville to Guilford Station, we had an instance of the daring exploits of the guerrilla Moseby, within whose domains we then found ourselves. Two clerks, belonging to the brigade commissary, rode off some distance from the troops to procure a supply of forage for the horses. Scarcely had they left the road over which our wagon train was passing, on their way to a farm-house across the fields, when, in going through a narrow strip of woods, they fell into the hands of Moseby. The party, consisting of the guerrilla chief and a dozen men dressed in Federal uniform, were mistaken for a squad of our own cavalry. Relieving the clerks of the pistols they always carried in their belts, but never used, the prisoners were ordered to remain seated on their horses, and observe perfect quiet. In a little while, placing our boys in the center of the squad, and intimating what would be the result in case of the slightest alarm, the guerrillas boldly galloped out into the road, riding some distance along with the train, and again taking to the woods on the opposite flank.

Excepting to disarm them, not the slightest indignities had thus far been offered, and Moseby seemed determined to convince his captives not only in words, but by actions, that he was not the style of person the Yankees represented him.

"Your papers speak of us as guerrillas, and every murder committed between the Potomac and the Blue Ridge is blamed on me or some of my men. These charges are all false. We are an independent command, to be sure, but a part of the Confederate cavalry, and only kill when we cannot capture, just as your men do. It is my business now to get all the information I can of your movements, and that is what I have been doing to-day. We have gone all along your trains, and from the marks on the wagons, and conversation with the drivers, I know how many corps are moving in this direction, and where you will probably bivouac to-night. If any horses should stray away from camp, or men either, for that matter, they may be among the missing in the morning."

Riding up to a house, partly hid in an apple orchard, another source from which Moseby derived his information was discovered. The farmer met him at the gate with every expression of hearty welcome. Two Yankee soldiers had been there an hour before, to whom he had given dinner, in the hope of getting some news out of them. "But they were a stupid pair," said the farmer, "and only knew that they belonged to the Eleventh Corps."

Moseby retained his prisoners until next morning, and then released them on parole. If he had not kept their horses, thus compelling the clerks to walk ten or twelve miles to overtake the brigade, so far as their experience went, the partisan chief might have received more credit for cleverness than he deserved.

SATURDAY MORNING, June 27.—Although orders to be ready to move were received on Wednesday, it was not until 10 o'clock Thursday that we broke up camp at Guilford Station. A march of six or eight miles brought us to Edward's Ferry, on the Potomac. Two o'clock we stood on the shores of Maryland. Not one single regret pained our hearts at parting with Virginia, and we shall be glad never again to set foot on her disloyal soil.

While the troops were crossing, rode up the river to Ball's Bluff, the scene of that wicked blunder in which the gallant California Senator (Colonel Baker) and nine hundred men were sacrificed to incompetency or treason. Passing through Poolsville, the Eleventh bivouacked at night near the little town of Barnesville.

Friday morning the troops were again on the march, moving toward Frederick City. The roads were in the worst possible condition, soft and slippery. But there were many points of special interest that helped, in no small degree, to vary the weariness of the way. First was the Sugar Loaf Mountain, whose graceful peak was in full sight almost from the moment of leaving Guilford Station. It must be said, however, that it had a grander view in the distance than when we came to climb up its steep rocky sides. After a march of two or three miles along the bank of Monocacy Creek, the troops began the ascent of the Kittoctan Mountain. Behind us was the Sugar Loaf and the country through which we had passed. In front were the South Mountain range, and the gap at Harper's Ferry, where the waters of the Potomac and the Shenandoah meet and mingle into one. At our feet lay Pleasant Valley, intersected by fields of ripening grain and green, waving corn, looking in the distance like a vast garden. The brigade halted last night outside the village of Jefferson. In company with Chaplain Howell, of the Ninetieth, found lodgings in the town, where we are now waiting the coming of the troops.

SATURDAY EVENING.—It was eight o'clock this morning before Baxter's Brigade, in rear of the Division, left Jefferson. The route was up the valley toward Middletown. Passing through the village, we are now in camp in sight of Mount Tabor Church, at the foot of South Mountain, near where the Eleventh marched up to take part in the engagement of 14th September last.

Monday, June 29.—There was such a falling off of startling rumors yesterday, and everything wore an aspect so peaceful and Sabbath-like, that every one imagined, holding as we did all the passes of South Mountain, and guarding all the avenues leading to Baltimore and Washington, that the army might rest some days in Pleasant Valley. But the call of the bugle dispelled the delusion; and at the hour we had appointed to hold religious services, the Eleventh marched to Frederick. The distance was only completed with the last ray of daylight; and yet so charming was the weather, and in such fine spirits were the troops, that the eight miles were made with scarcely more apparent fatigue than has often been seen in a simple change of camp.

At four o'clock this morning the column was again in motion, moving toward Emmettsburg. Everywhere along the route the troops were greeted with demonstrations of delight. It was so new to us, who had always been received with frowns, or a look of contempt, or in sullen silence, to be met with smiles of welcome, that the enthusiasm of the citizen was communicated to the soldier, and for miles a prolonged cheer rose from the moving ranks. Late in the afternoon, the First Corps entered Emmettsburg. One week ago, the finest half of the town was destroyed by fire, certainly the work of an incendiary—

but whether a rebel spy, or a home rebel sympathizer, does not yet appear.

Two miles from town we passed the Catholic College of Mount St. Mary, a large, imposing stone edifice, at the foot of the Blue Ridge, and surrounded by everything in nature to make it attractive. Taking advantage of a moment's halt, a party of three or four rode through the capacious gateway, and up to the main entrance of the building. We were cordially received by the president, and escorted through the several parts of the college. With characteristic hospitality, a collation was in preparation for us, but the column had moved on, and we were obliged to decline. Immediately in the town are the buildings and extensive grounds of the Sisterhood of St. Joseph, the headquarters of the Sisters of Charity in the United States. The regiment is now bivouacked a short distance to the west of Emmettsburg, on the road leading to Cashtown.

VII.

CHAPTER I.

HOOKER DISPLACED BY MEADE.

WHILE the Army of the Potomac was resting under the shadow of South Mountain, on the 28th of June, the supreme command of its forces passed from General Hooker into the hands of General George G. Meade.

Those were days when official jealousies and personal animosities—home-bred traitors—greatly interfered with the efficiency of the army. There had never been anything but bad blood between Hooker and General Halleck. "If the general-in-chief had been in the rebel interest," said Hooker, "it would have been impossible for him to have added to the embarrassment he caused me, from the moment I took command of the Potomac Army."

A garrison of ten thousand men had been placed at Harper's Ferry. There was nothing for them to do; they covered no ford of the river, nor were they of the slightest defense to the Cumberland Valley. Having sent the First,

Third, and Eleventh Corps to Middletown, on the flank of Lee, Hooker proposed, with the Twelfth Corps and the force at Harper's Ferry, to fall upon the rebel rear, destroy the bridges Lee might have laid across the Potomac, and intercept the commerce Ewell had established in grain, horses, and cattle, which he was sending into Virginia in large amounts. But Halleck refused to allow the withdrawal of those troops, and General Hooker asked to be relieved; declaring that he would rather go into the ranks as a soldier, than to stand at the head of the army and be thwarted at a time when it was necessary for every man to be used for the safety of the country and the destruction of the rebels.

On the morning of June 30th, leaving our bivouac near Emmettsburg, and filing out into the road to Gettysburg, the First Corps crossed from Maryland into Pennsylvania, the Eleventh Regiment halting near the house of James Wolfred. Two miles from Emmettsburg, an old tree, growing in a fence corner, was pointed out as marking the State line. As the three Pennsylvania regiments of the Second Brigade passed that boundary, a new class of emotions was awakened in every heart, that could only find expression in the hearty cheers there given for the good old State.

The order announcing the change of commander was here read to the troops. Cut off from all sources of information, the movements of the rebels only came to us in vague and unreliable rumors. Now the reports were more explicit. Lee had indeed penetrated far into the interior of Pennsylvania. Carlisle and York were already in possession of his forces, and a large body was marching against Harrisburg. It was a perilous adventure, in such a moment as that, when every man felt the impending crisis, to remove from the command one who knew so well not only the qualities of his own army, but the designs and purposes of the enemy, and supersede him by another who had all that to learn.

Unaccounted for, and to them unaccountable, the removal of General Hooker was accepted by the rank and file as the expression of doubt and uncertainty, in the high places of government, as to the issue before us; and with an army less patriotic or less intelligent, the effect would have been full of disaster. But there comes an hour, in the experience of every true soldier, when he feels that victory depends not so much upon the commander as on himself—on his own fidelity to duty. Such an hour came to the Army of the Potomac, and each man was nerved for the work before him.

The right wing of the army, consisting of the First and Eleventh Corps, under command of General Reynolds, continued its leisurely movement toward Gettysburg. There was nothing in the clear blue sky of that first morning in July to indicate what the day would bring forth. If anything could suggest peaceful thoughts to armed men, it was the country through which we were passing, so like a paradise it seemed to the forsaken regions south of the Potomac, almost every acre of which had been furrowed by battle, or trenched for the burial of the dead. With what hearty State pride each one beheld the lofty mountains — the broad plains — the flowering valleys of Pennsylvania. No wonder the Southern soldier, remembering to what he must return, was loathe to leave those fair fields.

While General Reynolds was approaching the town, Hill's Corps, of the rebel army, was moving in the same direction from Chambersburg, and Early's and Ewell's Corps from Carlisle and York. Buford's cavalry occupied Gettysburg the last day of June, and on the first of the new month, in a reconnoissance out on the Chambersburg pike, encountered Heath's Division of the rebel advance.

Robinson's Division was three miles to the rear when the first artillery report broke the stillness of the morning air, and rolled away in echoes among the surrounding hills. How that first gun — the invariable prelude to battle — always startles the nerves, and sends the heart on a double-quick motion! But as cannon answers to cannon, the nerves become accustomed to the unusual sound, and the heart comes back again to its steady beat.

It was not known that a considerable force of the enemy was in our immediate vicinity; and the party in front of the cavalry was regarded as an advance guard, sent forward to watch the movements of the Federal commander. Presently long lines of infantry began to develop themselves, and Buford sent word that the enemy was in heavy force. Wadsworth's Division of the First Corps was in the advance, then came Doubleday, and last Robinson. Placing himself at the head of Wadsworth's column, General Reynolds pushed rapidly forward, moving across the fields to the left of the Emmettsburg road and taking position on Seminary Ridge, half a mile west of Gettysburg.

There were other eyes than those of General Reynolds that saw the advantages of that commanding ridge. Scarcely had our troops reached the ground, when Heath's Division, having driven back the cavalry, turned upon Wadsworth, and in desperate charges vainly endeavored to drive him from the ridge. In the first volley from the rebel line General Reynolds fell mortally wounded, dying in the arms of his attendants before he could be removed from the field.

The firing of the first gun in front closed up the straggling ranks of the rear division. Aidde-camps were seen riding along the column, delivering orders to the several commanders, and urging forward the troops.

"Step out lively, men," said one. "General Reynolds has been wounded, and every man is needed at the front."

Those were troops not to be disheartened by disaster, and as they neared the battle-field, a firmer and a steadier step struck the ground.

Nobly did the First Division maintain its lines, inflicting heavy loss upon the rebels, and before its supports came up capturing General Archer and his entire brigade. The death of General Reynolds placed General Doubleday in command of the First Corps and General Howard in command of the right wing of the army. Strengthening Wadsworth's line with the Third Division, Robinson's Division was held in reserve behind Seminary Ridge. While the troops of the First Corps were thus disposed, the Eleventh Corps marched through the town and formed on the right. The outlines of the battle of Gettysburg at this moment began to be seen. Hill was in front of the First Corps with thirty thousand men, and Ewell was approaching our right flank with thirty thousand more.

"Tell Doubleday to fight on the left, and I will hold on to the right," said General Howard to Buford's adjutant, who rode up to tell him of the advance of Ewell.

Robinson was getting into position near the Seminary when Doubleday observed a dangerous gap between himself and Howard. The Eleventh Pennsylvania and the Ninety-seventh New York were at once pushed forward some distance beyond the railroad embankment to occupy the space. A little later, the rest of the Second Brigade was sent forward, and at last the whole division. Not a single regiment remained in reserve, and from left to right the line was enveloped in fire and smoke.

The enemy was striking his heaviest blows on the left, and changing front, Robinson took position on a ridge running parallel with Seminary Ridge, four or five hundred yards further west. It was now noon, and the battle grew fiercer with every hour. Gallantly the rebels came against our front, and as gallantly were they driven back.

"We are Pennsylvanians, and have come here to stay," was the shout that followed every repulse of the enemy.

There seemed to be no end to those Southern ranks, as there was no exhausting the persistent courage with which they continued the attack. Quick as one line was swept away another and a stronger line took its place. Baxter had just repulsed one of the enemy's severest assaults, when a North Carolina brigade veered round for a charge on our right flank. The Ninetieth Pennsylvania and the Twelfth Massachusetts met the North Carolinians with a musketry fire that doubled up their ranks and sent them streaming back toward the left in defenseless confusion. It was our time to charge; and rushing upon those broken ranks with the spirit of men who had everything at stake, the Eleventh Pennsylvania and Ninety-seventh New York brought back with them four hundred prisoners, and the flag of the Twenty-third North Carolina Regiment.

The record of one hour on that ridge is the record of the three hours the troops maintained their position. Now repelling the fierce attacks of a greatly superior force in front; now changing to the right and then again to the left; and when the enemy's ranks were broken, charging upon him, capturing his colors and his men. Shot and shell were every moment lessening the number. But the brave fellows were fighting on their native soil; *they had come there to stay*, and closing up the gaps, they fought on. When the ammunition began to fail, wounded men, carried from the field, passed their cartridge-boxes to the front. More than one volley that shattered through those rebel lines was supplied from the unexpended powder and ball taken from the persons of dead comrades.

Toward three o'clock the First Brigade moved to the front. The battle was now raging with greater fury than ever, and the Eleventh was hurried to the railroad embankment, a short distance to the left, to support Stewart's Battery.

The enemy, coming from the direction of Chambersburg, was gradually extending his line on the left so as nearly to touch the Emmettsburg pike. For six hours the First Corps, numbering in all only eight thousand men, had contended with Hill's Corps, full thirty thousand strong. A new danger now threatened them. The Eleventh Corps, that for some time gallantly held its own, suddenly broke, precipitating Ewell's Corps upon our right flank. Neither courage nor valor could avail against such fearful odds. Overwhelmed in front, and sorely pressed on either flank, the Union lines gave way in defeat and retreated through Gettysburg to Cemetery Hill.

Early in the day the surgeons had taken possession of the Lutheran Church, near the center of the town, for Division Hospital. Basement and auditory, chancel and choir, the yard in front, and the yard in rear, were soon crowded with the brave men of the Second Division, wounded and dying. We were going in and out among these, when the broken and flying battalions of the Eleventh Corps came streaming in from the right. It was a sight never to be forgotten. Crowding through the streets, and up the alleys, and over fences in utter ignorance of whither they were going, every moment increased the confusion and dismay. To add to the terrors of the hour, the enemy gained possession of the town, and firing rapidly into our retreating ranks, shot and shell mingled their horrid sounds with the groans of the dying thus stricken down.

But that retreat was not all confusion. The same noble corps that had so successfully maintained its ground on the left, when resistance was no longer possible, fell back in solid phalanx. And though

> "Cannon to right of them,
> Cannon to left of them,
> Volley'd and thunder'd,"

shoulder to shoulder they marched, rank after rank halting to fire upon the advancing foe, and then closing up again with daring coolness.

In marching through Gettysburg to his position on the right, General Howard placed Steinwehr's Division of the Eleventh Corps in reserve on Cemetery Hill. Twenty-four guns in position, with a strong infantry support, was not only a grateful covering for our retreating forces, behind which they could reform their broken lines, but also arrested the further pursuit of the victorious Southerner, and saved the Federal army from utter ruin.

CHAPTER II.

ARMIES CONCENTRATED AT GETTYSBURG.

Defeated on our own soil, and held in the town a prisoner, never did the cloud that hung over the nation seem so dark and threatening as at the close of that first day of July.

Generals Longstreet, Ewell, and Hill were quartered in the village, indicating that the entire rebel force was concentrated at Gettysburg. But there was no one to tell us of the Union army, whether its other corps were near enough to come to the support of the First and the Eleventh holding Cemetery Hill. Baltimore and Washington were within two days' march; and for anything that we could learn, there was nothing to prevent the entire accomplishment of the bold plan of invasion marked out by the Southern leader.

Elated with the success of the first day, the enemy in town passed the night in riot and feasting. But with the morning of the 2d of July, that dawned as brightly as though no disaster had befallen the cause of Liberty and Humanity, —came preparations for renewing the conflict. Two lines of battle were formed in the streets, and a force of pioneers removed all the fences and whatever else obstructed an easy access from one side of the town to the other. If we could have known that throughout the night one corps after another had been arriving until the line of the Federal army stretched from Round Top on the left to Culp's Hill on the right, we would have accepted that bright morning as the harbinger of final success.

General Meade was laying out a battle line along the banks of Pipe Creek, ten miles nearer to Baltimore, where he intended to concentrate his army and await the approach of General Lee. But the first gun fired in front of Gettysburg decided the battle-field. The Third and Twelfth Corps arrived on the evening of July 1st; the Second and Fifth between midnight and daylight of July 2d, and the Sixth Corps, after a march of thirty miles, between ten o'clock and noon.

"Your troops occupy a strong position at the upper end of the town, on the road leading to Baltimore," said a Confederate captain, who came into the hospital. "But I'm sure they won't be there long."

No word that a single man had been added to the brave few that bore the brunt of yesterday's fight, came to our ears; and when the battle commenced, shortly after noon of Thursday, it need not be concealed that there were painful fears of the issue. Hour after hour passed slowly away without a moment's lull in the roar of artillery and the rattle of small arms. Not until the darkness of night closed in between the two armies did the noise of battle cease.

The fiercest fighting was on the rebel right, in the vicinity of Round Top. Heavy columns of Confederate troops were seen moving rapidly in that direction, and long lines of ambulances had been passing to and from their hospitals all afternoon. The surgeons of the Eleventh, as indeed nearly every surgeon belonging to the Second Division, with all the medical stores, fell into the hands of the rebels when they occupied the town. We could not but think of our wounded, thus unprovided for. But the army,—did it hold its position throughout the fight, or were its ranks broken and scattered, was the thought that engrossed every other.

Later in the evening we inquired of an officer gathering up the stragglers that were hanging about the hospital, how the battle had gone. He was not at all inclined to be communicative, and only in answer to a direct question did he say that we still held our lines unbroken.

There was a faint dawning of hope. We knew that nothing less than the entire Potomac Army could resist such an attack as had been made during the day by the combined Southern forces. And though the contest was still in doubt, it was encouraging to think that our men were not contending against the fearful odds of the first day's battle.

Daylight of Friday, July 3d, the fighting that had ceased with the darkness of the night before, was renewed on the right of the line. During the previous evening, while the enemy was making his attack near Round Top, and the right had been weakened to strengthen the left, Early's forces broke through the lines, and took possession of a part of our defenses.

The Federal battle-line in its shape resembled a horseshoe. It was the inner circle, of which the rebel line was the outer circle, giving to General Meade immensely the advantage of position, in the facility with which reinforcements could be sent from one part of the field to the other. The threatened and broken right was now reinforced, and after a stubborn resistance, maintained from dawn until eight o'clock, the rebel troops, that shouted aloud over the success of Thursday night, with scarcely more than half their number left, fell back to their original line.

Then the firing ceased, and for hours there was an ominous quiet. It was not the quiet of inaction, but like that which precedes the storm. It was beyond human endurance that such fighting as had characterized the last two days could continue longer. And there was a changing of troops and a moving of artillery that indicated preparations for the final assault.

The enemy was boastful as ever. Our taciturn friend of the day before, accompanied by one or two others, came again into the hospital. They had been making observations from the church steeple, and the prospect of success made him more talkative.

"Everything," said he, "is going just as we wanted it. Longstreet has succeeded in reaching a position for which he was manœuvring all yesterday."

It was one o'clock before the silence that had lasted from the forenoon was in the least disturbed; and then it seemed as though ten thousand furies were let loose at once. Shells of all sizes and shapes went howling over the town like demons escaped from perdition, tainting the very air with sulphurous smoke and smell.

On the right and on the left, the enemy had vainly endeavored to pierce our lines. This attack in the center—a point upon which he had concentrated one hundred and fifty guns—was the last and most furious of all.

"If we cannot drive them from that hill we are gone," said a rebel officer.

From the spire of our church hospital we watched those rebel lines moving from the direction of Seminary Ridge to the attack of Cemetery Hill. In splendid order did they come, three columns deep, with every flag unfurled and flying in the breeze. For some minutes not a shot had been fired from the Cemetery, and the daring Southerners, counting largely on the effects of the terrific cannonade, marched with quick step across the several intervening fields. As they advanced nearer our lines, the prolonged shout was heard—so different from our own distinct cheer—that ever presaged a rebel charge. But a sheet of flame ran along Cemetery Hill, and everything was hid from sight by dust and smoke.

It was a fearful afternoon. The wounded men lying in the yard, and able to help themselves, crawled into the house. It seemed safer there, because less distinctly did the unearthly sounds that filled the air strike upon the ear. The rebel troops in line of battle in the streets, crouched closer to the earth, and for six hours we waited as men might be supposed to wait the striking of the knell of time.

Toward evening, when the fury of the battle had spent itself, there was evident uneasiness among the Confederates. No shouts of victory ran along their lines; there were no congratulations among officers and men, so natural if success had crowned their efforts.

Details of men were employed in loading into wagons the spoils of the first day's fight. The few of their wounded brought into the Second

Division Hospital were quietly removed, and by nightfall, scarcely a Southerner was to be seen, not even the paroling officer, who for two days had been busy taking the name and rank of each prisoner.

There was a complacent smile on the face of every Federal soldier; and when one ventured the belief that Lee was preparing to fall back, a brave Michigan volunteer, whose right arm had been amputated near the shoulder, held up the other, as he said:

"This is all I have now, doctor, but for a victory here, I would give this one, too!"

The signs of uneasiness so apparent early in the evening, increased with each hour of the night. Intense interest in the passing events drove away every feeling of weariness; and from a window that overlooked the street there were anxious witnesses of all that occurred. Now a passing wagon train, now a squadron of cavalry, and again the steady tramp of infantry, arrested the attention. Nor did we fail to observe that all these were moving in the same direction—not *toward* our lines but *from* them.

A little after the dawn of July 4th, a small party of Confederate cavalry rode rapidly through the street, hurrying up, in an excited manner, some lagging footmen. Scarcely had they passed when the sharp report of a rifle was heard, followed by another and another in quick succession. Looking in the direction from whence the firing came, a good strong line of Federal skirmishers was seen advancing boldly through the street.

One clear, shrill cheer was given, which, quick as thought, was repeated by a hundred voices. Instantly houses that had been closed for three days and looked deserted, were thrown open, and doors and windows crowded with faces beaming with hope and joy. Many of the wounded in hospital crawled to the doors as best they could, and though in some instances only in feeble strains, welcomed the morning with shouts of victory.

CHAPTER III.

GETTYSBURG UNDER REBEL RULE.

During the three days that the rebels held possession of Gettysburg, for representatives of Southern chivalry they displayed the grossest ruffianism. Stores were broken open and pillaged of their contents, and private cellars robbed to replenish their knapsacks. They came into the hospital, taking from the wounded men shoes or caps, or whatever article of clothing suited their fancy. Two soldiers fought over a sword taken from the side of a captain too badly wounded to offer resistance, and the dispute was only settled by the interference of an officer who, happening in at the moment, appropriated the coveted weapon to his own use.

The quartermaster of an Alabama brigade made himself especially conspicuous on the streets for loud talking and boisterous threats of firing the town, and making of Gettysburg a second Fredericksburg. On the night of the 3d of July, he invited himself to lodge in the house of one of the citizens. True to the instincts of genuine Pennsylvania hospitality, in the general rejoicings of the following morning, the *host* did not forget his *guest*. Two armed Union soldiers were shown into his room, and a few minutes after, the quartermaster was seen on an involuntary march up street, with a captor on either flank.

It had often been a question with those of us who had never seen them put to the test, whether the women of the North were as earnest sympathizers in the triumph of their cause as those we had met in the South. At Culpeper, and Warrenton, and Fredericksburg, the devoted attention of the Southern women to their sick and wounded was marked and apparent. It was something more than the natural expression of kindness that everywhere dwells in woman's heart; and seemed to us to come from sympathy for the *cause*, as well as for the sufferers in that cause.

But nothing we had ever seen could exceed the devoted attention of a few noble women of Gettysburg. From that first dreadful day to the last, they were angels of mercy, always coming at the auspicious moment; braving alike the bullets that were flying through the streets, and the shells that were bursting overhead, and the leering look and coarse remark of an exultant foe, to carry comfort and succor to the wounded and the dying.

Fears were entertained that the rebels might turn their guns against the town, and at an early hour on the morning of July 4th, all the wounded were removed three miles to the rear on the Baltimore pike, where general hospitals, well provided with medical stores and rations—such as the men greatly needed—had been established.

Leaving the wounded comfortable in their new quarters, we went in search of the regiment, from which we had been separated since the morning of July 1st. The army was in the same position it had maintained during the last two days. Robinson's Division was to the left of Cemetery Hill, the Eleventh connecting with Hays's Division of the Second Corps.

When the Eleventh Regiment entered the

battle of the first day, on Seminary Ridge, there were present two hundred and twelve officers and men. By the time it reached Cemetery Hill it numbered only seventy-nine. In the last hour of the first day's fight, General Paul, of the First Brigade, was severely wounded, as were also Colonel Leonard, of the Thirteenth Massachusetts, and Colonel Root, of the Ninety-fourth New York, who successively succeeded General Paul in command. The Eleventh Regiment was then transferred from the Second Brigade to the First Brigade, and Colonel Coulter placed in command.

Taking position on Cemetery Hill, on the evening of July 1st, the three Divisions of the First Corps were arranged with Wadsworth on the right center, Robinson on the left center, facing toward the Emmettsburg road, and Doubleday in rear of Robinson. The First Corps was under command of General Newton, Captain of Engineers in the three months' campaign, and under whose guidance the army of General Patterson, with a vanguard from the Eleventh Regiment, made its first crossing of the Potomac.

Longstreet's attack, in the vicinity of Round Top, was on the afternoon of July 2d. The lines of the gallant Third Corps, that bravely met the furious assault, first bending beneath the heavy pressure thrown against them, at last broke, and were driven in. Then a part of the

Second Corps, sent to the help of the Third, was also compelled to fall back. Generals Hancock, of the Second, and Sickles, of the Third Corps, were both wounded and carried from the field. General Newton ordered the Second and Third Divisions of the First Corps into the gap. The Third Division, taking the lead, were ordered to charge the rebels still coming on, and threatening to turn our left flank. A moment later the order was countermanded. But it was too late. The cheers had been given, and the ranks were flying across the field. The four guns lost by Hancock were recaptured, besides two other guns and a large number of prisoners taken from the enemy.

"When my men returned," said Doubleday, "they apologized to me for not halting at the command, and I accepted the apology."

Friday morning, Robinson's Division was massed in rear of Cemetery Hill, ready to push forward to the support of the Twelfth Corps, then engaged with the enemy near Culp's Hill,— the same enemy encountered the previous night by Wadsworth's Division and the single brigade of General Green, of the Twelfth Corps.

The troops that were seen from the church spire, on the afternoon of July 3d, moving up in such splendid order to the attack of Cemetery Hill, were the Divisions of Pickett, Wilcox, and Pettigrew.

"I anticipate an attack on the Cemetery from the enemy's forces massed in the town," said General Meade to Robinson. "Place your troops so that if our line gives way you can strike the enemy on the flank."

The division moved out at the moment that the rebels turned one hundred and fifty guns upon our position. "Never were troops exposed to such a fire of shot and shell," said General Robinson, "and yet the movement was made in perfect order, and with little loss."

For some minutes our guns had remained quiet, the cannoneers laying close to the ground, watching the steady approach of the enemy, and awaiting the word to send their double charge of grape and canister into those compact columns. At last it came; and the quick discharges from Captain Ricketts's Battery, and the guns of the Eleventh Corps, tearing great rents in Pettigrew's ranks, sent them back a broken and disorganized mass. Wilcox fared no better. But Pickett's Division, living through all the terrible storm, was moving onward with furious threatening against our left.

Robinson's Division, ordered to the threatened point, moved over ground plowed in every square inch by exploding shells, and taking position on the right of the Second Corps, the First Brigade met the shock of Pickett's wonderful charge, and shared in the last repulse of the sanguine Southerner.

Ten of the Eleventh Regiment were counted among the dead that lay on Seminary Ridge and in front of Cemetery Hill. Sixty were seriously wounded, and sixty taken prisoners. On the evacuation of the town by the rebels many of the latter returned to the regiment; while others, carried to Richmond, lingered days and weeks in Libby prison and on Belle Island, to die at last of disease or starvation.

In every former battle there were to be found those always ready to evade duty; men who seemed to have a greater fondness for the wagon train or the hospital than a place in the ranks. But there were no stragglers at Gettysburg. "No soldiers ever fought better, or inflicted severer blows upon the enemy."* "Not a single case of faltering came to my notice."†

As illustrating the spirit that ruled the hour, was a private in Co. K, who had been with the Eleventh ever since its organization. Mentally defective to a slight degree, Lacock was never intrusted with a gun; but strong as an ox, he was placed among the pioneers, and armed with a spade. Catching the enthusiasm of the men around him, with his spade on his shoulder, John

---

* Gen. Robinson's Report.
† Col. Coulter's Report.

bravely marched with the regiment, not only in the thickest of the first day's fight, but during the second and the third day. Passing unharmed through all, it deserves to be told that the sturdy fellow held fast to his spade.

In Pickett's charge, two of his three brigade commanders were killed, and the other seriously wounded. Fourteen field officers were killed, and only one out of the whole number escaped unhurt. Two-thirds of his men were killed, wounded, and captured, and of the thirteen standards that his regiments carried on that afternoon, only two did not fall into our hands.

CHAPTER IV.

THE RETREAT AND THE PURSUIT.

EMMETTSBURG, July 6.—Yesterday morning the pickets sent in word that the rifle-pits and breast-works in front had been abandoned during the night, and that the rebels were in full retreat. The entire army was at once put in motion. We are bivouacked on Wolfred's farm, near our resting-place of last Tuesday, thus far on the way in pursuit of the running foe. Never has this army come out of a battle in such high spirits. Every man is enthusiastic at the hope of overtaking Lee before he crosses the Potomac, and at once and forever finishing up the rebellion. The Eleventh is under command of Captain Bierer, of Co. C, the colonel having been left behind wounded.

Our friends of the Ninety-seventh New York have just received Colonel Wheelock with three uproarious cheers. The colonel was taken prisoner during the first day's fight, but escaped from his captors night before last. He reports great demoralization throughout the enemy's ranks, and the road strewed with his wounded and stragglers. Our cavalry is following close in the rear. Couch and the Pennsylvania militia are on the right flank, cutting off almost every possible chance of Lee's escape.

Foot of South Mountain, July 8.—Four o'clock on the morning of the 7th, we left our bivouac at Emmettsburg, marching briskly along the Frederick pike. Crossing Kittoctan Mountain some time in the afternoon, we turned off the smooth pike into a narrow country road that brought us to another, and, as we thought, the steepest part of the same range of hills. General Robinson halted the division on the mountain summit, and after half an hour's rest, massed the several regiments and read to them the dispatches from Washington, announcing the surrender of Vicksburg to Gen. Grant.

"Soldiers, the news of your glorious victory at Gettysburg has been telegraphed to the West. I propose three cheers for Grant and his army, feeling assured that while we shout their victories from this mountain top, they are shouting our victory along the Mississippi Valley."

Three o'clock this morning we were again under march, and are once more bivouacked at the foot of South Mountain, in sight of Mount Tabor church.

JULY 9.—Late last evening, with not more than an hour's rest after a long and severe march, Robinson's Division was ordered to cross South Mountain, and take position to the right of Turner's Gap. General French has destroyed the enemy's pontoon bridge at Williamsport, and it was thought Lee might make a desperate effort to secure this pass in order to protect his flank. In this position, a short distance below the old Mountain House, we have been resting all day, while one continuous stream of artillery, infantry, and cavalry has been passing along the National pike, in the direction of Hagerstown. Everything reminds one of last September. Over this same mountain, and along this same road, and with much of the same spirit, we were then, as now, in close pursuit of the rebels. Let us hope for a more decisive issue.

BENEVOLO, July 10.—The division left South Mountain at six o'clock this morning. Wonderful indeed are the recuperative powers of the soldier. Footsore and tired, when the hour for bivouac comes, if the sky should be overcast, and rain threaten, he *may* take time to pitch his shelter tent; but more frequently, with only a blanket wrapped around him, he stretches himself on the ground, to sleep soundly and well.

> "Weariness
> Can snore upon the flint, where resty sloth
> Finds downy pillows hard."

Next morning the fatigue of the former day is forgotten, and with spring and elasticity in his step, he takes his place in the ranks, ready to move forward at the word of command. So the few hours of rest enjoyed by our boys yesterday imparted renewed vigor, and when they started off this morning it was on a quick and steady march. We passed through Boonsborough and on toward Hagerstown, following after the rebels, with whom we have been skirmishing all day.

Three or four houses and a small, neat church make up this little town of Benevolo. Our troops are in line of battle about half a mile to the front, in expectation of an engagement.

"We had hard work to save our church from destruction the other day," said a gentleman living on the adjacent lot. "A party of rebels determined to tear out the upper corner for the sake of the money they were told that we always place under the corner-stone of our churches. I suppose they would have persevered in their attempt had not our cavalry come up so near behind them."

All the vandals are not found in the ranks of the Southern army. After the battle of Cedar Mountain a party of Irish soldiers visited a beautiful frame church, that graced the north slope of the hill, and forced out the corner-stone, not for the money beneath it, but for the bottle of whiskey which they avowed was always sealed up in the corner-stone of churches.

FUNKSTOWN, July 12.—Early this morning, the enemy disappearing from our front near Benevolo, the whole of the forces moved forward. Every day we have been coming nearer to the main body of the rebel army. Lee is now in line of battle across Antietam Creek, with his left resting on Hagerstown, and his right extending to Downiesville. The different corps of the army are coming up in quick succession, and going into position. The First and Sixth Corps are on the right, the Fifth and Third Corps in the center, and the Second and Twelfth Corps on the left. Buford reports that the enemy has a strong position, which he is fortifying and rendering stronger. Our troops are in excellent spirits. The hard rains of the two or three days past have swollen the Potomac almost to flood-hight, and with his bridges destroyed, there is every prospect that the most of Lee's army will fall into our hands.

The citizens of this village are not a little alarmed that the two hostile armies should have met so near their doors, while they look on with wonder at preparations making here in the rear for the battle in the front. The three churches of the place are fitted up for hospitals. Medical wagons are unpacked, and the amputating tables set up, and as our battle line is in easy sight on the other side of Antietam Creek, ambulances to bring off the wounded are all in readiness to proceed to the field on the discharge of the first gun.

When we came to count noses, after leaving Gettysburg, Dixie, one of our colored servants, was missing. He is a boy about sixteen years old, the former slave of a doctor living in Fauquier County, Va., but always regarded at headquarters as the personal property of the chaplain. Dixie was last seen on Seminary Ridge a moment before the troops fell back, and no one could tell what became of him. He was given up for lost, when but a little while ago he walked into the hospital, attired in a full suit of rebel gray, even to the cap. It is a wonder that some of the provost guards did not arrest him as a genuine "Johnnie," for he looks quite as white as many we have taken from their ranks, excepting, perhaps, that his hair is a little more inclined to curl.

This is his story. Lost in the confusion of the first day's fight, Dixie found himself among the rebels. "Dey war all too busy a-fightin' to mind a darkie. So I slid down into a deep gully washed out on de side of a hill by de rain, and laid quiet till it was nearly dark. Den I come out and looked around. Heaps ob dead war lyin' dar on de ground, and so many ob de wounded was cryin' for water. I 'spected if de rebels catch me wid dem blue clothes on dey would take me back to Virginny. I seed a dead man jist t'other side ob me wid dese clothes on. I took dem off de man and slipped into 'em; den I went back to my hidin' place, and lay till mornin'. Arter awhile, a company came out to gadder up de wounded and bury de dead. Dey hollered at me:

"'Hallo, darkie, where do you belong?'

"I told dem I b'long to an officer in de Second Virginny, and had lost my reg'ment. Byme-by de firin' commenced agin, and I went back and laid low in de hole."

Knowing the keenness of Dixie's appetite from an experience running through many months, we interrupted him in his story to inquire where he got his rations.

"Dar was plenty ob habersacks laying about full ob hard tack, and I helped myself."

"How did you know when to come away from there?"

"I kept near de party dat was buryin' de dead. One evening a captain came an' told 'em to go to dar reg'ment—dat de troops was gwine to leave Gettysburg. I went a little way wid 'em, until I seed a chance to go to one side, and get back to my hole in de ground. Next mornin' eberybody was gone. Presently some ob our own men come out dar, and tell me which way de corps was marchin'. I'se been gainin' a little on it ebery day since."

NEAR WILLIAMSPORT, July 14.—After all our marching and planning, the rebels have eluded us. With his army little better than a mob, General Lee has succeeded in making a safe passage of the Potomac. Where his capture was regarded with so much certainty, there could not be anything else than great disappointment at this unexpected result. Citizens along the route to this place tell us that if an attack had been made yesterday thousands of rebels would have fallen into our hands, as the troops then on this side of the river were entirely without artillery, and with but little ammunition. Another of those mistakes has been made so fatal to the permanent success of the Potomac Army. Never were men more eager to be led forward, and never did an opportunity, to all appearances, so favorable for utterly routing Lee present itself. If to that council of war, said to have been held night before last, where all the generals present, excepting Wadsworth (representing the First Corps in the temporary absence of General Newton) and Howard, voted against an attack, General Meade had invited representatives from the rank and file of his army, a different result would have been reached. Nothing now remains but to follow the enemy through Virginia, where the advantage of roads, position, and everything else will be in his favor.

CHAPTER V.

MARCHING THROUGH LOUDON VALLEY.

The halt of the army at Williamsport, after it was definitely ascertained that Lee had crossed the river and was pushing toward Martinsburg, was only a few hours.

The Federal commander was much in the same position that McClellan found himself after the battle of Antietam. The question of pursuing the enemy through the valley of Virginia was then thoroughly discussed; and because of the difficulty of supplying an army with only a single track railroad from Harper's Ferry to Winchester, it was pronounced impracticable. General Meade therefore determined to adopt the plan of the previous year, which was to move upon the enemy's flank through Loudon Valley. Pontoon bridges were ordered to be thrown across the Potomac at Berlin, and on the morning of July 15th the entire army was moving toward that point.

CRAMPTON'S GAP, July 15.—Crampton's Gap is the most southerly pass of the South Mountain. Here we are encamped for the night, after a march from Williamsport of twenty miles. Leaving the column still moving onward, and riding off to the right of Keedysville, we paid a visit to walnut grove, our camping ground of last fall, and to the house of Mr. Rowe. There were mutual congratulations over the victory of Gettysburg, and mutual regrets that Lee should have escaped. A large force of the enemy marched down the river and crossed at Shephardstown. They gave a pitiable account of the condition of the rebel army; and in such haste were they to have the Potomac between themselves and the Yankees, that they did not even stop to plunder —a thing they dearly love to do, and in which they are completely versed.

On our way back to the regiment we passed over the right of Antietam battle-field. Prolific nature and industrious man have greatly changed the face of the ground during the past few months. Tall grass waves over spots once worn bare by the friction of cannon wheels, or the tread of shifting infantry. The broken fences have been set up in the old lines; while the Dunkard church—around whose doors was the fiercest fighting between Hooker's Corps and Stonewall Jackson, and whose walls were pierced with many shells—still bearing the scars of battle upon it, has been refitted, and resounds again with prayer and praise.

During the fiercest fighting of September 17th, near this spot, a soldier, mortally wounded, was carried by his companions. They laid him at the foot of a tree, and were vainly endeavoring to stop the blood flowing from a gaping wound.

"It's all of no use," said he. "I am dying." With some effort he drew from his pocket a Bible, and handing it to the nearest friend, said: "Give this to my wife. Tell her that I died trusting in Christ as my Saviour; and that this book has been to me a comfort and solace in all the trials of soldier-life. To my children I send a father's last blessing." Still addressing his friend, he added, "Now pray with me." And there, on the battle-field, amid bursting shell and flying shot, those men knelt down, and commended their companion to the care of God. Afterward he said, "Sing." There was a moment's pause, as though one was waiting for the other, when the dying man commenced, faintly—

> "Jesus, lover of my soul,
> Let me to thy bosom fly."

But before the verse was ended the pulse had ceased to beat, and the tongue of the singer was silent in death. Did the victorious general, falling at the head of his charging column, die more heroically than this nameless and unknown soldier? No, not unknown! To-night he marches the streets of the New Jerusalem, the loved companion of its blessed inhabitants.

A sad fatality has attended the Hoffman family, whose house was occupied as brigade hospital during the battle. Returning to their home after the last of the wounded were removed, in a few days a malignant fever carried off one and another, until of father, mother, two daughters, and an equal number of sons, not one remains.

WATERFORD, VA., July 18.—For the third time we crossed the Potomac, and are again in Virginia. The pontoon bridges were laid at Berlin last night, and the crossing commenced early this morning. There is no enthusiasm among the men; nor will they be persuaded that we shall be more successful in the pursuit of Lee south of the Potomac than we were north of it.

The district surrounding Waterford is the most loyal of Virginia. Captain Steel's Rangers, a body of troops that often measure arms with Moseby's guerrillas, are from this neighborhood. The gallant captain and a part of his men arrived in town to-night, to the evident gratification of the citizens.

HAMILTON, July 19.—We marched eight miles to-day from Waterford to Hamilton. There is an air of quiet repose about these little towns, nestled in this verdant valley, quite refreshing. Why a town should be built just in the particular locality you find it, would be hard to tell. But the suddenness with which you come upon them, and the unexpected places in which they are to be found, adds all the more to their beauty and attractiveness. Another thing is also to be observed—that every mile we make southward marks a change in the sentiments of the people. Loyalty to the Government increases as you move toward the Potomac, and decreases as you recede from it. The hospital steward of the Ninetieth New York asked permission of the lady of a house, near where we halted, to bring into her room, until the ambulances came up, a sick man, who gave out on the march.

"No," was the curt reply. "Sick or well, no Yankee shall come into my house with my consent."

The sick man was taken in and made comfortable, without the consent of the amiable madam.

MIDDLEBURG, July 20.—As early as four o'clock this A. M. the Eleventh Regiment, leading the First Corps, was moving in the direction of Middleburg, sixteen miles distant from Hamilton.

The march was drawn out until late in the afternoon.

One thing that has greatly relieved our journeys through this part of Virginia, is the abundance of good water. Loudon Valley is the great highway to the ocean for all the streams rising in the Blue Ridge. Clear running water met us all day long at every step, and in one instance offered no little impediment to our progress.

A large stream, that flows into the Potomac, under the domestic name of Goose Creek, where the main road to Middleburg crosses it was once spanned by a substantial stone bridge. But our friends from Richmond, after they themselves had made a safe passage, turned round and destroyed it. Nothing was left for us but to ford Goose Creek, as we had more than once forded other creeks. With the water three and a half feet deep, the crossing was not made without the occurrence of many ludicrous scenes. Some of the men were content to remove only shoes and stockings; others doffed coat and breeches; while many more, discarding every particle of Uncle Sam's uniform, excepting the cap, undertook the transit in the uniform provided by nature. One missed his footing and became an involuntary immersionist. Another let fall the bundle of clothes he seemed most anxious to keep dry; or, stepping into a treacherous hole, for a moment man and bundle both disappeared. Escaping all the perils by water, the first step up the slippery bank was often a false step, letting down the too confident soldier into a bed of soft mud, or sliding him back into the stream. All these mishaps were signals for expressions more witty than polite: and for bursts of laughter more vociferous than musical.

Our present encampment is in sight of the handsome town of Middleburg. The citizens of the place showed their utter contempt for us by retiring to their houses and closing every door and window. Not a white person was to be seen, and but for the negroes that met us on the street corners, we might have thought the town uninhabited.

Another reason for the unusual quiet of Middleburg has just been discovered. Between one and two hundred rebel wounded from the field of Gettysburg are quartered in the town, and it was very desirable that they should remain undiscovered by the prying and curious Yankees. Liberal supplies of stores, stolen from Maryland and Pennsylvania, were also left for their subsistence. General Newton has very properly ordered this supply to be considerably lessened. It may be gratifying to some loyal Pennsylvania farmer to know that a part of his smoked hams, recaptured from the rebels, is now filling the haversacks of Pennsylvania soldiers.

JULY 23.—Just as we had ceased to wonder at

our long delay in one place in the pursuit of Lee, the bugle sounded the assembly, and at seven o'clock yesterday evening the march was resumed, Robinson's Division in rear of the corps, and the Eleventh in rear of the division. We had not proceeded more than a mile or two before it was known that guerrillas were following after our wagon train, and fears were entertained of an attack. The regiment halted along the road-side until the wagons passed, when we fell in behind them, thus marching until daylight this morning. After a rest of three hours at White Plains, the column moved on to Warrenton, where we are now in camp, with the prospect of remaining for some days. Our friends— the Fosters—are still at the Plains. But a shadow has fallen upon the hearth-stone. The son, a lieutenant in Major Moseby's Partisan Rangers (so they speak of Moseby and his men), is now a prisoner in Washington, confined in the Old Capitol.

BEALTON STATION, July 26.—All our pleasant imaginings of a quiet time at Warrenton were suddenly dispelled yesterday morning by orders to march. "What does all this mean?" "Where are we going?" were questions asked in no amiable mood. "Our supplies have been cut off at Catlett's Station," said one. "Bragg has reinforced Lee, and the rebels are coming down the Manassas Gap Railroad to Bull Run," said another. Toward noon we reached Warrenton Junction, to find that the supplies were not cut off, and that Lee had no intention of coming to Bull Run. It was satisfactorily explained that we had moved to the railroad junction, to be nearer our base of supplies. Wagons were again unpacked, tents pitched, and arrangements made for a long stay at Warrenton Junction. Near sundown, when we were listening for the bugle to sound retreat, it sounded to march. "Where now?" all were ready to ask. "It is only a change of camp to get a better supply of water." But an order assigning the Eleventh Regiment as rear-guard of the wagon train, was the end of all further speculation. A little after midnight we bivouacked at Bealton Station, where we are awaiting further orders.

JULY 26, Evening.—The only move we have made to-day was to join the rest of the brigade, from which we were separated last night by the wagon train. With our tents pitched, we find ourselves comfortably located, and will accept Bealton Station as the resting-place we have been looking for since we left Warrenton.

MONDAY, July 27.—A train of cars came from Alexandria, loaded with material for building the bridge at Rappahannock Station. One brigade of our division is now at the river, three miles distant. It seems to be the purpose to cross at the earliest practicable moment. But that cannot be for several days to come. Our men are sadly in want of clothing, and many of the troops that have joined us since the last battle are unarmed. All these wants must be supplied before we can advance.

FRIDAY, July 31.—During the last four days Bealton Station has grown into quite a business center. Half a dozen trains arrive daily, loaded with all kinds of army supplies. New clothing and equipments have been issued, and the rest enjoyed since Sabbath has had an improving effect upon the men.

While the First Corps was marching through Loudon Valley, in the rear and on the flank of the army, the other corps had been pushing rapidly forward toward Manassas Gap, in the hope of intercepting Lee at Front Royal. The Third Corps reached the Gap on the 23d of July, the day of our halt at Middleburg. We were then in advance of the rebels, and it was expected that the error committed at Williamsport would be atoned for at Manassas Gap. But instead of attacking with his usual earnestness, General French wasted a whole day in reconnoitering the position. When the Gap was at last forced, it was only to find that he had been baffled by a small rear-guard, General Lee, in the mean time, making good his escape. Scouts report that the Southern army is now in position near Culpeper, while our own lines stretch along the north bank of the Rappahannock, from Kelly's Ford on the left to Sulphur Springs on the right. A large cavalry force, under command of General Buford, is collecting here, which looks as if the pursuit of Lee was still to be kept up.

SATURDAY, August 1.—Across the Rappahannock. At five o'clock this morning we left Bealton Station and marched to the river. As soon as the pontoon bridges were laid, the cavalry crossed in force, and afterward Robinson's Division of infantry. The Eleventh was at once placed in position on the knoll next to the river, and every man set to work throwing up intrenchments. The cavalry continued the march toward Culpeper, in which direction there has been severe fighting all afternoon, but with what result we cannot tell.

SUNDAY, August 2.—The warmest day of the season; not a breath of air stirring; not a tree to protect the men from the scorching rays of the sun. All work on the intrenchments suspended because of the heat.

The fight of yesterday was a serious affair. Encountering a force of rebel cavalry at Brandy Station, Buford opened the engagement, pressing the enemy back near to Culpeper, when a heavy reinforcement of infantry fell upon the Federal flank, compelling a retreat to Brandy Station, with considerable loss. The entire rebel army is concentrated in the neighborhood of Culpeper; and it is possible that the fight may be renewed at any hour. No troops are here but those belonging to the First Corps. We must make our intrenchments count in the place of men.

Monday, August 3.—The railroad bridge across the river was completed to-day, a locomotive passing over to try its strength. Everything is quiet on the plain below. Our position is the same as yesterday, excepting that the Eleventh was moved further to the front this afternoon. We are now on the hill occupied during the engagement of last August, and which our boys claim especially as belonging to them. Here are the breastworks thrown up nearly a year ago. They have been strengthened this afternoon, and if the enemy should attack us again in this place, he will have a greeting quite as warm as on the former occasion.

Tuesday, August 4.—We had about made up our minds that an opportunity would be afforded to test the strength of our intrenchments and our ability to hold them. The day passed quietly enough until two o'clock P.M., when the discharge of a cannon out in front brought every man to his feet. A few steps from our tent and the whole plain was visible. The rebels had planted a battery on the crest of a slight eminence, a mile distant, and opened a rapid fire on the pickets, at the same time they advanced a strong line of skirmishers. For a time everything looked as though a general engagement was inevitable. Our guns replied to the enemy; the cavalry formed in line of battle on the plains, and the Ninetieth Pennsylvania reinforcing the Eleventh on the top of Hartsuff's Knoll, the men took their places in the intrenchments. After two hours of brisk skirmishing, all the time gradually advancing, our cavalry compelled the enemy to withdraw. The plain is now quiet, but the troops are ordered to remain in the intrenchments.

CHAPTER VI.

OCCUPYING THE LINE OF THE RAPIDAN.

When General Meade reached the Rappahannock, he proposed at once to follow up the pursuit of Lee, rather than to wait for the rebel general to rest his men and recruit his army. But orders from Washington directed Meade to assume a threatening attitude along the Rappahannock, but not to advance beyond it. The operations on the south side of the river, during the first days of August, were in obedience to General Halleck's orders.

The campaign was now at an end. Throughout the month of August the army remained in undisturbed quiet, receiving daily accessions to its numbers from the draft that had been made in the several Northern States. Some of the drafted men were good and reliable soldiers; but the vast majority that first reached the army were hired substitutes, adding nothing whatever to its material strength. They deserted every day by scores, before they had time to learn the number of the regiment to which they were assigned, or even the letter of the company. The division guard-house became an indispensable institution, often containing at one time a hundred prisoners. Courts-martial were in perpetual session, and the shooting of deserters an ordinary affair.

The mortality among the conscripts, even of the better class, was fearfully great. Coming to the front in the heat of July and August, and taking their places by the side of men who had been inured to the service, they broke down on the march, or yielded to the first attack of diseases incident to camp life.

Toward the 1st of September, the numerical strength of the army was greatly diminished by sending detachments of troops, first to South Carolina, and then to New York to enforce the draft. But the army of General Lee had undergone a like depletion, Longstreet's Corps having been sent to the Southwest to reinforce Bragg.

Without waiting for instructions from Washington, General Meade abandoned the line of the Rappahannock, and advanced to the Rapidan. The rebel army was found on the south bank, in a position so strongly fortified as to defy an attack in front. The country south of the river was almost unknown, and before a flank attack could be made—the only one promising any success—it was necessary that the territory should be explored by our cavalry.

Meanwhile the disaster of Chickamauga occurred, and the Potomac Army was further weakened by the departure of the Eleventh and Twelfth Corps to Tennessee. With the army thus reduced, the attack on the enemy's flank was abandoned, and General Meade occupied the line of the Rapidan, as he had before occupied the line of the Rappahannock.

THURSDAY, September 24th. —Moving from camp near Culpeper, the First Corps has taken the place of the Twelfth Corps, next to the river. The regiment is doing picket duty at Raccoon Ford. The history of the Eleventh marks each distinctive step of the war. First we did picket duty on the Potomac; then, advancing southward, on the Rappahannock, and now on the Rapidan. Will it come our turn, in the course of events, to picket the James?

A part of the day has been spent with two men who are to be executed for desertion. One is an Irishman, and the other a German. The German has been in this country only two or three months, and is to be pitied as the victim of circumstances. The case of the Irishman is one of the many impositions practiced upon the government. A citizen of New York, he sold himself for a substitute in Boston, and then took advantage of the first opportunity to desert.

SUNDAY, September 27.—Broke up camp at noon, and after marching an hour through the woods and over the rocks that skirt the base of Pony Mountain, halted in our present bivouac near Mitchell's Station, the railroad crossing of the Rapidan. The wherefore of these short and frequent moves is not quite plain to us. One thing, however, is apparent—our friends across the river do not mean that we shall come to their side of the stream, for, as usual, they are busy ditching and intrenching a position that nature has already rendered next to impregnable.

THURSDAY, October 1.—These mellow, autumnal days slip away almost imperceptibly. September is gone, and we have entered upon October. So little has been accomplished since the battle of Gettysburg, that we fear to think the fall rains will soon commence. Virginia mud will be worth more to Lee than fifty thousand men. The cases of Sullivan and Von Henike are still in suspension. But another German, named Schmidt, a conscript belonging to the Ninetieth Regiment, has been added to the condemned, and will be shot to-morrow.

FRIDAY, October 2.—Private Henry Schmidt was executed in presence of the entire division. It is well when a man is to be ushered into eternity, whatever is the nature of the crime for which he dies, that all the arrangements should be solemn and impressive. The troops were drawn up on three sides of the open grave, with space enough between the regiments in front for the funeral cortege to pass through. After the lines were formed, the slow notes of the band playing a funeral dirge, gave warning that the procession was approaching. The provost marshal of the division entered the arena, followed by an ambulance containing the condemned and a Catholic priest. Arrived at the grave, the coffin was placed at its side. The priest and the prisoner knelt a moment in prayer, then taking a seat on the coffin, the hands and feet of the condemned were pinioned, a bandage placed over his eyes, and all was ready for the execution. The commands were given in a clear, steady voice, "Ready—aim—fire!" Half a dozen balls entered the body near the heart, and without a movement of limb or muscle, the deserter was dead. Schmidt had been in the country only a few months. He was a stranger in a strange land. The friends he left behind in the fatherland will never know what has become of him, and there will be none to mourn his ignoble fate.

WEDNESDAY, October 7.—Most of the regiment has been detailed for special picket duty. The Rapidan in front is so narrow, that the pickets of the two armies approach within a few yards of each other. With rare exceptions the utmost good feeling prevails, and a regular exchange of newspapers, coffee, sugar and tobacco is kept up.

FRIDAY, October 9.—The quartermaster is busy issuing eight days' rations to the men, always a sure intimation of a speedy move. Yesterday morning, as division officer of the day, Colonel Coulter had a short interview with a Confederate captain, stationed on the south side of the Rapidan. The rebels fired on our pickets stationed near the house of Dr. Stringfellow, and the meeting was in the interests of the family, who were in continual alarm for their personal safety. The officer said that the firing was unauthorized, and had occurred through the removal of the old pickets and the substitution of others not acquainted with the order against picket firing. The fact of the interview was signaled all along the rebel lines, and read at our own stations. For some time the signal officers have thought themselves in possession of the key to the enemy's signals, and this slight event, apparently so accidental, has proved the surmising to be true. General Meade and staff spent the day at the signal station on Pony Mountain. The discovery of yesterday has doubtless much to do with present preparations for an advance. What a little thing sometimes develops great issues!

SUNDAY MORNING, October 11.—Late on Friday night, orders were received indicating the character of the move for which preparations had been making during the day. Buford's Division of cavalry was to cross the Rapidan at Germania Ford, and, marching up the south bank, uncover the fords of Morton and Raccoon, at which points the First Corps was to cross and move against the enemy's right, while the Sixth Corps was to attack his left. The infantry forces were to march as noiselessly as possible, and to be at the localities designated before daylight, so as not to awaken the suspicion of the enemy, or reveal the movements of the cavalry.

Leaving camp at two o'clock Saturday morning, long before the hour appointed Robinson's Division was massed in the woods in front of Raccoon Ford, awaiting the approach of Buford. Hour after hour wore away, but no sign of our horsemen. A little after dusk yesterday evening, the cavalry still failing to appear, the division moved back to Culpeper pike, in sight of Stevensburg, where we remain in bivouac. It is rumored that while Meade is operating here on the enemy's left, Lee is moving up toward our right. However that may be, the movement on this side of the Rapidan extends to the whole army, and no longer looks like an advance.

MONDAY MORNING, Oct. 12.—Yesterday afternoon the First Corps marched to Kelly's Ford, on the Rappahannock, the Eleventh in rear of Robinson's Division. No time was lost on the way, as it soon became known that the pickets had been withdrawn from the Rapidan, and the rebel cavalry was in close pursuit. Twice the regiment was halted to meet an expected charge of the enemy. As the sun was going down the men waded waist-deep through the waters of the Rappahannock, and formed in line on the north bank. Our batteries were unlimbered and placed in positions commanding not only the river ford, but all the opposite plain. General Baxter was ordered to keep a watch on the road over which we had come, and have a care lest we did not fire into Buford's men, who might find it necessary to fall back in this direction. The large brick-mill and neat dwelling-houses at the ford, the river-hills, and the broad, green plain on the opposite shore, seen in the lingering twilight of yesterday evening, made up a picture the mind will long retain.

MONDAY EVENING.—The sharp firing heard all day, at short intervals, on our right, is certain evidence that the enemy, as well as ourselves, is making rapid moves. For several hours we have been in readiness to march. Just now an order was received for the wagons to proceed to Bealton Station, and the drivers are already in the saddle.

The individuals who suffer most in these excited army movements are the sutlers. A large train of them had ventured to the front with a heavy stock of goods. Halting with us here at Kelly's Ford, they have been doing a brisk trade. There is great alarm among them as they make for the rear; and great sport among the boys as one wagon after another (from whose wheels the pins have been secretly removed) breaks down, leaving their contents to the mercy of a hundred sly and roguish soldiers. That hurrah, this moment heard, is everywhere understood to mean "cleaning out" a sutler's establishment, and never fails to bring forth a large body of recruits.

CENTERVILLE, Wednesday, Oct. 14.—For the last thirty-six hours we have had scarcely more than time to breathe. Monday midnight the division left Kelly's Ford for Warrenton Junction. All manner of rumors were in circulation as to the doings of the rebels. Some had it that they were moving in large force far up to our right; others again, that they were coming down from Warrenton. The latter report seemed the more probable; because from the Ford to the Junction was all the way at a run, and with scarcely a halt. Robinson's Division was the first to reach the threatened point, and without a moment's delay artillery and infantry were formed in line of battle.

If any one imagines it to be an easy thing to move an army, he should have seen the sight that here presented itself. Not far in the rear was heard the roar of cannon; but louder than this came the rumbling of hundreds of wagons, that in every direction skirted the horizon, and covered the plain. By every avenue troops were pouring in, until the eye wearied of the watching. Waiting in line of battle for two hours, Robinson moved on to Catlett's Station, and then to Bristow, where, foot-sore and tired, we bivouacked for the night.

Early this morning the division was again in line, moving toward Manassas. A courier reported Manassas Junction occupied during the night by a force of the enemy. Skirmishers were thrown out on either flank and in front. Slowly and cautiously the troops advanced, halting occasionally that the skirmishers might enter some copse of woods, or turn some angle in the road far enough in advance to give the main column notice of danger. But not a foe was to be seen to dispute our march. Over Manassas plains and across Bull Run we continued to these hights of Centerville, within whose fortifications we are ordered to halt. Thousands of armed men, and bristling cannon, and white-topped wagons crowd the roads below. What it all means is to us a profound mystery.

CHAPTER VII.

FROM THE RAPIDAN TO CENTERVILLE.

The reason of the retrograde march soon became apparent. As already stated, General Meade determined to assault the enemy's right in the vicinity of Raccoon and Morton Fords. From the hights of Pony Mountain and Slaughter's Hill the country had been carefully studied, and the plan of attack thoroughly discussed. But the last view from those look-outs presented a new scene to the eyes of our signal officers. It told that a movement of vast magnitude—the very counterpart of our own—was in progress on the south side of the Rapidan. Lee was as well satisfied that he could turn the Federal right, and break our communications with Washington, as Meade was that he could turn the rebel right, and break Lee's communications with Richmond; and the singular coincidence occurred of the two armies moving to attack one another at the same time, and on the same though opposite flanks.

Confident of the enemy's intentions, General Meade determined to select his own battleground. The cavalry was thrown out to watch Lee's movements; Pleasanton occupying the ground between the Rappahannock and Culpeper, and Gregg guarding the fords near and above Warrenton. The commanding general looked to Gregg for the earliest information of the whereabouts and the doings of the enemy on his right.

The Federal army was that moment en route for Warrenton Junction, along which line it was intended to await the approach of the Southerners. But no word coming from Gregg that would indicate the appearance of the enemy on the Upper Rappahannock, and Pleasanton reporting that Lee was concentrating around Culpeper, the troops were halted, and three corps moved back to Brandy Station.

A reconnoitering party kept on to Culpeper, but without meeting any force of the rebels. It began to be thought that General Lee had countermanded marching orders, and that his troops were going back into the old position along the Rapidan. Thus passed the 12th of October until ten o'clock at night, when word came in from Gregg that his cavalry was attacked by an overpowering force of the enemy, and driven from their defenses with great loss. He was then within five miles of Warrenton Junction, hard pressed by Ewell, with whom he had been contending since eleven o'clock A.M.

It was a critical moment. On our right flank were the advancing columns of Lee's entire army, while our own corps were distributed, one at Freeman's Ford, three at Brandy Station, across the Rappahannock, and one at Kelly's Ford. The darkness of the night favored the concentration of our troops, and the correction in part of Gregg's error. But Meade was compelled to move further in toward his base, in order to get the army together and recover a position on the line of his communications.

The First Corps came to Warrenton Junction, by way of Bealton, without opposition. No enemy showing himself, after a halt of two hours the troops were pushed on to Bristow Station, and then to Manassas. Not a living thing was to be seen moving over those broad plains, on which had settled down the very silence of death. Far to the left great clouds of dust were driving along by the blustering October winds. Lee was still moving over the Warrenton pike, with the hope of occupying Centerville, and thus compel Meade to open his communications with Washington by first attacking that strong position. The First Corps continued its steady and rapid march, reaching the hights of Centerville at noon of October 14th.

Although a day behind the rebels in the start of that exciting race, we were now several hours in advance. General Ewell, whose corps led the opposing army, in his eagerness to strike our flank, left the plain road over which he was marching, and penetrated a section of country lying between the railroad and the Warrenton turnpike. It proved a *terra incognita*, in which his entire corps was lost. Heath's Division came up with the rear of the Federal army at Bristow, and following close after it to Kettle Run, the skirmish assumed the outlines of a fierce battle, Heath losing five pieces of artillery, two stands of colors, and five hundred prisoners.

There was something too threatening in those fortified hights of Centerville, bristling with artillery and crowded with infantry, for General Lee to come further north, and his troops halted south of Bull Run. The Federal army now well in hand, General Meade at once countermarched his troops, ready to accept battle wherever the enemy might offer it.

Cub Run, October 15.—Three hours after reaching Centerville Robinson's Division moved back along the Warrenton turnpike to Bull Run. The Eleventh formed in line to the left of Stone Bridge, extending some distance down the stream. Along this same road the army has twice retreated in rout and confusion. The extreme care with which the pickets were stationed; the strict orders given to the men; and the low tone of voice in which all commands passed down the column, betokened danger, and seemed to point to the possibility of a third engagement on this ill-fated field. No fires were allowed to be kindled, and with blankets spread on the ground, we went to sleep, watching the bright stars that shone in the overhanging sky. The night passed without the firing of a shot; and this morning the Eleventh moved to the hights of Cub Run, where we still remain in line of battle, with several large guns in position on the hill above us.

FRIDAY, October 16.—No change since yesterday. The troops are in line of battle awaiting the movements of the enemy, who is reported as massing large forces directly in front.

To know the meaning of Despair and Hope one must have such an experience as was this day afforded at the division guard-house. The execution of Harrison, convicted of desertion at the battle of Fredericksburg, was fixed at twelve o'clock noon. We called to see him at ten o'clock. His countenance was haggard and careworn. It was hard for him to realize that he must die so soon; but he saw no avenue of escape, and had given up all hope. Some time was spent in writing to his mother, begging her to forget the manner of his death, and to believe that he never intended to desert. His personal effects were given into our keeping, together with messages for several absent friends. It was now past eleven o'clock. The ambulance in which the condemned was to ride to the grave, and also containing the coffin, had driven up along the roadside; while the beating of the drums, that announced the forming of the division to witness the execution, could be distinctly heard. Everything was ready to carry out the sentence of the court-martial, and the officer only delayed for the word of command. Presently there came the sound of a horse's hoofs clattering over the hard stony road. It was an aid from army headquarters, not to order the procession forward, but bearing in his hands a commutation of the death penalty. The complacent smile on the face of the rider betrayed the nature of his message before it was read aloud in the hearing of the prisoner. Harrison looked at the officer for a moment with a vacant stare, and then exclaimed, in a wild and hurried manner:

"Read it again, won't you? Does it mean me? Are you sure there is no other Harrison in the army? Am I really to live?"

His tongue refused to say anything more. Nerves strung to the utmost tension now relaxed; and, prostrate on the ground, the reprieved man gave expression to feelings too deep for words in tears of joy. Saw Harrison an hour ago. That look of fixed despair was gone. The light of hope was in his eye, giving him the appearance of quite another being.

MONDAY, October 19.—General Lee refuses battle, though offered to him on the field of Bull Run. He is now retiring in the direction of the Rappahannock, but will hardly be permitted to do so in undisturbed leisure. Five o'clock this morning the First and Sixth Corps were moving toward Gainesville and Haymarket. The route was across Bull Run and along the Warrenton pike. Leaving the regiment halted near the Henry House, took a hasty ride over the ground of the second Bull Run battle. It did not look as though the foot of a human being had passed over it since the day of the fight. Boxes half filled with ammunition, and others again entirely empty, knapsacks stuffed with clothing now rotten and musty, and haversacks containing the moulded remains of the last scanty issue of rations, lay scattered about just as we had seen them during the engagement. From the spot where the regiment halted on the night of August 29th, we rode to the extreme right of the line, where the division was sent to the support of Heintzleman. Coming back over the same path traversed by the Eleventh in its rapid move to the left, we stood on Bald Hill, and looked down into the woods out of which poured the rebels, and over the fields through which they came, on the afternoon of the 30th, in such overwhelming masses. The field presented a loathsome sight. Human bones, washed from their shallow graves by the rains of the past year, covered the ground, telling more plainly than the living tongue can tell of the horrors of war. The Eleventh is bivouacked between Gainesville and Haymarket.

TUESDAY, October 20.—After my note of yesterday was made, and toward the dusk of evening, we became aware that the enemy was in our front, but in what numbers it was impossible to tell. A heavy detail of pickets from the Third Division, and a battery of four guns, advanced through Haymarket, and formed in line. Presently the battery opened a quick fire, lasting for several minutes. Then all was quiet for an hour. Another rail was added to the camp-fire, and the men laid down to wait the developments of the morning. But the discharge of a single musket, that soon multiplied into volleys, brought every man to his post, ready to meet the danger. Again the noise in front ceased, and after extinguishing the fire whose genial warmth was so needful to our personal comfort, the men once more lay down to sleep. To any one who had seen the dead of the battle-field arranged in rows for burial, those ranks of men, wrapped up head and foot in blankets and ponchos, would have suggested the thought of dead men awaiting sepulture. This morning brings the report that the attack of last night was made by a party of guerrillas who drove in our pickets, capturing thirty or forty prisoners and so exciting the rest as to cause them to fire upon each other. The Eleventh is now advanced a mile beyond Haymarket, supporting a force of cavalry sent out toward Thoroughfare Gap.

These rapid marches that we have been making for the past few days have been particularly hard on the conscripts—the "conneys," as the boys call them for short. They have not yet learned to march with the same ease as the old soldier, and many of them present a pitiful appearance in their efforts to keep up with the column. One man particularly, who complained of a stiff knee, awakened our sympathy as he hobbled along under a heavy knapsack and gun. After earnest solicitation, an ambulance driver agreed to haul his knapsack, and when not overcrowded with sick, allow the fellow to ride. But from the first, the doctors suspected that it was all pretense, and that the man was playing a part. Yesterday evening, after the regiment halted for the night, to be certain of his case, the soldier was taken into a tent and chloroform administered. He had complained that the knee-joint was so rigid from a hurt received in youth that it would not bend. But it was found uninjured, and flexible as the other. Tying the foot back so as to bring the limb in a kneeling posture, the conney was aroused to consciousness. One look at the laughing spectators, and another at his knee, was enough. He was heard to say, as he left the tent, "Played out!" This morning he was in the ranks, sound and well.

THOROUGHFARE GAP, October 21.—The First Corps commenced moving late on Tuesday. Cavalry scouts reported a large body of the enemy concentrating at White Plains, with the intention of falling upon our rear, should we keep up the pursuit of Lee to the Rappahannock. New tactics must now be resorted to by the enemy. Occupying this mountain pass, as we do, it would be a hazardous adventure to attempt its passage. This is an interesting spot to the Eleventh Regiment, not only because several companies were stationed in this vicinity, guarding the railroad, in the spring of 1862, but it is the scene of our first severe battle. As soon as it was known that the march was not to be resumed this morning, in company with Major Keenan, we passed through Chapman's mill, the strong barricade of the rebels, and on to the hill above, across which our men drove the astonished enemy.

"I was standing here by this rock," said the major, "hurrying up the men of Co. K, when I was shot. I saw the soldier as he raised his gun and aimed directly toward me, and felt confident that he would hit me. But there was such a brief moment between the look and the shot, that perhaps I confound the thought that he was taking sure aim with the fact itself. I was near enough to the fellow to see his face, and it is singular how his features remain fixed in my mind. I believe now that I could distinguish him from a regiment of Southerners, though they do look so much alike."

Friday, October 23.—Yesterday and to-day have been days of quiet and rest. We who are in camp, trusting to the vigilance of a strong guard of reliable pickets to keep off the roving bands of guerrillas that infest these mountains, have given ourselves up to discussing the various rumors of the hour, exciting enough to arouse the utmost stoic. Rosecrans, whose very name hitherto has been a talisman of strength, has been relieved from the command of the Cumberland Army. General Thomas succeeds Rosecrans, while to General Grant is given the command of the department. In the wake of this dispatch comes the rumor that General Meade has been removed from the Army of the Potomac, and that General Sedgwick is to be his successor. There is the usual excitement among the troops always attendant upon a change in army commanders. Some are loud in their defense of Meade, while others again, with equal warmth, condemn him. One thing is certain, General Meade has added nothing to his fame since the battle of Gettysburg, and it is questionable if he has the same hold upon the troops now that he had then.

CHAPTER VIII.

GETTING BACK TO THE RAPPAHANNOCK.

On the 25th day of October the Federal army was concentrated at Bristow Station. General Lee rapidly retired before our advance, but at the same time effectually destroyed the Orange Railroad from Bristow to the Rappahannock. A further pursuit was impossible until this main artery of supplies was repaired, and to this one object all the resources of the army were applied.

In the mean time, the Confederate army strongly fortified the defenses at Rappahannock Station, and confident in the belief that General Meade could not make another advance during the season, had gone into winter quarters on the south bank of the stream. But our cavalry, without waiting on the tardy movements of the infantry, penetrated the enemy's lines, felt the strength of his position, and learned the points of attack and defense.

The relation of that army to our own was such as to warrant the belief that by marching three corps to Kelly's Ford, and thence across the Rapidan at

Germania Ford, while the two remaining corps moved by way of Rappahannock Station, the rear of the rebel army could be reached, and Lee's line of communication with Richmond severed.

The new movement was at once inaugurated, and with a degree of spirit that of itself insured success. The First, Second, and Third Corps were to cross at Kelly's Ford, and the Fifth and Sixth Corps at Rappahannock Station. The preliminary move concentrated the corps at Catlett's Station, and on Saturday morning, November 7th, the army was again in motion.

NEAR MORRISVILLE, November 7.—Six o'clock this morning the Eleventh Regiment was bringing up the rear of Robinson's Division. It was understood, before leaving Catlett's, that a grand movement was in contemplation that might take us further south than the army had yet essayed to go. We are now within five miles of the river at Morrisville, a cluster of houses near the junction of the roads leading to Kelly's Ford and Falmouth. A part of our forces have already reached the river, as heavy firing is heard in that direction. The night air is cold and chilly, reminding us of the comforts of stoves and fireplaces that we had gathered around us during our stay at Bristow.

BRANDY STATION, Sunday, November 8.—The clear, shrill blast of the bugle, sounding from brigade headquarters at four o'clock this morning, cut short our slumbers, and from the land of dreams brought us back to the realities of a fall campaign. Half an hour later, the Eleventh was leading the division in the march, and the division leading the corps. The direction in which the army is moving, and the prospect ahead, always make a difference in the conduct of the men. At other times lively and hilarious, awake to everything that can provoke a criticism, and ready to laugh at it, when the enemy is in front, and a battle imminent, a quiet that of itself becomes solemn possesses the most garrulous. Every one is in communion with himself; and what thoughts are born of those silent moments; what high resolves are formed, or what earnest prayers go up to Heaven, are only known to Him who can read man's heart. It was so this morning. The troops were marching toward the river through a deep pine forest, the slow firing in front telling of the presence of the enemy, and for more than an hour scarcely a word was spoken that disturbed the current of our meditations.

The fight of yesterday afternoon was for possession of the river crossing, in which the enemy lost a pontoon bridge, four pieces of artillery, and twelve or fifteen hundred men in killed and prisoners. On our arrival at the river hill, the Third Corps was passing over under cover of the artillery, and toward ten o'clock all the troops were across moving up the south side to Rappahannock Station. The passage of the river at Kelly's Ford flanked the strong position at the railroad bridge, causing the enemy in front of the Fifth and Sixth Corps to fall back to Culpeper. The army, thus united, moved to Brandy Station in long battle lines, sweeping across the entire plain, and presenting a sight of great animation. Here we are in bivouac, with our faces toward Culpeper. The Eleventh occupies a part of the grounds of John Minor Botts. In our frequent marches over this disputed territory, the troops have often been compelled to make a detour of many weary steps to save passing through the fields of this important individual. During the late retrograde, three thousand rebel cavalry halted for the night on Auburn farm, burning up the fence-rails, and appropriating to their own use a plentiful supply of corn and oats. The soldiers have never had the same respect for Botts that army commanders appear to entertain; and no tears are shed over the losses that are said to make the irate old Virginian more crusty than ever.

Near Liberty, Tuesday, November 10.—Yesterday passed in comparative quiet until an hour before sundown, when with an alarming suddenness the whole army was in motion. It only made the excitement greater to observe that instead of moving to Culpeper, we were taking the backward track toward the Rappahannock. Artillery and wagons made the most of the good roads, as the very spirit of Jehu took possession of the drivers.

"Another race for Manassas," whispered the brigade commissary, as he rode past to take charge of his supply train.

When we reached the north bank of the river it was discovered that only the First Corps was on the wing, and that instead of Manassas as its destination, the corps was to be placed along the line from the Rappahannock to Warrenton Junction. A detachment of four regiments and a section of artillery, under command of Colonel Coulter, is stationed at this point, reached last night at ten o'clock.

It is the intersection of three roads, one leading to the upper fords of the river, another direct to Warrenton, and a third running parallel to the railroad, and at present used by our trains in conveying supplies to the front. From the location of Liberty, the special duty of the detachment, as may be inferred, is to fill up a gap through which Stuart or Moseby might fall upon our wagons, or capture the stores at Bealton Station, two miles distant.

FRIDAY, November 13.—Our camp is in the midst of a pine forest, whose trees have been cut out to make room for the quarters of officers and men; while a fence, constructed of green pine boughs, incloses the entire space. Just now the weather has all the genial warmth of a Northern Indian summer; and if soldier life were ever like that we have been living for the past few days, war would not be a frightful thing. There is only enough of actual danger to make the pickets watchful, and prevent the men from straying too far from camp. Passing down the several company streets this evening, beginning with Co. A on the right, and ending with Co. B on the left, you might notice at the head of each street, except one, comfortable board shanties, the quarters of the several line officers. The exception is Co. G. Our boys have come to believe that in some way or other the movements of the regiment are connected with the building of Captain McGrew's quarters. For a long time past it has been observed that at the moment the captain has finished fixing up for a lengthy stay in camp, orders to march have been received. Neither officers nor men have the slightest disposition to leave Liberty; and as a condition that he will be in no hurry to complete his house, Captain McGrew is the guest of all the other companies, entitled to the choice seat at table, and the extra blanket at night.

SUNDAY, November 15.—A heavy rain last night, with thunder and lightning. To-day the weather is cool and cloudy. Most of the Eleventh is out of camp on special duty, giving to our quarters an unusual quiet. A soldier belonging to the

Ninth New York died suddenly this morning, and was buried an hour ago. There is something touchingly sad in these army funerals; not that they are wanting in feeling, or in any of the respect which the living everywhere pay to departed friends. But do the best we can, and it is only a rough sepulture. A blanket is at once winding-sheet and coffin. Sometimes in an obscure corner of the camp, and again along the roadside, a square trench receives the remains. A rude board, unskillfully inscribed with name, company, and regiment, may tell who lies there, but far more frequently even this is wanting; and there is nothing to distinguish the grave of a brave soldier from the common earth that surrounds it.

WEDNESDAY, November 18.—There has been no little excitement in camp during the last three days. Sunday morning one of our men went to a farm-house near by to purchase something for the mess. The farmer would not allow him to alight; but pointing to three horses tied up at a residence quarter of a mile distant, told him they were Moseby's guerrillas, and to make his way back to camp as fast as possible. The farmer himself has been suspected of belonging to Moseby, and was given to understand that he would be held responsible for attacks on the pickets, or any of the men near his premises, which may have been the reason of his anxiety for the safety of Mike. From the manner in which both rider and horse came panting into camp, the farmer's instructions must have been obeyed to the letter. A party went out in pursuit of the guerrillas, scouring the country for several miles. The road they had taken was readily shown by those of whom inquiry was made; but in every instance certainly the wrong one, for nothing could be seen of the flying horsemen. Monday morning the whole field and staff of the Eleventh, with the addition of several cavalrymen, renewed the search, with no better success. To-day the picket line was secretly extended, taking in several of the suspected houses, and the three gentlemen who have been prowling about our camp since Sunday, were taken prisoners. They were on foot when captured, and armed with navy revolvers. Guerrilla warfare is little better than cowardly assassination. If General Meade will send the prisoners to the detachment stationed at Liberty for proper punishment, the census of Virginia will be reduced by three before morning.

Thursday, November 19.—Expecting a speedy move. The paymaster has been here to-day, paying off the regiment for the months of September and October. Then there has been a canceling of the conditions between Captain McGrew and the line officers, and the headquarters of Co. G are nearly completed. It happened in this wise: The captain's negro man, lost during the night of our march to Liberty, and carrying with him the entire commissariat of his master, suddenly turned up to-day, minus everything but a handleless coffee-pot. The captain insisted on including Bob in the liberal conditions made for his own easy subsistence. But the party of the second part strongly demurred, saying many things of the looks and habits of the African in question neither complimentary nor polite. The result was a dissolution of the social compact between the Captain of Co. G and the other line officers of the Eleventh Regiment.

The delightful fall weather still continues. When the sun goes down, the frosty evening air is tempered by the huge fires burning throughout the camp, and around which the men gather in groups. The conversation is more generally retrospective than prospective; suggested, possibly, by the presence of one whose arm or leg has not quite recovered from some serious wound, and who now, in the midst of attentive listeners, recounts the mishaps of past battles. Noble, of Co. A, and Murdock, of Co. E, were both reported killed, the latter at Thoroughfare Gap, and the former at Bull Run. Noble was left on the battle-field nearly a week. Toward evening of the day of the fight, a Confederate soldier came along and placed near him a haversack tolerably well filled, and a canteen of water. Fortunately for Noble, he had fallen near a clump of bushes, which afforded ample shade during the heat of the day. With his haversack and canteen, he began to calculate that although a Minie ball had penetrated his side, producing a painful wound, and entirely disabling him, his chances for living were still tolerably fair. Next day another rebel soldier passing that way, gave it as his opinion that the sergeant would die in exactly three hours; and lest they should fall into more worthless hands, relieved him of haversack and canteen. Then he was compelled to beg of those that lingered around the battle-field for the sake of the spoils. One gave him a drink of water, another a cracker, and a third put a blanket under his head. Two days later three or four Virginia soldiers came along in company, one of whom wanted his shoes.

"No," said Noble; "these are all I have, and you can't get them." "But see here, Yankee," replied the Southerner, "you'll die anyhow to-morrow. My shoes are all worn out; yours are good, and I will have them." He then stooped down and began to untie Noble's shoes. "No doubt," retorted the wounded Federal, "you are a brave fellow. Only a brave soldier like you are would take the shoes from a man unable to help himself. You always bring up the rear-guard in time of battle, don't you?" The companions of the Confederate, who had been looking on all the while, raised a loud laugh, and the Virginian walked away, leaving the sergeant in possession of his shoes. On the sixth day, one of our ambulances, sent out under a flag of truce to bring off the wounded, passed near him. He called to the driver and begged to be taken up. But the ambulance had already a full load, and the driver said he would take no more. The offer of money, however, touched the fellow's heart sooner than the wounded man's condition, and a comfortable passage was secured to one of the Washington hospitals.

Sergeant Murdock was reported killed at Thoroughfare Gap. He was shot through both legs at the moment our men were retiring from the hill from which they had driven the enemy. After laying for some time in a partially unconscious state, he became aware of some one coming toward him. It was a rebel picket, feeling his way slowly over the rough and uneven ground. The Southerner had raised his gun, ready to shoot, when a groan brought him to the side of the wounded Federal. Between the two thus introduced, there sprung up the most kindly feeling, and in his new friend Murdock found a protector against several fellows of the baser sort, who shortly after arrived, plundering the living as well as the dead. From Thoroughfare Gap he was conveyed to Warrenton, the rebel general hospital, and was there on the 26th of the following September, when the town was captured by our cavalry. A week or so prior to that attack, a visit from the Yankees was hourly expected. Then came wild stories, that Washington and Baltimore were in possession of Southern troops, and that Lincoln and his Cabinet had fled to Philadelphia. The Yankees were entirely forgotten, and everybody gave themselves up to the joys of the hour. One fine afternoon, a number of ladies were visiting the hospital. Some young Southern beaus, who had been watching from the cupola of the building a squadron of cavalry going through the quick evolutions of the drill, came down in apparent alarm, and announced that the Yankees were approaching the town in force. Of course the ladies were frightened, and the gentlemen too, not in the secret of the joke. But, alas for the jokers, the cavalry force they had supposed to be their own, were genuine Yankees, and in less than half an hour the town was in our possession!

FRIDAY, November 20.—Yesterday afternoon a young lady, attended by an ancient negro, came into camp, asking the services of a physician in behalf of her mother. It was too late an hour in the day at once to accompany the lady to her home; but after leaving explicit directions how to find the house, she was dismissed with the assurance that the doctor would see her mother in the morning. The lady was sincere enough to say that guerrillas were frequently seen in the neighborhood in which she lived, and begged of the surgeon not to come alone. It would be better to come in such numbers as either to overawe an attack or be able to resist it. It cannot be said that no suspicions were entertained as to the designs of the fair visitor. Some accused her of acting the part of a spy, and regarded the guerrilla story as made up to deceive. Others declared that the intention was to invite all the mounted officers belonging to the regiment out of camp, and then make a wholesale capture of them. It was at last decided that if guerrillas were so near camp we had better know it; and if the young lady were an accomplice, she ought to be secured before imparting to them any knowledge she might have gained by coming within our lines.

Fully armed and equipped, a party of ten, under command of Captain Haines, started this morning through the woods and over the fields, two miles beyond the picket lines, to the residence of Mrs. Kelley. It is an old Virginia mansion, large enough in its dimensions to recall the halcyon days of Virginia hospitality. Within and without everything indicated taste and refinement. The captain had observed the precaution of posting a part of the escort outside of the house to give alarm in case of danger. Thus secure in the enjoyment of the conversation of two intelligent ladies (the mother did not prove to be seriously indisposed), interspersed with delightful music by the younger, an hour passed rapidly away. It was like suddenly transplanting us from the roughness of soldier life to all the kindly endearments of home. As we bid adieu to those who had made us so happy, and turned our faces campward, we laughed at our unfounded suspicions, and sincerely wished that the doctor might have many such patients.

SATURDAY, November 21.—It is a serious question whether, after all, the pleasant termination of yesterday's adventure was not owing more to good fortune than prudence. The events of to-day have almost confirmed the first suspicions entertained of the young lady who visited our camp on Thursday, and that a few hours ago we were so ready to laugh away. A party of guerrillas, variously estimated at seventy-five to one hundred and fifty strong, just now attacked a supply train, under escort of a small cavalry force. The guard was overpowered, and taking refuge in flight, fell back on the first line of pickets. The guerrillas were dressed in blue overcoats, and before they could be distinguished from our own men, succeeded in capturing five or six of the infantry pickets. The alarm soon became general, and the whole detachment was speedily under arms. But after robbing their prisoners of money, overcoats, and haversacks, and with eighteen mules and four horses, Moseby was off as suddenly as he came. A cavalry force was sent out in immediate pursuit, and a second squadron is preparing to follow.

Was the young lady an accomplice of these thieving fellows, and did she really intend to lead us into the hands of this party, whose arrival she had calculated a day too soon? Appearances are certainly much against her, and in the absence of positive proof, we have concluded to decline the very polite invitation to call again!

SUNDAY, November 22.—Three or four of the guerrilla party that entered our lines yesterday have been captured. It scarcely admits of a doubt that these robbers are citizens of the immediate vicinity, so familiar with every nook and corner that their capture in any numbers is next to impossible. Those captured to-day were taken in the very act of changing the attire of the soldier for that of the farmer.

An hour after sundown orders were received to be ready to march to-morrow morning. The men are now engaged in cooking the extra rations that have been issued, and a buzzing noise is heard throughout the camp, in strong contrast with the former repose of the day. For some reason, as yet unexplained, General Meade's late crossing of the Rappahannock, though a complete surprise to the enemy, resulted in nothing more than the army occupying its old position around Culpeper. It was a small advantage to be purchased at the loss of a good many lives; and in the opinion of leading generals, a great mistake was committed in not following out the original plan of pushing across the Rapidan and attacking the rebel rear. The order received this evening does not give the line of march; but it is intimated, now that the railroad is finished to Brandy Station, that the Rapidan is to be forded at several points, and an earnest effort made to reach Gordonsville.

CHAPTER IX.

THE MINE RUN CAMPAIGN.

RAPPAHANNOCK STATION, Wednesday, November 25.—The entire army has been halted here at Rappahannock Station since Monday, awaiting the holding up of a cold, drizzling rain that commenced falling on Tuesday morning. The sky is clear now, and with the stiff wind that has been blowing since noon, the roads must become at least passably good in a few hours. There is no longer any secrecy about the contemplated move. A Washington paper received this afternoon gives the whole programme. General Meade's scouts report that the lines of the enemy are so formed as to leave uncovered all the lower fords of the Rapidan; that Ewell's Corps is next to the river, and Hill's Corps in the vicinity of Orange Court House, leaving a space between them of seven or eight miles. Our present object is to gain this interval, prevent a union between Ewell and Hill, and give them battle in detail. Whatever is done must be done quickly. There is not an hour to spare. It is late in the season, and bad weather and bad roads may be expected any moment.

SOUTH OF THE RAPIDAN, November 26.—The moon was shining in a cloudless sky when we left Rappahannock Station this morning. After crossing the river on the railroad bridge, the Division marched down stream. It soon became known that the First Corps was to cross the Rapidan at Culpeper Mines, while the other corps crossed at the several different fordings above. We of the Eleventh did not forget that it was the national thanksgiving day on which the movement was inaugurated, and our trust is that God will hear the prayers this day offered up in behalf of our cause. Our thanksgiving dinner was eat during a halt near Richardsville; and though it consisted only of the plain fare Uncle Sam furnishes his men when on a march, it was with a relish, and, let us hope, with becoming thankfulness. It was dark before we reached the Rapidan River. Pontoon bridges were at once constructed, and the corps crossed to the opposite hights recently occupied by the enemy. The bivouac of the Eleventh is near the Culpeper gold mines. The hour is one for thought and reflection. We are further advanced in this direction than any of the infantry troops have yet marched. If the movement proves a success, all will be well; if it should result in failure, it may be a great calamity. The men are in good spirits, and enthusiastically cheered the dispatch received from army headquarters that Grant had gained a decisive victory over Bragg.

FRIDAY, November 27.—The march was resumed this morning at five o'clock, over a country entirely unknown, whose hills and ravines had never before been pressed by such an army. In two hours we struck the Germania and Fredericksburg road. Our movements became more cautious as we were advancing through the dreary and uncertain region of the Wilderness. Scarcely had we entered its thick growth of dwarfed oak, when far to our right was heard the slow and measured reports of artillery. We knew they were signal guns, and that however Meade might have deceived the enemy in the crossing, his presence south of the Rapidan was fully known. Pursuing the Fredericksburg road within five miles of Chancellorville, the Eleventh halted in front of the Wilderness Tavern, a tall frame building, and one of the bygone celebrities of this remarkable country. There was some confusion in front, a part of the ambulance train of the Second Corps having been decoyed from the right road, and two or three of the drivers murdered. Near the tavern is the residence of Major Vincent of the rebel army. To this house Stonewall Jackson was conveyed after the battle of Chancellorville. Some distance beyond we left the old turnpike and marched along the Orange and Fredericksburg plank-road. We are now halted at Parker's store, where the whole corps is concentrated on the extreme left of the army. There must have been severe fighting by some of our forces during the afternoon. It is nearly dark, but from the direction of the river every once and again comes the sound of cannon.

SATURDAY, November 28.—Two hours after dark last night Robinson's Division, following the Orange plank-road half a mile beyond Parker's store, turned abruptly to the right into a narrow country road, leading through a thick forest. The march was continued for more than an hour, when we halted at the junction of a broader and more clearly defined highway. The division was formed in line of battle, with the Eleventh on the right. "Colonel," said General Robinson, "tell your men that the Second Corps is on the left, and the Fifth Corps in front. Instruct the pickets not to fire without first giving the challenge." The night passed without alarm, and at daylight this morning the division, continuing its march through the woods, was massed with the rest of the First Corps near Robertson's tavern, on the old Orange turnpike. Two hours later a general advance was ordered. The army is now in position along Mine Run. Colonel Coulter is in command of the division reserve, consisting of the Ninetieth Pennsylvania, Sixteenth Maine, and Twelfth Massachusetts, leaving the command of the Eleventh to Major Keenan. The enemy's pickets occupy an opposite crest of hills, so singularly shaped as to make them look like the angles of a fort, while between us and them is a low marshy ravine, through which Mine Run flows to the Rapidan. Heavy skirmishing has been going on all day, and there is every appearance of another Sunday battle. A cold drizzling rain has been falling for several hours, making us fearful of the effect it may have on these Virginia roads.

An incident occurred this morning which clearly shows the vigilance of the troops here marshaled. Shortly after the Eleventh had taken its position on the extreme left of the line, a body of skirmishers was seen advancing across the fields. The rainy weather made the atmosphere dull and hazy, and for a time it was doubtful whether they were friends or foes. The skirmishers finally halted, and an officer came within speaking distance. "Who are you?" "First Corps," was the reply. "Who are *you?*" "Fifth Corps." "All right," said Major Keenan, "come on." Assured that there was no deception, the officer advanced, saluted the major, and informed him that the Fifth Corps was approaching to form on the left of the First Corps.

SUNDAY, November 29.—Although there has been considerable activity in the shifting of divisions and brigades, no change has been made in our battle-line, nor has there been any general advance upon the works of the enemy. The Eleventh has been on picket duty out in front of the lines since early this morning, meeting with no other casualties than private Swartz, slightly wounded. This evening the Eleventh was added to the division reserve.

MONDAY, November 30.—Marching from our position on the left, the division formed in line to the right of the Orange pike. Later in the day General Robinson was directed to advance his pickets across a small stream (a branch of Mine Run) directly in front, and build two bridges for the passage of artillery and troops in column. A small force of the enemy occupied the overlooking crest, and though they stubbornly resisted, a detachment of the Ninety-fourth New York drove them away. Large working parties are now engaged constructing the bridges.

Back at the hospital, the day has been one of suspense and anxiety. Several times reports came to the rear that the troops were in the act of attacking the rebel fortifications, and from the position the enemy occupies, fearful losses were anticipated. There is more news here than reaches the front. This hospital, from its location, happens to be the rendezvous of the newspaper reporters, and already the gentlemen of the press are predicting a retrograde move on the part of Meade. The fight of the Third Corps, Friday afternoon, with a part of Ewell's forces, not only delayed the Second Corps in its march to occupy the interval between Hill and Ewell, but revealed the point of Meade's strategy. Falling back from the commanding position at Robertson's tavern to that of Mine Run, by Saturday morning the breach in the rebel line was closed, and whatever we do now must be done against a force quite as large as our own.

General Warren marched to-day to the extreme left of the line, and will attack the rebel right to-morrow morning. The weather has grown intensely cold, causing much suffering among the troops, especially to those on the picket line, where not a spark of fire is allowed to be kindled. Three men of the last relief were frozen to death at their posts.

TUESDAY, December 1.—Last night General Robinson was ordered to suspend all operations on the bridges in front of his line, and to withdraw the pickets across the run. From early morning until this hour (noon) the men have been waiting in battle-line for the sound of Warren's guns on the left as the signal of a general charge. Not a sound, not even the crack of a rifle has been heard in that direction. Something has gone wrong, too late to be corrected. The men are nearly out of rations, and our supply trains are on the other side of the Rapidan. In another day we must either go back for supplies, or the trains must be moved to the front. The former is far more likely, in the present precarious state of the weather, than the latter.

FOUR O'CLOCK P.M.—The First Corps is ordered to march, by way of Robertson's tavern, to Germania Ford.

NORTH SIDE RAPPAHANNOCK, NEAR KELLY'S FORD, December 3.—One week ago the grand movement of the Army of the Potomac was inaugurated. This evening we are back within a few miles of the starting-point. However much was intended, very little in fact has been accomplished. My last entry was on Tuesday afternoon, at the moment the corps began its move for the river. We bivouacked at midnight overlooking Germania Mills, crossed the Rapidan at daylight Wednesday, and took position to cover the crossing of the Fifth and Sixth Corps. The division remained at the ford until noon of Wednesday, when we marched to Stevensburg.

The rations of the men were entirely consumed, and every haversack was empty. "Twenty-five cents for a hard tack," was the offer made after the first hour's march. "Fifty cents for a hard tack," became the cry as the march continued. "One dollar for a hard tack," but even that did not bring it at the hour of bivouac. The time was in the memory of some of those same men, who now clamored so loud for hard tack, when the commissary of Camp Wayne was treated to a shower of the vilest epithets for offering them such fare. "Soft bread! soft bread!" was then the cry. The crackers strung upon a rope, and with which they garlanded the neck of his horse, and at last the neck of the commissary, was their estimate then of that for which they now clamored so furiously. The officers were in the same hungry plight as the men. Imagine the headquarter's mess of the Eleventh, composed of a colonel, a major, two doctors, and a chaplain, sitting down on the ground, ten o'clock at night, to a supper made up of one dish only—a plate of fried liver. But we were better off than brigade headquarters. Their last meal was taken in the morning, and consisted of stewed dried apples.

Even the brigade commissary was on short

allowance, as the novel mode to which he resorted to supply himself will fully attest. Riding off some distance from the troops to a finelooking residence, he represented himself to the family as an officer of Stuart's cavalry, disguised in Yankee uniform, the better to watch the movements of the Yankee army. Without a question, he was taken into their confidence. All the information they had was readily communicated; and, better still for the captain, preparations were at once made for dinner. An old colored woman, who overheard the conversation, unperceived by the family started off in all haste for the nearest body of soldiers. She was not long in finding some one to listen to her story, and a lieutenant and a squad of men were dispatched to make the arrest. The squad arrived at the house as the officer was sitting down to the table. Expostulation was useless. They had no time for delay, and he yielded himself a prisoner to the guard. Taken before the corps commander, of course he was recognized as Captain Bucklin, Commissary of the Second Brigade; but it was Captain Bucklin without his dinner.

This morning, before the march was continued, a ration of fresh beef was issued, and in the strength of that one meal the men journeyed to our present halting-place. An hour ago the wagons came up with full supplies. There is just now a savory smell throughout the camp of broiling beef and boiling coffee, by no means unpleasant to the olfactory nerves, as the hospital steward likes to say.

SOUTH SIDE RAPPAHANNOCK, December 4.—Unexpectedly to all, the first sound that disturbed our camp this morning was the bugle note to pack up. We were again to cross the Rappahannock. Last evening, hungry, tired, and cold, the men waded three feet deep to the north bank. To be called upon so soon to repeat the cool operation, was well calculated to ruffle the not very even temper of the soldier; and terrible maledictions were called down on the heads of all in authority. But it must be confessed that there was less grumbling to-day than last night—the difference, possibly, between stomachs full and stomachs empty.

TUESDAY, December 8.—Without waiting for orders, the men have gone into winter quarters. Substantial log-cabins, with fire-places and chimneys, have been constructed by all the companies. At headquarters we have our wall tents, but no fire-places. The fire is on the outside, and a picture of our present home would show to good effect. About a mile from the Rappahannock, and within a few yards of the road leading from Kelly's Ford to Stevensburg, would be seen four tents, two on a line, and one on each flank, facing inward. Between the tents and the road is a fence of pine boughs; on the other side of the road are the quarters of the men. The fire that burns night and day in front of the tents deserves to be noticed because of its royal back log, ten feet long and three feet in diameter, the contribution of a noble old white oak tree that has lived in these forests since the days when the red man claimed them as his own.

CHAPTER X.

ANOTHER CAMPAIGN COMPLETED.

The advance on Mine Run completed another campaign of the war. The operations of the year had been on a scale of vast magnitude. Beginning at Chancellorville, seven months before, they had extended twice across Virginia, through a large part of Maryland, into the interior of Pennsylvania, and back again within a day's march of the place of commencement. But in its bearing upon the great issue—the destruction of the rebel army—it was easy to see, looking out from our winter quarters on the Rappahannock, that the campaign had not fulfilled all its promises.

It must be said, however, that a better spirit prevailed throughout the army at the close of this campaign than had marked the close of the last. There had been, during the year, a gradual dying out of the ruinous partisan spirit once so prevalent. Without losing the least respect for the genius and ability necessary to command the army, each man had more respect for his own well-performed duties. The lesson had at last been learned that the strength of the army was not in McClellan, or Burnside, or Hooker, or Meade, but in the intelligent patriotism of the rank and file.

There was also to be noticed an increasing confidence in the integrity of the government, and in the justice and humanity of those principles lying at the base of the great conflict. The prophetic spirit of that strangely popular song,

"John Brown's body lies mouldering in the grave,
But his *soul* is marching on,"

now sung more than ever, possessed every heart; and though it might seem a long and wearisome way to the end, the *ultimate* triumph of the national cause was the accepted faith of the army.

The troops once in winter quarters, no further general movement could be expected before the beginning of May—five months in the future. But with that very month would commence the expiration of the term of enlistment of a large proportion of the old regiments, and before the next spring campaign fairly opened, the government would lose one-half of its most available force. It was well for the nation that the patriotism of the army was equal to the emergency; and when those men were asked to re-enlist for a second term of three years, if, in yielding to the request, there was less enthusiasm manifested than at the first enlistment, the veteran volunteer proved that he had lost none of his devotion to country.

It was provided, in addition to the liberal bounties that a generous people could well afford to pay to their noble defenders, that each veteran volunteer should be granted thirty-five days' furlough; and that where three-fourths of a regiment re-enlisted, such portion of the regiment should go home in a body, taking with it arms and equipments. The gallant old Eleventh was among the first of the Pennsylvania regiments to answer this new call of the government, just as it had been among the first to answer the nation's call at the end of the three months' campaign.

During the three weeks that intervened between the inception of this third term of service on the part of the Eleventh, and its entire completion, in the shiftings of the several corps, and the changing of the picket lines, marching from Kelly's Ford to Culpeper, and from thence to

Mitchell's Station, early in January the regiment encamped on Cedar Mountain. We were again upon our first battle-field; the circle was now complete, and from that field, after spending a few days at Culpeper, it was proper that the Eleventh Regiment should take cars, on the 5th of February, for Alexandria.

Five days later the regiment was in Camp Curtin, Harrisburg. From that point the men separated, in companies, and in squads, and singly, to meet again at the end of the veteran furlough.

VIII.

CHAPTER I.

LIEUTENANT-GENERAL U. S. GRANT.

OLD Time, unaffected by the joyous meeting of long absent friends, and heedless of the fresh griefs to be experienced at another parting, abating nothing of his rapid flight, hurried away through February and March at his usual gait.

The veteran furlough ended, the Eleventh once more rendezvoused at Camp Curtin. From thence over the familiar route through Baltimore, Washington, and Alexandria, and along the Orange Railroad by the old camping grounds of Manassas, Bristow, Rappahannock and Brandy Station, on the last day of March, after an absence of fifty days, the regiment rejoined Baxter's Brigade at Culpeper.

During the several weeks of our Northern sojourn a large number of recruits had been added to the regiment, which now, in dimensions, looked somewhat like its former self, numbering over five hundred men present for duty. Many vacancies were filled among the commissioned

PROMOTIONS IN THE ELEVENTH. 319

officers, and such a general reorganization effected as told favorably in the subsequent campaigns.

Lieutenant Absalom Schall was promoted to be captain of Co. C, vice Captain Jacob J. Bierer, honorably discharged; Lieutenant James Chalfant, captain of Co. F, vice Captain E. H. Gay, deceased; Lieutenant Andrew G. Happer, captain of Co. I, vice Captain Thomas, mustered out of service; Jesse Lauffer, captain of Co. K, vice Captain John Read, killed at Antietam; Lieutenant John P. Straw, first lieutenant of Co. B, vice Lieutenant George Tapp, discharged on account of wounds; Sergeant Enos E. Hall, first lieutenant of Co. D, vice Lieutenant Chalfant, promoted; Lieutenant Samuel J. Hamill, first lieutenant of Co. E, vice Lieutenant Piper, promoted; Lieutenant Robert Anderson, first lieutenant of Co. F, vice Lieutenant Kettering, discharged; Lieut. W. A. Shrum, first lieutenant of Co. I, vice Lieutenant Painter, discharged; Quartermaster Sergeant Samuel W. Phillips, second lieutenant of Co. B, vice Lieutenant Straw, promoted; Sergeant James Moore, second lieutenant of Co. D, vice Lieutenant Cross, discharged; Hospital Steward James J. Briggs, second lieutenant of Co. E, vice Lieutenant Hamill, promoted; Sergeant Samuel McCutcheon, second lieutenant of Co. F, vice Lieutenant Anderson, promoted; John Brenneman, second lieutenant of Co. G, vice Lieutenant Liedtke, discharged.

While the Eleventh was enjoying its well-earned rest from active duties in the field, and thus preparing for the future, great and important changes, materially affecting the army, were taking place at Washington. General U. S. Grant had been confirmed Lieutenant-General, and was invested by the President with the chief command of all the national forces.

To those who had known of the petty jealousies and personal ambitious aspirations, often interfering with the wisest plans, and threatening the most fatal consequences to the army and the country, the revival of the rank of Lieutenant-General, that placed Grant over all other generals, and out of the reach of envy or interference, was accepted as an assurance that the same spirit which had induced more than three-fourths of the army to re-enlist for the suppression of the rebellion pervaded every department of the nation.

Three days before the Eleventh returned to the front, General Grant established his headquarters with the Army of the Potomac at Culpeper, and the work of getting ready for the spring campaign was at once commenced. Speedily armed and equipped, the new recruits were drilled four to six hours each day, making such proficiency in the manual of arms, and in the various evolutions of regiment, brigade, and division, that by the time the spring suns had dried up the roads, recruits and veterans were one in everything except the actual experience of the battle-field.

Instead of the five corps with which General Meade had conducted the latter movements of his last campaign, the army was consolidated into three corps—the Second, Fifth, and Sixth—commanded respectively by Hancock, Warren, and Sedgwick. In this new organization the old First Corps was merged into the Fifth Corps, of which Wadsworth's Division was the first, Robinson's Division the second, Crawford's Division the third, and Griffin's Division the fourth. Retiring from the command of the First Corps, with which he had been associated since the death of the lamented Reynolds, General Newton expressed his regrets in an eloquent farewell address, in which the former services of the men were acknowledged and appreciated:

"In relinquishing command, I take occasion to express the pride and pleasure I have experienced in my connection with you, and my profound regret at our separation. Identified by its services with the history of the war, the First Corps gave at Gettysburg a crowning proof of valor and endurance in saving from the grasp of the enemy the strong position upon which the battle was fought. The terrible losses suffered by the corps in that conflict attest its supreme devotion to the country. Though the corps has lost its distinctive name by the present changes, history will not be silent upon the magnitude of its services."

In all this new-modeling and reorganizing of his forces, General Grant had not overestimated the prowess of his antagonist. The army of General Lee, composed of the Corps of Ewell, Hill, and Longstreet—the latter just returned from Tennessee—lay along and near the south bank of the Rapidan, with its flanks well protected by the natural defenses of the country, and its front secured by strong artificial intrenchments. The Federal commander could discover no secret or untried route leading to Richmond. The opposing armies were to meet somewhere, as they had often met before, and the result of the campaign, as seen from the beginning, was a question of martial endurance.

The stirring address of General Meade, issued on the 3d of May, was followed by the bugle note to march. At midnight the Fifth Corps was leading the army over the Stevensburg pike toward the Rapidan. The Sixth Corps followed after the Fifth; while the Second Corps, keeping down the north bank to Ely's Ford, was intended to strike the plank-road near Chancellorville, each corps commander hoping to evade an engagement in the forlorn region of the Wilderness.

THE SPRING CAMPAIGN BEGUN. 323

Crossing the river at Germania Ford, and marching two or three miles toward the Wilderness Tavern, five o'clock P. M. the Fifth Corps halted for the night, the Eleventh bivouacking in an open field, and furnishing the picket detail for the brigade. To our right, and sometimes apparently in front, during most of the night, dull rumbling sounds were heard, such as indicated that the enemy, too, was moving. Five o'clock next morning the march was resumed, carrying us out to the old turnpike, in sight of the Wilderness Tavern. With every passing moment it became apparent that our further progress was to be contested.

General Lee, ever watchful, and tracing in the outlines of the opening campaign the energy of the new commander, was coming against Grant in two columns, one along the Orange turnpike, and the other by way of the Fredericksburg and Orange plank-road. The rebel general was intent on accomplishing what Grant was manœuvring to avoid,—to intercept our southward march, and, by striking his blows on the flank, entangle the Federal army in the Wilderness.

The advance division of Ewell's Corps, that reached Parker's store, immediately in front of Warren's left, was the first to become engaged with parts of the First and Fourth Divisions. The Fifth Corps, halting all its regiments, and concentrating on the turnpike, prepared for a vigorous defense. The Sixth Corps was hurried to its place on the right, and the Second Corps, marching rapidly along the Chancellorville plank-road, hastened to extend our position on the left.

Sights not strange to the veteran soldier, but new and exciting to the recruit, were now to be witnessed. Divisions and brigades, advancing at a double-quick, were forming in line of battle, or massing in reserve. Hundreds of pioneers, with axes and shovels, were felling trees and throwing up earthworks, behind which scores of cannon, unlimbered and charged with shot, presented a threatening array.

The first attack of the Fifth Corps, led on by Wadsworth and Griffin, drove Ewell from all his positions, and far in from our front. But meeting heavy rebel reinforcements, by a sudden turn the enemy rallied, and Wadsworth and Griffin were compelled to give way to the enemy. Baxter's Brigade, with the Eleventh in front, marched in quick time to the extreme left at the moment to support the wavering lines of the two divisions, and hold in check the advancing rebels.

The storm of battle had again broken out in the Wilderness, and was sweeping along the lines with increasing fury. Lee's intention was now more apparent than ever. It was to turn Warren's flank before Hancock, who was marching from Chancellorville, could come to his

BATTLE OF THE WILDERNESS.

relief. He had so far succeeded in his design that Hill's Corps, overlapping Warren, was already confronting a part of Hancock's lines, vainly endeavoring to force him back to the river.

Baxter's Brigade was again ordered to the left, and together with Griffin's Division, marched to the support of Hancock.

It was six o'clock in the evening, and the dense undergrowth through which the troops had to feel their way made it prematurely night. The Eleventh, marching by the flank, soon engaged the enemy's skirmishers, keeping up a brisk fire until total darkness ended the contest. Uniting with Hancock, and throwing out a strong line of pickets, the position was maintained until the morning of the 6th of May.

At the close of the first day's fight the line of the Federal army extended along the Germania Ford and Chancellorville road, with the right near the river, and the left near the Brock road leading to Spottsylvania. During the night it was determined to make a simultaneous attack on the enemy's left by Sedgwick, and on his right by Hancock. Shortly after daylight Hancock's advance was undertaken by the Fourth Division of the Fifth Corps and Baxter's Brigade. It was a bright May morning, and as the troops marched through the thick growth of hazel, the rays of the sun, that here and there penetrated the deep shade of the Wilderness, were reflected as well from the unsheathed swords of the officers as from the muskets of the men.

The first shock of battle fell unexpectedly on the enemy, causing his lines to give way in rout and confusion. No time was lost by Hancock in following up so great an advantage, and occupying either side of the plank-road with his forces, the men pushed steadily onward. In that gallant advance General Baxter was severely wounded and taken from the field, leaving the command of the brigade to Colonel Coulter, and the command of the Eleventh to Major Keenan.

Quick to see the danger that threatened his right flank by Hancock's valorous assault, General Lee hurried forward the troops of Longstreet's Corps, then arriving on the ground, and placing himself at the head of one of the brigades, dashed forward into the wide and extending breach in his lines.

It was not a broad, open country in which the men were fighting, where the movements of the enemy could be seen and promptly met by counter movements. But every one knew from the galling fire poured in that the enemy, reinforced, was assuming other and more advantageous positions. Presently the whole front lighted up with deadly volleys, and coming down on our first lines with the force of an avalanche, the divisions of Longstreet swept Hancock back over the ground taken from Hill, across the plankroad, and to the shelter of the shallow earthworks that the troops had left in the morning. Sedgwick on the right, at the instant of moving out his lines, received the advance of Ewell, who had anticipated the Federal attack. After a fierce conflict, repulsed at every point, the rebel general slowly retired. Several hours later, coming once more against Sedgwick, the whole Sixth Corps was thrown forward, driving Ewell far back in the Wilderness, and firmly holding the ground thus won.

It was now noon; and from right to left there was a lull in the battle. Each army, half exhausted, as if by common consent was reposing a moment to gather new strength for a more decisive blow. Four o'clock P.M. there came a sharp rattling of musketry and a quick succession of artillery reports from the left of the lines. It was quiet no longer. Longstreet had again moved up to assault Hancock in the most fearful attack of the day, and made with a vehemence that threatened to ruin our left and drive us into the Rapidan.

But foreseeing where the blow would fall, the left had been strongly reinforced by Gibbons's Division, to whom Colonel Coulter was ordered to report his brigade. The charge of the rebels, though at first successful, met by the timely arrival of Gibbons, was handsomely checked, and the enemy at last forced back across the Brock road. Foiled a second time in his attempt to turn our flank, and in each instance suffering severely in killed and wounded, Longstreet withdrew, and, to all appearances, the second day's fight in the Wilderness was over.

General Lee had promised to drive Grant across the Rapidan in three days. The advantage of the fighting thus far had been with neither army; but to accomplish his undertaking the rebel general saw how much still remained to be done, and in the very last hour of day, while many a soldier was looking forward to a night of rest for weary and aching limbs, the battle broke out afresh far to the right.

With all the stealth and quiet with which the twilight was coming, a heavy rebel column, moving out from behind its intrenchments, fell upon Ricketts's Division, holding the right flank of the Sixth Corps. Impetuous and sudden, the enemy's assault was successful, completely turning our flank and cutting us off from Germania Ford; and but for the promptness of officers and men, might have crowned the day with irretrievable disaster. But fresh troops strengthened the yielding line, until the enemy, first completely checked, and then put on the defensive, gave up the contest.

Colonel Coulter's Brigade, a short time before united to the division, from which it had been separated for nearly two days, at the beginning of the last attack was ordered into position on the plank-road, in rear of army headquarters. It was the direction in which the rebels were bearing down with such frightful rapidity, until arrested further toward the front.

The Federal battle-line, after two days of wave-like advancing and receding, excepting that the right was thrown somewhat back, occupied the same ground on which the conflict had begun. There was no difficulty in tracing that line through the most intricate and deeply-tangled portions of the battle-field. It was not the marks of blood only that guided us over those six miles from left to right, but a line of prostrated human forms, here dead, and there dying; here still and uncomplaining, and there wild with the delirium of fever and the agony of pain. Scattered all along the way, from the Brock road to the Wilderness Tavern, lay one hundred and fifty-seven killed and wounded belonging to the Eleventh.

During the quiet of the early afternoon the roads had been given to the ambulance corps that came upon the field, rapidly loading up the wagons with maimed and bleeding forms. The wounded of the Fifth Corps were placed under charge of Surgeon Anawalt, with directions to cross the Rapidan and proceed to Rappahannock

28*

Station, where cars were in waiting to convey them to Washington. But before the first carriage of the long line had made half the distance to the ford, the rebel assault on the right cut us off from the river. The confusion was only for a moment.

"Doctor," said an aid-de-camp from General Warren, "you are directed to take your wounded men to Fredericksburg."

Turning short in the road, and pushing forward as fast as a care for the comfort of the men would allow, a little after midnight Fredericksburg received its first installment of wounded from the Wilderness battle-field.

The 7th of May dawned clear and bright. Several hours of undisturbed quiet, in rear of army headquarters, prepared the Eleventh and the rest of the brigade for a change of position to the support of Ricketts's Division on the extreme right. A fierce and determined effort was to be made to retake the ground lost on the previous evening; and as we marched to our place early in the morning, batteries were already wheeling into line, preparing to open the attack by a shower of grape-shot and shell. But when at last all was in readiness, and with the first volley of our numerous cannon a heavy body of skirmishers advanced, it was found that we were only beating the air. The rebels had retreated from our front, and nothing remained but the line of rifle-pits from which Ricketts had been driven to tell the story of their last successful charge.

Traversing each of the roads leading southward, the cavalry were employed in developing the meaning of General Lee's sudden and unexpected retreat. He had failed to make such an impression on the Union lines as in any degree to compensate him for his own severe losses, and observing the movement of our wagon trains and ambulances toward Fredericksburg as a new base of supplies, Lee became alarmed for the safety of his right flank, and was marching with all speed to secure the high grounds around Spottsylvania Court House.

In rapid pursuit came the Army of the Potomac. The Fifth Corps again took the lead, with Robinson's Division in front. Filing out from the grounds near the Lacey House, and marching past the Second Corps, ten o'clock P.M. of the 7th we struck the Brock road and pushed on to Todd's tavern. Few and short were the halts of that long night march, that tested to the full the endurance of every man.

Five o'clock of the next morning the division was within three miles of Spottsylvania. But the enemy moving on a shorter parallel road further to the west, with a start of several hours, headed us in the exciting race for position. Crossing our path was the narrow little river Ny, and in our front, disputing all further progress, were the rebel skirmishers.

Time was now more precious than life; and without a moment to refresh themselves after the fatigues of a ten hours' march, the division was pressed rapidly forward, meeting in what was reported as only dismounted cavalry, Hood's splendid Division of rebel infantry. In charging over the rough and difficult ground, and through Alsop's farm, though many fell out of the ranks from utter exhaustion, the troops steadily advanced, driving back the enemy's skirmishers and pushing on within seventy-five yards of his intrenched position. At every step the rebel fire was becoming more and more destructive. At last it could not be endured, and retiring first to the edge of the woods, and then to the rear of Alsop's house, temporary defenses were thrown up, behind which the troops took shelter.

General Robinson, while gallantly leading the charge across Alsop's fields, was severely wounded, and carried from the field, the command of the division devolving upon Colonel Coulter. "The disabling of General Robinson at this juncture was a severe blow to the division, and certainly influenced the fortunes of the day. The want of our commanding officer prevented that concert of action which alone could have overcome the enemy in front."*

But above the loss of General Robinson, the

---

* Coulter's Report.

Eleventh felt the loss of Major John B. Keenan, shot dead at the head of the regiment while by word and example he was cheering forward the men. Identified with the Eleventh from the beginning, and in every time and place displaying all the generous qualities of the true soldier, the commanding officer could well say, not only for himself, but for the regiment, that "long acquaintance led to a full appreciation of Major Keenan's character. He was brave, cool, and courteous, and by his personal exertions and bold example nobly sustained his command."

The rapid arrival of fresh troops enabled us to hold the line on Alsop's farm. But when the day closed Robinson's Division was nearly without an organization. In three days it had lost General Robinson, all of its brigade commanders, and not less than two thousand officers and men. What still remained of it was temporarily attached to the other divisions of the corps. The First Brigade, Colonel Lyle, was transferred to the Fourth Division; the Second Brigade, Colonel Coulter, to Crawford's (Third) Division; the Third Brigade, Colonel Bowman, was retained by General Warren under his own supervision.

CHAPTER II.

IN FRONT OF SPOTTSYLVANIA.

NEAR LAUREL HILL, Monday, May 9.—The remainder of yesterday, until eight o'clock P.M., was spent in strengthening our intrenchments near the Alsop mansion. Then the Eleventh was ordered some distance further to the right, passing the rest of the night and until noon of to-day in erecting defenses in front of the new position. This afternoon Robinson's Division was broken up, and the brigade reported to General Crawford, of the Third Division, near Laurel Hill. We were at once placed on the right of the line, the Eleventh (under command of Capt. B. F. Haines) connecting on the left with the Pennsylvania Reserves. The Fifth Corps is now in the center, with the Second on the right and the Sixth on the left. The enemy holds strong and solid intrenchments just over against us, that can only be taken by the most determined valor.

TUESDAY, May 10.—Our men bivouacked last night behind a range of formidable breastworks; and but for the active preparations going on around us, all pointing to an early attack on the enemy's lines, we might have slept in undisturbed security. When the order came this morning for a general assault along the whole front of the Fifth and Sixth Corps, there was a determined expression on the face of every man, answering to the desperate work before him.

"You will advance your entire brigade in support of the line of skirmishers, and carry the rifle-pits now in front. Go on until you come upon the enemy's intrenchments, and hold on firmly to all you get. Take the first line of rifle-pits at all hazards."

There was no mistaking these orders sent from General Crawford to Colonel Coulter. Throwing out the Ninety-seventh New York as skirmishers, and placing the Eighty-third New York and Eleventh Pennsylvania on the left of the line, the Eighty-eighth Pennsylvania and Twelfth Massachusetts on the right, and forming the left wing of each regiment in rear of the right wing, the two lines of the brigade moved out to the attack.

The first forward step developed the well-directed fire of the enemy, but through a shower of bullets, for more than a quarter of a mile, the forward step was maintained. Still moving on up the slope of Laurel Hill, the summit was at last gained, and the line of rifle-pits that crowned its crest gallantly carried. Beyond a reach of broad open ground were now to be seen extensive earthworks filled with artillery. Advancing within a hundred yards of these intrenchments all further progress was impossible. The troops had fought their way to that point, not with enthusiastic cheers, but with steady and persistent determination. Colonel Coulter reported to General Crawford that he had taken the rifle-pits of the enemy, but could go no further.

"Tell the colonel to hold the line where he is," was the reply.

And though the rebel artillery swept the area in our front, and a severe musketry fire was concentrated upon the men, the line was held from noon until five o'clock. Two brigades of Gibbons's Division, Second Corps, then came to our relief, and Coulter's Brigade retired twenty or thirty yards to the rear. With the line thus reinforced, an hour later there was a second attempt to carry the enemy's position; but no advance could be made beyond the ground already secured. At dusk the Pennsylvania Reserves were sent to the right of Gibbons, and Coulter's Brigade ordered back within the breastworks, where we are at present resting. When we marched out from these defenses this morning the brigade numbered nine hundred men. Two hundred and twenty-nine have been killed and wounded in the narrow space in our front of less than half a mile.

THURSDAY, May 12. — Another unsuccessful

attempt has been made to dislodge the enemy from Laurel Hill. Yesterday and last night were occupied in remodeling and extending our defenses. After dark, in the midst of a heavy rain-storm, the Second Corps commenced moving toward the left, leaving our brigade on the extreme right flank. This morning dawned with fierce fighting in front of Spottsylvania, the roar of musketry passing slowly from left to right until every part of the line was engaged. At the hight of the battle, Coulter's Brigade was ordered to the support of the Pennsylvania Reserves, who were seen a moment before to pass over the intrenchments to attack the rebels in front. The Reserves hardly reached the crest of the hill until the same staggering fire that told so fearfully upon our ranks on the morning of the 10th, was again experienced. The enemy was as strong and watchful as ever. Following after the first line, and a little to the right of its former position, the brigade advanced a short distance beyond the Reserves, the men protecting themselves from the rebel fire by the peculiar formation of the ground. Toward noon we were again withdrawn to the intrenchments, but leaving behind on that fatal hill, as an additional sacrifice to its evil genius, seventy-five men.

SATURDAY, May 14.—The uncertainty hanging over all our movements since we crossed the

Rapidan, and which has been a serious check to the *esprit de corps* of the army, begins to clear away. The troops had not ceased cheering over Hancock's successes on the left, in capturing Johnson's entire Division, when Grant's dispatch to the Secretary of War, in which he proposes to "fight it out on this line if it takes all summer," aroused them to the highest pitch of enthusiasm. Now we have the congratulatory order of General Meade, stating in brief what has already been done, and what there remains yet to do. On the heels of this comes a rumor that Sheridan's cavalry is operating in rear of the rebel lines, tearing up the railroads and burning depots of supplies. But these successes do not make us insensible of our own great losses. The Fifth Corps, as it is now seen, looks scarcely larger than did Robinson's Division ten days ago.

Since crossing the Rapidan we have lost Generals Hays, Wadsworth, Sedgwick, Stevenson, and Rice. A Pennsylvanian and a resident of Pittsburg, General Alex. Hays was a personal friend of the officers of the Eleventh, admired by all as a brave and accomplished soldier. At Mine Run, as the troops were in line of battle, awaiting the word to charge the enemy's works, the general remarked: "I don't like the look of things around here. This is the only place in Virginia where I have not wanted to fight."

It is not a little singular that he should have met his death so near that same locality. The rebels have lost Generals Jenkins, Jones, Gordon, and Perrin. Longstreet was severely wounded on the evening of the 6th; and it is rumored that J. E. B. Stuart was killed in a fight with Sheridan. There is a spirit of hopefulness throughout our ranks that will carry the men along with their indomitable leader.

NEAR SPOTTSYLVANIA, May 16.—Leaving the Twelfth Massachusetts and Eleventh Pennsylvania on the picket line in front of Laurel Hill, the rest of the brigade, following in the wake of the division, on the evening of the 14th moved toward the left. It was a dark, rainy night, and the muddy roads and swollen streams made the march full of weariness to men already worn down with incessant labors. Yesterday afternoon, the two regiments left on picket having rejoined the brigade, we were placed in position near the Anderson House, holding now the extreme left of the army, as we formerly held the extreme right. It is a relief to know that we are quite out of the Wilderness; but the ground in front is rough and uneven, covered with a heavy growth of timber. On every commanding position is a rebel fortification, from which defiantly floats the Confederate flag.

THURSDAY, May 19.—During the last three days the lines of the army have been several times changed to meet the impetuous assaults of the rebels, who seem stung to the quick by operations in their front and rear. Tuesday afternoon the brigade crossed the River Ny, and moved up nearer Spottsylvania, taking position to the left of the First Division, and in support of Cooper's Pennsylvania Battery. All night long the men worked with pick and shovel—tools with whose use they have grown familiar—intrenching themselves on their new ground. It was a wise precaution; for with the morning of the 18th the rebels opened a heavy cannonade. But the shells buried themselves in the newly constructed sand-banks, or harmlessly ricochetted from the fallen timber in our front, while a squad of riflemen, hiding behind the logs, and picking off with unerring certainty every gunner that showed himself above the parapet, kept in silence one of their most effective batteries.

Toward 10 o'clock P.M., making a sally on the pickets in front of our brigade, the rebels pushed back the line for more than a hundred yards. While bringing up supports, and in the act of advancing the troops to re-establish the picket lines, Colonel Coulter was shot through the body and taken to the rear. Apparently satisfied with testing the strength of the force in his front, the enemy retired, and everything remained quiet until a few hours ago. A part of

Ewell's Corps, crossing the Ny at a point above our extreme right, moved down to the Fredericksburg road, thus seizing the main line of our communications. The Eleventh was hurried along for two miles toward Fredericksburg, at a double-quick. But the work of driving back Ewell was accomplished by Tyler's foot artillerists; and leaving it to others to keep up the pursuit, we returned to our intrenchments on the left. The brigade is under command of Colonel Bates. of the Twelfth Massachusetts.

ACROSS THE PAMUNKEY, May 28.—The events of the last nine days, though so full of significance, have been crowded upon each other in rapid succession. Noiselessly as the Second Corps, preceded by a large force of cavalry, marched some distance to the rear of our position in front of Spottsylvania, at midnight of the 20th, it did not escape the notice of the men. It was the beginning of another move by the left flank. Next morning the Fifth Corps was following the Second, in easy supporting distance, over the road leading to Guinney's Station, where we bivouacked on the night of May 21st, driving away a small body of rebel cavalry. On the morning of the 22d, Colonel Bates's Brigade was ordered to make a reconnoissance toward the Telegraph road, three miles from the station. It was a slow and cautious march, our flanks well protected by trusty skirmishers. Not an enemy was to be seen; he too was moving southward. Some hours later, striking the Telegraph road, the Fifth Corps marched to Bowling Green, the county seat of Caroline County. The dreary Wilderness, and the scarcely less dreary region of Spottsylvania, where for two weeks, day and night, we had been fighting or intrenching, were left behind us, and the beautiful county of Caroline, without a mark of war's ravages upon its fair face, was a feast to the eye and a joy to the soul. Quitting our bivouac near Bowling Green early Monday morning, and passing in the march the Second Corps halted at Milford, the Fifth Corps reached Jericho Ford, on the North Anna River, near the hour of noon. The enemy was not expecting us so high up the river; but Hancock's guns, afterward heard further to the left, gave warning by their thunders that the rebels had neither been deceived by our movements nor surprised at our advance. Unconquerable as ever, their gray-clad legions formed in battle-line across our path to Richmond.

The Fifth Corps crossed the North Anna at Jericho Ford without opposition, and marching a short distance down the south bank to a copse of woods, formed its battle-line with Cutler on the right, Griffin in the center, and Crawford on the left. Time was when the first thing to be done after a halt was to make coffee, in whose grateful fumes all weariness was forgotten. Now the first thing the men do is to intrench. We had but commenced this necessary work when the center division was furiously assaulted by a heavy rebel column. The attack soon spread all along the line. But with intrenchments incomplete, the rebels were repulsed at every point, leaving in our hands not less than a thousand prisoners.

Tuesday morning an interval of three miles was discovered between Hancock on the left, who had bravely fought his way across the river at Chesterfield bridge, and the Fifth and Sixth Corps on the right. The First Regiment of Pennsylvania Reserves was sent down the stream with orders to form a connection with the right of Hancock's line. Moving stealthily along the rocky bed of the river, concealed from view by its high bank, the regiment reached Quarrel's Ford, to find all further progress impossible, and the enemy closed in upon its rear. General Warren then ordered Crawford to advance his entire division to find the lost regiment, and to complete the connection with Hancock. With the Second Brigade on the left, the Eleventh marching next to the river, our line was advanced against a desultory fire from the rebel pickets. The Reserves were found in communication with Burnside's troops, just arrived, and posted on the north bank. The uncovering of Quarrel's Ford, thus effected, made a passage for the Ninth Corps, whose divisions at once passed over the river, and filling up the gap, by nightfall Crawford had returned to his place on the right.

After two days of unsuccessful effort to carry the enemy's position, Thursday night, under cover of the thick clouds that were scudding the sky, the Fifth Corps recrossed the North Anna. Daylight of Friday, following after the Sixth Corps, we were marching down the north bank. Traveling eastwardly for two or three hours, the impression became general that the army was making a retrograde movement. Again we changed course to the westward, and at last to the southward, bivouacking at night five miles from the Pamunkey. This morning when we came to the river it was spanned by pontoon bridges; the cavalry and the Sixth Corps were already on the opposite side, and filing down the slippery banks, made so by half an hour's rain, and over the trembling foot-walk, the Army of the Potomac was again on the Yorktown Peninsula.

SUNDAY, May 29.—There has been nothing of the quiet or sanctity of the Sabbath in any of our movements to-day. From early morning until this late evening hour, cavalry, infantry, and artillery have been marching, now cautiously in line of battle, and again flying in squadrons, or quickly moving in columns of division.

Leaving our bivouac at an early hour, the corps began its advance toward the Chickahominy, Crawford on the left, Cutler in the center, and Griffin on the right, and thus forming the left of the army. The route has been along the Grove Church turnpike, the enemy's skirmish line falling slowly back as we continued forward. The entire army is to-night in battle-line near the Chickahominy River. On the left of the Eleventh are the Pennsylvania Reserves. Near the camp-fire where we write, a group of officers and men are recounting incidents that occurred two years ago, as the army of General McClellan marched over this same ground to the battle of Mechanicsville. There are frequent shots on the outlying picket posts, that seem to speak of the probabilities of to-morrow; but there is no flinching anywhere among the troops. We have fought our way once more to the gates of Richmond, and this time with a persistency that must sooner or later carry us through them.

NEAR COLD HARBOR, Monday, June 6.—This is the eighth day of the battle of Cold Harbor, and the end is not yet. With the first dawn of Monday, May 30th, starting from beds on the ground, and shaking the dew from their blankets, the ranks of the Fifth Corps were formed for a speedy advance. Crawford's Division moved directly forward across the road to Shady Grove Church for the Mechanicsville pike, driving back in its progress a body of rebel cavalry. But it soon came to be known that there was something more than horsemen in our front—that the whole of Ewell's Corps held a position to cover all the approaches to the upper bridges of the Chickahominy. Detaching a division from his left, and marching it in rear of his line of troops, the rebel general had attempted to seize the Mechanicsville pike, and thus strike our undefended flank.

The movement was at once detected, and a brigade of the Reserves sent out to meet it. Penetrating as far as Bethesda Church, the Reserves were met by the head of the rebel column as it emerged from a narrow strip of woods, and the fierce encounter in which we are still engaged was there begun. Soon the whole division moved to the left, and around that quiet church, hitherto resting in undisturbed repose in a grove of beautiful oak trees, for many hours there was an angry clashing of arms, and a thundering of artillery. The rebels came to the attack in double lines, exposing themselves with reckless daring to the unerring fire of our batteries, whose shot and shell made great and frequent gaps in their ranks. Six o'clock in the evening the conflict extended along the whole front of the Fifth Corps, the enemy concentrating all his efforts to carry that portion of the line. But the troops of those war-tried brigades were immovable, and despite the most passionate and earnest charges, in which the Confederates revealed the spirit that inspires men fighting in the last straits, those lines maintained an unbroken front, and when night closed down upon the battle-field the position was securely held.

Tuesday, the 31st, was comparatively quiet until late in the afternoon, when the battle broke out afresh still further to the left. It was Sheridan's cavalry fighting for the important point of Cold Harbor, that was only wrested from the enemy after a severe struggle. June 1st the Eighteenth Corps arrived from Butler's Department, and formed in line to the left of the Fifth Corps. During the night of the 31st the Sixth Corps had also been moved to the left, and on the morning of the 2d of June the Fifth Corps was the extreme right of the line, which now extended from Cold Harbor to Bethesda Church.

In forming this new line there had been more or less of fighting at different points; but true to the promises of these preparatory moves, Friday, June 3d, witnessed the contest renewed with a fierceness beyond all precedent. Hancock's first gun on the left was speedily answered from the extreme right, and everywhere along the extended line there were the sounds of desperate battle. Late in the afternoon the Eleventh was sent out on the picket line. It was taken by the enemy to be an advance of the division on his position, and subjected the regiment to a fire so direct and certain that in hardly as many feet across the open ground four of the men were killed and a number wounded. No impression whatever was made upon the rebel position on the right, and scarcely any on the left, where the fighting was more severe. The night of the 3d and most of the 4th of June were occupied by the troops in throwing up intrenchments, as though the enemy's works were to be carried by regular siege.

The showery afternoon of Saturday was followed by a dark and cloudy evening. It was one of those nights when the soldier feels like early wrapping himself up in his blanket to rest; and it was a fitting night for the enemy, ever watchful and sagacious, to make a furious attack upon our lines. Deeper than midnight thunder peeled forth the cannon; while the burning shells, coursing through the air, looked like angry meteors escaped from their orbits. The assault did not reach the front of the Fifth Corps; but as the men stood in their places, ready for the word of command, they joined in the loud hurrah that told again and again of the repulse of the foe. The attack had been deferred too long. If we could not drive the Southerner from his strong earthworks, we were not to be driven from our own. Behind its intrenchments either army was unconquerable. Last night was not unlike Saturday night in the black clouds that hung over the army. Under cover of its darkness, again the enemy sallied forth, this time, as before, on our extreme left. In the midst of the heavy cannonading we drew in our picket lines, and leaving the position near Bethesda Church, the corps marched slowly toward the left.

The Eleventh is now on the right of the line, which rests near Gaines's Mills, while the left extends to Cold Harbor. The troops of the Second and Eighteenth Corps are between us and the enemy. Whether the corps are thus massing for a final assault upon the rebel lines, or a new flank movement is to be inaugurated, will soon be known.

SOUTH OF THE JAMES, Thursday, June 16.—It has a strange sound to say south of the James. From the point where we entered the Peninsula to that of our exit is fifty miles. We could have made the distance in two days' march, if nothing had opposed our progress, whereas it has consumed nearly three weeks. In less than two years history has so far repeated itself as to reenact nearly all the prominent scenes of the first Peninsular campaign. Chickahominy Swamps, Gaines's Mills, Cold Harbor, Harrison's Landing —names familiar, and of enduring associations, for the moment pushing aside Antietam, Fredericksburg, Chancellorville, Gettysburg—claim again their first absorbing interest.

Five days were spent in comparative quiet near Cold Harbor, the men working in details at digging rifle-pits and throwing up intrenchments. Saturday morning, June 11th, the march of the Fifth Corps began, Crawford's Division leading the corps, and itself led by Wilson's Division of cavalry. The route was down the Peninsula, and the purpose to effect a crossing of the Chickahominy at Long Bridge. The Confederate general was also extending his line eastward, and on the morning of the 13th, when the brigade reached the bridge, a force of the rebels already held possession. It was only a small force, however, that quickly retired at our approach. Crossing the Chickahominy and filing out into the New Market road, the division changed the direction of its march and moved toward Richmond. In less than an hour, and within a mile or two of White Oak Swamp, our line of battle was confronted by a line of the enemy. There was a mutual halt, each army again throwing up intrenchments and preparing for an attack.

While the Fifth Corps thus lay stretched across the only road by which General Lee could assail our flank, the other corps were crossing the Chickahominy at points lower down, and without opposition moving toward the James. When night came on our picket line was quietly abandoned, and falling into ranks, the Fifth Corps was bringing up the rear of the army. The march was continued all night and until eleven o'clock of Tuesday, when we halted near Charles City Court House.

This morning, all the wagon trains having passed on to the James River, we left our bivouac and marched to Harrison's Landing. The steamer John Brooks ferried the Eleventh across the magnificent river to Windmill Point. The men are now disembarking, and stacking arms on the nearest ground. The Army of the Potomac is at its watering-place, and ten thousand bathers crowd the beach.

CHAPTER III.

SOUTH OF THE JAMES RIVER.

THE Army of the Potomac had not yet reached its resting-place. The campaign north of the James, though bitter and bloody beyond anything that had ever preceded it, without any abatement of these terrible qualities, was to be continued over the territory south of it. A halt of an hour or two, and the bugle-note, familiar as ever, though echoed from strange and unknown surroundings, called the men into lines, and the march was continued toward Petersburg, now the objective point of the campaign.

Contending with an opponent ever on the defensive, and fighting always on his own ground, Grant had so far failed of his original intention to invest Richmond from the west, and connect his lines with those of Butler at Bermuda Hundred, that he now resolved to siege Petersburg, and thus cut off the rebel army, pent up in its capital, from all sources of supply except the solitary line of the James River Canal.

The Eighteenth Corps, that came in transports from White House Landing, on the York River, to City Point, on the James, and the Second Corps, the first to cross from the Peninsula, were already in front of Petersburg. The Ninth Corps was *en route* for the same destination, two or three hours in advance, when the Fifth Corps began its march from the river shore. Diverging to the left of the direct route, and following the road to Prince George Court House, the last rays of the setting sun had melted into twilight as we took our position on the left of the line now formed in front of Petersburg, the right of the Eleventh connecting with the Ninth Corps.

The golden moment to carry Petersburg by an unexpected attack passed away with the night of the 15th. It was then held by only a small force of home-guards. But clearly divining Grant's designs, Lee had crossed the James at Drury's

Bluff, and every subsequent hour witnessed a fresh arrival of his veteran divisions. The 17th was spent in adjusting our lines and preparing for a general assault on the following morning. Toward nightfall Crawford's Division advanced with the Ninth Corps, and gaining some ground in front, captured a number of prisoners and the battle-flag of an Alabama regiment.

The morning of June 18th opened clear and bright, revealing in its first light the spires of Petersburg, and wafting on its fresh, balmy air the sound of bells, ringing out their alarm in the ears of the anxious inhabitants of the beleaguered city. It was five o'clock, and orders having passed along the lines, from the right of the Eighteenth Corps, on the Appomattox, to the Fifth Corps, opposite Cemetery Hill, on the left, the skirmishers advanced to the grand assault. But the intrenchments, filled with armed men only the night before, and in whose front many a soldier expected to die, were now empty. The enemy had taken up a new line nearer to the city, and more securely defended than the outer line.

Instead of a general assault, as at first intended, a new order of battle was devised. The attack was to be made in columns at different points along the enemy's works. Speedily as possible the troops were distributed, and beginning on the right, the fearful work soon extended to all the corps. The Fifth and the Ninth, moving out from their intrenchments, and passing over ground whose surface was crossed by deep and numerous ravines, made their daring but unsuccessful assault against that part of the Confederate line afterward the scene of the mine explosion. The repulse of the Federal army was general. Enfilading fires of infantry and artillery swept through our columns, leveling the ranks and with frightful suddenness depleting our numbers.

The same persistency of purpose, seen in all the movements of the Federal army north of the James, was still apparent. Moving up to and beyond the abandoned works of the enemy, the morning of the 19th found the Union troops behind intrenchments as unyielding as those of the foe. The lines of the opposing armies, in many places, were scarcely a hundred yards apart, and for several succeeding days the conflict on either side was committed to the sharpshooters, who picked off every man that showed himself above the parapets. Men and officers lived in bombproof quarters, and moved to the rear, or from right to left, through covered ways.

As the line of earthworks became more systematic and complete, daily attempts were made to extend our left flank, and more certainly envelop the communications of Lee. But every day only brought out more clearly the conviction

EXPLOSION OF FORT PEGRAM.

that the enemy had lost nothing of his watchfulness, and that for every advantage gained we must pay the price in men.

The mining of Fort Pegram, opposite the Ninth Corps, began on the 25th of June. Its conception belonged to a Pennsylvanian—Colonel Henry Pleasants—and its entire construction devolved upon a Pennsylvania regiment. The want of entire success attending the enterprise does not detract in the least from its merits as a wonder of perseverance and industry. The length of the main gallery was five hundred and twenty-two feet, and that of the laterals forty feet. For want of wheel-barrows, the excavated earth was carried out in cracker boxes, and ingeniously concealed from the prying look of the enemy.

Through many discouragements, the mine was at last finished, and the 30th of July fixed for its explosion. It was to be the signal of another grand assault. Every gun along the whole Federal line was to open upon the enemy, while the Eighteenth Corps, on the right of the Ninth, and the Fifth Corps on the left, were to be drawn up in line of battle, ready to rally to the support of Burnside as soon as his divisions succeeded in carrying the crest of Cemetery Hill.

The orders were received the night before, and at the hour appointed—half-past three—the cannons were charged, and the troops formed in line.

A defect in the fuse delayed the explosion for more than an hour. It seemed almost an age to men eager to behold the result, and who stood with one foot advanced, ready to leap over the parapets at the first appearance of success.

At last it came—a low, rumbling sound, which made the ground to shake with a sudden tremor, and then a heavy report, that seemed like distant thunder. Quickly following was the more dreadful roar of hundreds of cannon, lighting up a line of miles in extent with a sheet of flame. Along the entire front the supports moved forward, while forth from their intrenchments poured the storming party of the Ninth Corps.

By the explosion of the mine a strong fort was converted into a deep and extended fissure, in which three batteries of the enemy and not less than two hundred of his men found a sepulture. Paralyzed by the disaster, and fearful of other explosions, for a time the enemy was powerless, and a gap was made in his lines through which we might have secured the coveted city. But it was only for a moment. The divisions of the Ninth Corps, pausing at the crater instead of pushing on to Cemetery Hill, gave the enemy time to recover from his surprise From right to left he gathered up his forces, and turning his guns upon the gap through which the confused masses of Union troops were vainly endeavoring to force their way, the crater became the burial place of more than two hundred rebels. Before the attacking column returned to the intrenchments four thousand men of the Federal army were killed and wounded.

The reverses in our immediate front did not prevent a gradual extension of our lines southward. For several days the Fifth Corps had been constantly veering toward the left, until toward the middle of August, the camp of the Eleventh was within three miles of the Weldon Railroad, one of the chief sources of supply of the Confederate army. The whistle of the locomotive and the rattling of the trains could be distinctly heard in their passage to and from Petersburg, now laden with commissary stores, and again with troops. A happy combination of movements calling the attention of Lee north of the James River, promised success to an effort to secure this road, and thus lessen the resources of the Southern commander.

The enterprise was committed to the Fifth Corps, throughout whose camps cartridge-boxes were replenished, and rations for four days issued to the men. The march began on Thursday morning, August 18th, Griffin's Division in the advance, and Crawford's following in his rear. Two hours of slow and steady marching brought us to the railroad, when, changing direction, and moving toward Petersburg, the work of tearing up the track was prosecuted with vigor.

The thin line of the enemy, met early in the morning, had fallen back before our advance, But the great clouds of dust, rising between us and the city, told of the approach of such a body of troops as would contest any further progress. It proved to be Hill's Corps moving down the railroad in line of battle, and presenting indeed a formidable barrier across our path. Securing the position we had already gained, at six o'clock P. M. the divisions of Crawford and Ayres were ordered forward. The enemy at once developed a strong line in front of Crawford, but it was a mere feint, for, massing to the left of Ayres, Hill fell upon that extreme flank with one of his strongest divisions, capturing many prisoners, and driving back the entire line.

It was now night, and the falling rain made it pitchy dark. There were few alarms until after daylight of the 19th, with whose first dawning the men of Crawford's Division began the erection of earthworks, to protect their flank and front. All forenoon reinforcements were reaching the enemy, and everywhere along the line he was testing the strength of our position. We might have concluded that a thorough examination only revealed the folly of assaulting a strongly intrenched line. But General Lee is reported as saying that the Weldon Railroad must be regained that day if it cost him one-half his army, and at four o'clock in the afternoon those rebel troops came rushing down upon us with yells and hurrahs, only a proper accompaniment for the volleys of their rifles.

There was a gap between the left of the main line of the army, resting on the Jerusalem plank-road, and the right of Crawford's Division, held by the Third Brigade, discovered by the enemy, through which he was pouring his regiments, until completely carrying away our right flank, he had swept quite into our rear, taking in his track nearly all of four regiments, the Ninetieth and One-hundred-and-seventh Pennsylvania, and the Ninety-fourth and One-hundred-and-fourth New York. It was a moment when confusion worse confounded had come again, threatening not only the loss of our hold on the railroad, but of most of the corps.

Fortunately Colonel Wheelock, for the time in command of Baxter's Brigade, with characteristic gallantry, ordered his command to change front, and charging upon the rebels at the same time that each regiment delivered a terrible volley of musketry at short range, retrieved the fortunes of the day. The enemy broke and fled with an astonishment equal to that caused by his own daring flank movement, leaving in our hands numerous prisoners, besides hundreds of our own men captured a moment before, and on their way to the rebel rear.

The standard of the Ninety-fourth New York,

wrested from the color-bearer as he lay on the ground wounded, was retaken by Captain James Noble, of the Eleventh, and restored to the regiment. Private George W. Reed, of Co. E, in a hand to hand conflict, captured the flag of the Twenty-fourth North Carolina Regiment, and was awarded a medal of honor by the Secretary of War.

Our front line had now given way, and though the Confederate loss in men was as great as our own, the grasp by which we held the railroad, the prize for which we had been contending, was considerably weakened. At that opportune moment reinforcements from the Ninth Corps came up. Our ranks were at once reformed, and by a charge full of the old enthusiasm, the lost ground was regained. The enemy fell back to the intrenchments from which he had so defiantly marched three hours before, disappointed and defeated.

The morning of the 20th of August found a strong line of earthworks along the entire front held by the Fifth Corps, and the gap through which the enemy executed his flank movement, filled by a division of the Ninth Corps. Heavy clouds poured forth a constant rain during most of the day, and though there was sharp firing among the skirmishers, the rebels seemed indisposed to repeat the assault of Friday. Sunday morning came, wearing a smile of loveliness on the clear sky and in the balmy air. The first look at the Southern lines revealed an intention to renew the attack. The Weldon Railroad was of too much importance to be yielded up without a further effort.

Half-past eight o'clock, treating us first to a storm of shell from well-posted artillery, Lee advanced his columns for a final assault. There was no faltering anywhere along that rebel line. But it was too late. Waiting behind earthworks that could not be stormed, our men reserved their fire until the furious foe came within the measure of certain death. Then cannon and musketry shot forth their contents, sweeping down whole ranks at each separate discharge.

It was too late. The Federals held secure possession of the Weldon Railroad. The rations in Lee's army were at once reduced from half a pound of bacon and a pound and a quarter of meal per man, daily, to one-fourth pound of bacon and three-fourths pound of meal.

CHAPTER IV.

ADVANCES AND RETROGRADES.

The days that followed the occupation of the Weldon Railroad were as prolific as ever in active movements against the rebels. Now north of the James, and again south of it; now in Butler's Department, and again on the left as far as Reams's Station and Rowanty Creek, there were advances and retrogrades, skirmishes and battles. The month of September and the greater part of October wore away in these various enterprises, and in extending the strong line of redoubts to Fort Dushane, the extreme southern flank held by Baxter's Brigade. Presuming still more upon the beautiful weather of that fine autumnal month, on the 27th of October a new movement was undertaken, having for its object the extension of our lines to Hatcher's Run. It was a blow threatening the Southside Railroad, and aroused all the vigilance of the Southern commander. The expedition was unsuccessful, and by the 1st of November, after an absence of six days, the corps were back again in the old camps.

The campaign that opened with the crossing of the Rapidan in May, ended with the expedition to Hatcher's Run. It had continued through six months, with an aggregate loss, on battle-fields, in skirmishes, on picket, and in the trenches before Petersburg, of a hundred thousand men. The organization, not only of single regiments, but of the entire army, was almost radically changed. New recruits that were coming rapidly to the front prevented the ranks of the Eleventh from falling at any time below two hundred; but they were strange faces. Five hundred men had been lost to the regiment during the campaign; many of them among the killed; more of them disabled by wounds, and still others of them in the hands of the enemy, enduring the horrors of Andersonville and Salisbury.

On the 5th of September Colonel Coulter recommended the appointment of Captain B. F. Haines to be major, vice Major Keenan, killed at Laurel Hill; Sergeant Harrison Truesdale to be first lieutenant of Co. B, vice Lieutenant John P. Straw, killed at Cold Harbor; Corporal Robert R. Bitner to be second lieutenant of Co. B, vice Lieutenant Samuel W. Phillips, discharged on account of disability; Sergeant Major John A. Stevenson to be first lieutenant of Co. C, vice Lieutenant John McClintock, discharged on account of wounds; Sergeant William H.

McLaughlin to be second lieutenant of Co. C, vice Lieutenant A. Schall, promoted; Second Lieutenant James Moore to be first lieutenant of Co D, vice Lieutenant Enos S. Hall, died of wounds; Sergeant James R. Brown to be second lieutenant of Co. D, vice Lieutenant James Moore, promoted. On the 13th of October Second Lieutenant James J. Briggs was recommended to be first lieutenant of Co. E, vice Lieutenant Samuel J. Hammil, discharged on account of wounds; Sergeant Daniel Bonbright to be second lieutenant of Co. E, vice Lieutenant Briggs, promoted. Immediate attention to these appointments was urged, because four companies were without commissioned officers in the field, and the other companies had but one officer each present for duty.

On the 1st of November Sergeant John Kyle was recommended to be first lieutenant of Co. I, vice Lieutenant W. A. Shrum, discharged on account of wounds; Sergeant Lewis Mechling to be second lieutenant of Co. I, vice Lieutenant Shrum, promoted. Again, later in the month, the heavy loss in officers continuing to be felt, Lieutenant John A. Stevenson was recommended to be adjutant, vice Arthur F. Small, discharged; Sergeant David Weaverling to be second lieutenant of Co. A, vice Lieutenant Allen S. Jacobs, promoted; Lieutenant William H. McLaughlin to be first lieutenant of Co. C, vice

Lieutenant Stevenson, appointed adjutant; Sergeant Henry D. Weller to be second lieutenant of Co. C, vice Lieutenant McLaughlin, promoted; Lieutenant Robert Anderson to be regimental quartermaster, vice Lieutenant Allen S. Jacobs, deceased; Lieutenant Samuel McCutcheon to be first lieutenant of Co. F, vice Lieutenant Anderson, appointed quartermaster; Sergeant James T. Cook to be second lieutenant of Co. F, vice Lieutenant McCutcheon, promoted.

The reorganizing of the broken ranks of the old Eleventh was not only necessary, but timely. A new raid was to be made by the Fifth Corps on the Weldon Railroad. Although our lines crossed it within six miles of Petersburg, it was known that the enemy was procuring large supplies for his troops by way of this road to Stony Creek, whence they were conveyed in wagons to Petersburg. The Fifth Corps, with the Third Division of the Second Corps, and Gregg's cavalry, were detailed effectually to destroy the road as far south as the town of Hicksford, on the Meherrin River.

The march commenced on Wednesday, the 7th of December. It was a dull winter morning as the troops filed out along the Jerusalem plankroad. Various indeed were the conjectures as to the probable destination of the column, carrying on the persons of its troops six days' rations.

At one time the movement was pronounced a reconnoissance toward the Southside road; at another we were certainly to effect a union with Sherman in Georgia.

The heavy clouds of the opening day realized the promise of a rain-storm which lasted until noon. Late in the afternoon the sun came out bright and warm, sending a spirit of cheerfulness throughout all the ranks. Crossing the Nottoway River—a little stream not unlike the Upper Rappahannock, that flows on toward North Carolina, and helps to form the Chowan River—nine o'clock at night, we bivouacked at Sussex Court House. A brick building, standing a short distance from the road, and of unpretentious size, was pointed out as the place where in other times Justice was dispensed according to the code of Virginia. Six other buildings, every one of them a good deal the worse for the wear, completed the ancient and insignificant town.

Thursday morning, with the first streak of gray dawn, the march was resumed. The quick ear of the troops, awake to the perils of the undertaking, that increased with every advancing mile, caught the first shot in front, that told of the presence of the enemy. It was Gregg encountering a party of rebel cavalry guarding the railroad bridge across the river. Driving away the guard and setting fire to the structure, the work of destruction at once commenced. The infantry struck the railroad four miles further south, and lending willing hands to the cavalry, by Friday night, from the Nottoway to the Meherrin, a distance of twenty miles, the Weldon Railroad ceased to exist.

Each division did its appropriate part; destroying all in its immediate front, and then moving alternately southward. The burning ties, aided by the nearest fence rails, cast a lurid light on the midnight heavens, telling to the Confederate commander the story of ruin wrought; while the heated rails, torn from the car track, that many strong arms made to take the shape and form of the distinguishing badge of the Fifth Corps, may remain to this day to tell by whom the ruin was wrought.

The country through which we passed differed but little in its general features from that in the immediate vicinity of Petersburg. There were no intrenchments to be seen, nor anything to intimate that two hostile armies were only a day's march distant. The plantations were large and frequent, with here and there fields of cotton, still carrying their small, imperfect crop.

The most noticeable feature to the eye of the soldier was the apparent plenty that dwelt in the land. Chickens and turkeys, that were thought to be extinct in Virginia, dwelt here prolific, in ease and security; while the lowing of the cow and the tinkling of sheep bells suggested that quieter days than those that came to us still dawned upon the world.

Breaking up our bivouac at Bellfield Station, two miles from the Meherrin River, the return march began in the early morning of December 10th. A cold, sleety rain had fallen during the night, softening the roads, and making the movement slow and heavy. Crawford's Division was the left of the column, with Baxter's Brigade and a squad of cavalry as its rear-guard.

Our destructive operations had not proceeded altogether unmolested. At different points the enemy showed himself, and as his cavalry were known to be following a short distance in our rear, every precaution was taken to defend the column against attack. Five miles from the place of starting, the troops halted in a thick woods, whose trees and overhanging branches were an agreeable shelter from the cold north wind that blew in keen and piercing blasts. Resuming the march, and as the rear regiments were moving out into the road, our cavalry guard, driven in by the rebels, came rushing through the ranks of the brigade in affrighted confusion, breaking its files, and throwing the whole line into disorder.

It was only momentary. A line of battle composed of four regiments—the Eleventh Pennsylvania and Ninety-seventh New York on the left of the road, the Eighty-eighth Pennsylvania and

Thirty-ninth Massachusetts on the right, each regiment deploying skirmishers in its front—was thrown across the track of the pursuing enemy. The cautious Confederates came near enough to reconnoiter our lines, but not near enough to exchange shots. Supported by infantry bayonets, the cavalry recovered their courage, and falling into ranks, the advance was continued.

Seven o'clock in the evening the rebel cavalry, that had followed us all day, was still hanging on our flanks, with the evident purpose of attacking some part of the column as we went into bivouac for the night. But there were counter-movements going on, quietly and secretly, that entirely defeated this purpose of our troublesome friends.

Halting near the camp of the division, by order of General Crawford, the Eleventh Pennsylvania, Ninety-seventh New York, and a part of the Eighty-eighth Pennsylvania, formed in ambush on either side and across the road. Favored by the darkness of the evening and the shadow of the pine woods through which a section of the road passed, the men crouched down behind the fences, and awaited the coming of the foe. The strategy was explained to our cavalry, who, first making a show of resistance, quickly retired, pursued by the rebels, fifteen or twenty of whom came within the ambush. It was a fatal trap for more than half the number that entered it. At a word, a volley of musketry issued from either side of the road, lighting up the darkness with a fitful glare, and carrying death and wounds to those fearless rebel riders.

"If you had delayed a day longer," said one of the wounded men, "you would not be marching back at your present leisure. A force is now in pursuit with orders not to permit a single raider to escape."

The knowledge of a pursuing foe had something to do with the early sound of the bugle on the following morning; and, while the stars were yet shining, the troops started off at a brisk walk over ground frozen hard by the cold that had increased with every hour of the night. Late in the afternoon, reaching the Nottoway River, a division of the Ninth Corps was found halted on the north bank. General Meade had read the signals of the enemy in front of Petersburg, and with the departure of the Confederate force to intercept our return, sent Park's Division to reinforce Warren. Three cheers from the south side of the stream greeted those on the north side; and crossing on pontoons that were soon made to span the river, two miles from its bank the army encamped until next morning.

By sundown of Monday we were back again in the old position on the Jerusalem plank-road. More than a hundred miles had been traveled in six days, and with a loss to the Eleventh of one man severely wounded, and two missing, the

Hicksford raid resulted in the entire destruction to the Confederates of the Weldon Railroad.

The Army of the Potomac quietly settled down into winter quarters. Dense forests, once so difficult to traverse, yielded to the sturdy blows of the axe, and numerous log cabins, similar to those erected north of the Rappahannock in the preceding winter, were now seen covering miles of territory where once stood the baronial dwellings of the Randolphs and the Tuckers, and around which transpired scenes and events that still live in story.

CHAPTER V.

EXTENDING THE LEFT TO HATCHER'S RUN.

THE advent of the year 1865, in the preparations throughout the camps of infantry and cavalry, gave notice of an early campaign. During the several weeks of comparative quiet that followed the expedition to the Meherrin River, the Eleventh was adjusting its broken ranks, and preparing for the next offensive movements against the rebels.

Major B. F. Haines was promoted to lieutenant-colonel, vice H. A. Frink, promoted to colonel of the One-hundred-and-eighty-second Regiment of Pennsylvania Volunteers; Captain John B. Overmyer was commissioned major; Lieutenant James Moore was made captain of Co. D; Lieutenant James J. Briggs, captain of Co. E, vice Henry B. Piper, discharged; Daniel Bonbright, first lieutenant of Co. E; and Sergeant Richard W. Morris, second lieutenant of Co. H.

Some time before the Hicksford raid, in December, the members of the Ninetieth Pennsylvania Regiment, who had re-enlisted as veterans, were transferred to the ranks of the Eleventh. Belonging to the same division and brigade, companions in the march from Washington to Petersburg, side by side these two regiments had fought in all the great battles from Cedar Mountain to the Weldon Railroad. The story of one, with but slight and insignificant changes, is the story of the other. It was eminently proper, at the close of the original term of enlistment, on the retirement of Colonel Peter Lyle and Lieutenant-Colonel William A. Leech, together with a number of the line officers—men who did their whole duty nobly and well—that what remained of the Ninetieth should be consolidated with the Eleventh.

With the opening of the month of February the wind began to blow warm from the south. Inspection of arms and accouterments had been a part of the daily drill for more than a week,

OPENING OF THE CAMPAIGN.

and on the evening of February 4th, when there commenced all along the lines a fierce bombardment of the rebel works—such as had not been heard since the close of the fall campaign—every man knew that the time to march had come.

Three o'clock Sunday morning, the shrill blast of the bugle gave notice that Gregg's Division of cavalry was in motion, moving down the Jerusalem plank-road. Two hours later, the Fifth Corps was following the cavalry, marching along the Halifax road, with Ayres's Division in the advance, Griffin next, and Crawford in the rear. Further to the right the Second Corps was moving directly toward Hatcher's Run. The Fifth Corps was intended to strike the enemy's right, and so made a detour to the left; while the Second Corps, marching along the Vaughan road, would strike the enemy's works on Hatcher's Run in front.

Leaving the old camp on the Jerusalem plank-road—which had already served as the starting-point for several important movements—the Eleventh marched in rear of the brigade. Through the stupid blunder of an aid-de-camp, the troops started out equipped for light marching, taking nothing with them but arms and accoutrements. In the afternoon a cold, pelting rain-storm set in, continuing through most of the night.

The bivouac on Dabney's plantation, across

Gravelly Run, presented a strange sight of men crowded together around the camp-fires, with no other protection than overcoats, and an occasional gum blanket. Sleeping on the ground, in a winter rain-storm, is not well calculated to make men amiable, and there was a disposition on the part of many to express their wrath in hard words. But there was also a vast deal of patient endurance among those men who covered up their heads in the capes of their overcoats, and with feet to the blazing camp-fire—that was made to burn despite the rain—slept on until morning.

Next day the march was continued, Crawford's Division crossing Hatcher's Run, and massing along the bank of the stream. The Federal battle-line was formed with the Second Corps on the right, the Fifth Corps in the center, and the cavalry on the left. Hatcher's Run flows in a southeasterly direction, and at its junction with Gravelly Run, forms the Rowanty Creek, a deep but sluggish stream that flows into the Nottoway River. The country around is low and swampy, cut up by ravines, and covered with forests traversed here and there by narrow country roads.

Early in the morning the Second Corps carried the first line of the enemy's works, and was firmly established on Hatcher's Run, the left connecting with the Fifth Corps. Two o'clock P.M. of February 6th, Crawford's Division recrossed

Hatcher's Run, and advanced three-fourths of a mile toward Dabney's Mill, with the intent of striking the Boydton plank-road. Baxter's Brigade was formed in two lines of battle, the Ninety-seventh New York, Sixteenth Maine, and Thirty-ninth Massachusetts in the first line, and the Eleventh and Eighty-eighth Pennsylvania in the second line.

Colonel Coulter had been breveted brigadier-general, and was in command of the Third Brigade. Lieutenant-Colonel Haines was serving on General Crawford's staff as Inspector-General, leaving the command of the Eleventh to Major Overmyer.

Moving forward a quarter of a mile further, the first line encountered Pegram's rebel division, and in a moment Crawford's troops were in the heat of battle. General Pegram was killed by the first volley from our guns, and the ranks of his division, missing the animating voice and cheering presence of their gallant leader, were pushed back in surprise and confusion.

In front of Crawford were the ruins of an old saw-mill and a broad swamp; to the right of his line was a strip of heavy forest. Moving a short distance by the right flank, the Eleventh threw up temporary breastworks within the cover of the woods. But Evans's Division was sent to the relief of Pegram, and no troops being on our right, in which direction the enemy was bearing down in large force, the defenses were abandoned, Crawford's line falling back some distance to the rear.

The momentary lull in our own rapid firing brought to our ears the sound of battle as it was raging on the right and on the left. Seeing the enemy halt in the works we had just abandoned, and encouraged by the report of heavy reinforcements coming up in the rear, Crawford's men rallied, retook the works from the enemy, and held them against a terrible fire.

The head of Ayres's Division, marching to Crawford's relief, was now in plain view. But before he could form his line on the right of the Eleventh, the enemy struck his flank, and threw him back on Hatcher's Run. Without support, and the last round of ammunition expended by the troops on the right, Crawford's line could maintain itself no longer, and went down with the giving way of Ayres.

Meanwhile Gregg, on the left, pressed on flank and in rear by the rebel cavalry, was also driven from his defenses, and forced to retreat beyond Hatcher's Run. The enemy, still further reinforced by Mahone's Division, followed the routed Federals with fiendish shouts. Another disaster on the left—"the bloody left," as the troops called it—appeared inevitable, as the men, lost in the woods, and entangled in the swamps and ravines, made their uncertain way to the rear. But the

BATTLE OF HATCHER'S RUN.

line of intrenchments thrown up by the Second Corps, on the evening of the 5th and the morning of the 6th, was a rallying point for the troops, and from behind those works a fire was poured into the eager Confederates that first halted their lines, and then sent them back to the cover of the woods. It was now dark night. The noise of battle had ceased, and secure within its defenses, the Federal line kept a firm hold on Hatcher's Run.

Early on the morning of February 7th, the enemy showed himself in front of our infantry and cavalry pickets, keeping up a heavy skirmish fire for several hours, but making no attempt to charge our lines. Toward noon Crawford's Division, supported on the left by General Wheaton, marched along the earthworks a mile to the right of the Vaughan road. Debouching from the intrenchments, the Thirty-ninth Massachusetts, of Baxter's Brigade, supported by the Eleventh Pennsylvania, was thrown forward as skirmishers. At the moment of marching out into comparatively open ground, as though possessed with the thought of testing the strength of our works across the Vaughan road, a line of the enemy's skirmishers was seen issuing from behind temporary works, and moving toward us. The contest between the skirmishers was short and decisive, resulting in the driving back of the rebels, and the capture of their defenses.

The Eleventh remained on the picket line until ten o'clock P.M., and without attacking the main line of the Confederates, Crawford retired behind Hatcher's Run, where the division bivouacked until morning.

Throughout the livelong night was heard the sound of the axe and the spade, as thousands of workmen threw up strong and enduring intrenchments. On the afternoon of February 8th, Baxter's entire brigade was sent out on picket. But the enemy maintained a sullen silence. Content to defend the Boydton plank-road against all attacks, Hatcher's Run was given up without a further struggle, and on the morning of the 10th, the Eleventh marched back to the old camp near Jerusalem plank-road, losing in the first campaign of the new year eighty-nine officers and men.

Two days later, the military railroad running from City Point was extended to Hatcher's Run, which thus became the extreme left of the Federal battle-line, a success of no little importance in the subsequent campaign.

CHAPTER VI.

FINAL CONCENTRATION.

The extension of the left flank to Hatcher's Run was followed by several weeks of almost entire inaction to the armies besieging Richmond and Petersburg. But it was not inaction after all; it was the labor of patient waiting. Sherman had completed his march from Atlanta to the sea, and turning northward, the tramp of his legions was heard moving across the Carolinas. A second attempt had reduced Fort Fisher to a Federal garrison, over whose parapets now waved the old flag, while a column of brave troops, thirty thousand strong, were marching inland from Wilmington and Newbern to join Sherman. One comprehensive mind was directing all the parts, and the Army of the Potomac, beginning the campaign on Hatcher's Run, was resting on its arms, awaiting the Lieutenant-General's final concentration.

For two or three days President Lincoln, and a party of ladies and gentlemen from Washington, had been the guests of General Grant. Before returning to the capital, the President was to review the army, throughout whose ranks active preparations were making for the event. General officers sent to City Point for dress-coats, and fancy horse trappings, that had been left there as of no use at the front; while the men, compelled to wear whatever the quartermaster provided, burnished their muskets, and rubbed to silvery brightness the brass plates of their accouterments.

Daylight of March 25th—the day appointed for the review—the troops were startled from their bomb-proof sleeping apartments by firing on the right. It was too early in the morning for a salute, and the practiced ear of the soldier detected in the *thud* of the distant guns something more than the noise of a blank cartridge.

The click of the telegraph at Crawford's headquarters, whose first anticipated message was an order to fall in line for review, told of the rebel attack on Fort Steadman, and an hour later the division was marching at a quick step to the right. Two divisions of the enemy, quietly massing in front of the Ninth Corps, burst upon our intrenchments, and capturing the fort, turned its nine guns upon the adjacent batteries. It was a brilliant achievement, but its success was short-lived. Rallying from all points of the Federal line, the daring enemy was pushed out into the space over which he came, now swept by the cross-fire of a score of batteries right and left of Steadman. There was no alternative but to surrender, and two thousand prisoners were sent to the rear. Thus the review was changed into a battle; and Crawford's Division marched back to its place on the left.

For three days after, the camps were all alive with preparations for a general move. But when the order came, on the 29th of March, there was nothing borne on the wings of the wind, or seen in the face of the sky, to indicate that the army was beginning its last campaign. Rumors reached us of the conference of generals at City Point, and the union of the armies of Meade and Sherman. But all that had been talked of many times before. The rank and file had grown incredulous. Four years of war, while it made the men brave and valorous, had entirely cured them of imagining that each campaign would be the last. Passing by the cooking apartment of regimental headquarters, a soldier struck his musket against the cracker-box, set up on a barrel to help the draught of the chimney.

"Don't knock dat chimbly down, please, sah," was the polite expostulation of the cook. "We'll be back here agin in a week, and I'll want to use it."

But Struthers was a false prophet. That was our last move from the old camp near the Jerusalem plank-road.

Wednesday morning, March 29th, as early as

three o'clock, the Fifth Corps was moving in the direction of Dinwiddie Court House. Sheridan's cavalry was in the advance, with instructions to find the enemy's right, and, if possible, force him from his intrenchments. Crawford's Division moved along the Halifax road, Baxter's Brigade bringing up the rear. Time was when the Eleventh alone would have made a show of resistance quite equal in numbers to that presented by the entire brigade. Neither through volunteering nor drafting could the ranks be kept up to more than a fourth of their original strength for duty.

By noon we had passed the line of earthworks on the left, and moving southward, crossed Rowanty Creek, below the junction of Gravelly and Hatcher's Run. Following the road to Dinwiddie Court House as far as the Quaker road, the troops turned up the latter, and crossed Gravelly Run. The line of the Fifth Corps was formed with Griffin on the right, Ayres in the center, and Crawford on the left. In front of the entire line were the enemy's skirmishers, disputing every step of our advance. But it was Griffin, near the old saw-mill, that had the sharpest engagement, inflicting a severe loss upon the enemy, and losing heavily himself. The left of the line, not thus delayed, swung around further to the front, until near its junction with the Quaker road. The brigade commanded by General Coulter was the first to lay its hands on the coveted Boydton plank-road, and by early evening a strong line of intrenchments was stretched across it.

The rain that commenced falling in drenching showers with the setting in of night, though it did not prevent the men from extending the defenses, confined the operations of March 30th to short advances and reconnoiterings along the plank-road as far to the right as Burgess's Mill. March 31st, the storm was over; but the whole country round was one vast swamp, holding fast in its quagmire everything on wheels. The only exception to the flat, marshy character of the ground was the line held by the enemy, running along the White Oak Ridge, whose tolerably good road crossed the Boydton plank-road near Burgess's Mill, and continued on to Petersburg.

General Lee was not ignorant of Grant's movements on the left, and with heavy reinforcements from Petersburg, was directing in person the operations in our front. Toward eleven o'clock a brigade of Ayres's Division was sent out against the enemy's skirmishers. The object was to discover with what force he held the White Oak road. Our troops had only advanced a few hundred yards, when the repulse became general, and Winthrop's Brigade returned.

Meanwhile, the rebels were also contemplating a forward move; and seizing that as a favorable moment, the Confederates fell upon Ayres, from the north and the west, breaking his ranks and forcing him back in confusion. Crawford's lines were also carried down in the assault, both divisions falling back on Griffin, who was in position along the bank of a small stream—a branch of Gravelly Run—west of the plank-road. Four hours later, with broken ranks reformed, General Warren advanced the entire available force of the Fifth Corps, driving the enemy back into his intrenchments, capturing almost the whole of the Fifty-sixth Virginia Regiment, with its complete stand of colors.

Sheridan and his cavalry bivouacked at Dinwiddie Court House March 29th. Next day a reconnoissance toward Five Forks drove back parties of the enemy's skirmishers, and developed a strong force in position, holding the White Oak road. Returning once more to Dinwiddie, the troopers awaited the coming of March 31st. Early Friday morning they were moving out along the several roads concentrating at Dinwiddie, to the attack of Five Forks. But there were counter-movements from the rebel side. As a military point, the Court House was all-important, and must not be left in the hands of the Yankees. Starting as early as Sheridan, the enemy met him in the way with cavalry and infantry.

The Fifth Corps was distant several miles from

where the opposing forces first exchanged shots. But the sound of battle could be distinctly heard, and toward evening the receding noise suggested the driving of our cavalry before the enemy. Later in the day an officer of Sheridan's command, cut off in an attack, found his way within the lines of the Fifth Corps, confirming the suspicion that the cavalry had been driven back to Dinwiddie.

Army headquarters were all astir, and orders quick and fast were transmitted to Warren. At one time a brigade is ordered to be sent down the White Oak road, and at another time down the Boydton plank-road. One order directs Warren to open communications with Sheridan; by another he is told to halt his troops at Gravelly Run. Eight o'clock, it was intimated in a confidential note that the Federal battle-line would be contracted, and an hour after Warren was directed to draw back two of his divisions within the Boydton plank-road, sending the remaining division to report to Sheridan.

One o'clock A.M. of April 1st, it became known that Sheridan could not maintain himself at Dinwiddie without reinforcements, and as these could only reach him from the Fifth Corps, its commander was urged to use every exertion to get troops to him as soon as possible. The bridge across the swollen stream of Gravelly Run, now too deep for infantry to ford, had to be rebuilt, and with the first order to send troops to the relief of Sheridan, a pioneer force was set to work spanning the creek.

Two o'clock A.M., the bridge was completed, and Ayres's Division reported to General Sheridan. The enemy that had driven Sheridan back to Dinwiddie retired from his front during the night and early morning of April 1st. Withdrawing from White Oak Ridge in line of battle, first Griffin and last Crawford marched in the direction of the Court House, and by ten o'clock A.M. Sheridan was reinforced by the three divisions of the Fifth Corps.

CHAPTER VII.

FIFTH CORPS WITH SHERIDAN.

THE movement of the Fifth Corps to Dinwiddie Court House was a part of Grant's general plan, and placed Warren under the immediate orders of General Sheridan, with whom he was to co-operate.

Eleven o'clock of April 1st, the three divisions of Griffin, Ayres, and Crawford were in position near Gravelly Run, looking toward the White Oak road. The thick fog had cleared away, and long lines of cavalry, soiled with mud, but with spirit and daring in every look and movement, were seen marching in the direction taken by the retiring Confederates. Two hours later General Warren was ordered to move his corps to the front, the enemy having made a stand which promised to be obstinate, behind formidable intrenchments at Five Forks.

Up to this moment General Lee seems to have been in strange ignorance of the doings on his right. Assured that with a knowledge of the danger imperiling his flank would come reinforcements, or a retreat, Sheridan, anxious to improve the golden opportunity, was impatient at the slightest apparent delay.

The roads were heavy with mud, and the men worn down by four nights of marching and battle. It may have looked like slow plodding, as the troops crowded through that narrow lane, leading past Gravelly Run Church to the White Oak road. But they were doing all that men depending upon their own legs alone could do, and when they merged out into the open ground upon which they were to act, the compact lines of the old Fifth Corps told that the lessons learned in the van of many important army movements, since the crossing of the Rapidan a year before, were not quite forgotten.

The right of the battle-line was given to Crawford's Division, and the left to Ayres, Griffin forming his ranks behind Crawford. A hurried survey of the ground in front enabled General Warren to explain to his division and brigade commanders the part that each one was expected to perform. The cavalry was to attack in front, while the infantry, crossing the White Oak road, was to carry the enemy's flank and rear.

The lines moved out in splendid style. But a faulty calculation as to the exact position of the enemy's left flank, and the difficult nature of the ground over which the troops were moving—through bogs, and tangled woods, and thickets of pine—threw Crawford too far to the right. The assault intended to be made by the Third Division, supported by Griffin, as a consequence fell upon Ayres.

The first volley from the muskets of the infantry was the signal of attack for the cavalry in front. It was now four o'clock in the afternoon, and though assailed on the flank and in front, and threatened in the rear, the enemy made a bold and gallant defense. Griffin came into the gap between Ayres and Crawford, while the latter, wheeling to the left, crossed the Ford road, a country highway running through the center of the enemy's position and directly in his rear. It was not intended that the Federal line should take such a formation, but it was this form alone that made the battle of Five Forks such a complete victory. Staggered at first by the heavy fire that struck their left flank, and unable for the thick woods and bushes to see the foe with whom they were contending, Ayres's men faltered a moment. But it was only for a moment. Recovering from their surprise as they neared the enemy's intrenchments, they charged his works at a single bound, capturing hundreds of prisoners and several flags. Joined by Griffin, who had also wheeled to the left, both divisions went sweeping down the line of rebel works toward Five Forks. The cavalry was already on the right flank, and it only needed Crawford to close in upon the Ford road to cut off every avenue of escape.

Crawford's line was formed with the First Brigade on the right, the Second (Baxter) on the left, and the Third (Coulter) in the rear. The Third Brigade was soon ordered to the front, to fill up the gap between our own and the Second Division, bringing it next to the Eleventh Regiment, holding the left of Baxter's second line. The fire of the enemy now became severe, especially on Crawford's center and left. But shouts and cheers, rising above the din of clashing arms, were heard from every part of the field.

The moment had come for the final charge, and riding to the right, Warren directed Crawford to move down the Ford road, and attack the enemy in rear of his fortifications. The advance was given to General Coulter, the other two brigades marching in near support. Across the road, and in a position to defend all its approaches, was a rebel battery of four guns and a strong line of infantry. Against this force the division was pressing down, meeting in its ranks a rapid and destructive fire, from which the troops were at first disposed to shield themselves in the woods on either side of the road. But the enthusiasm of certain success carried them onward.

Coulter was handsomely sustained by Baxter, and when the men of the Third Brigade shouted over the taking of the battery whose terrible execution could be seen in the breaks in their ranks, so near was the Eleventh to its old commander that not only did it join in the cheer, but charging the enemy's line of infantry, Sergeant H. A. Delavie, of Co. I, seized the flag of the Thirty-second Virginia Regiment from its retreating bearer, and waved it aloft over the enemy's captured works.

A short distance beyond where the guns were taken, Crawford connected with the First and Second Divisions, and without halting for an instant, the lines of the Fifth Corps, as they bore down on Five Forks, moving through the rifle-pits and over the intrenchments of the enemy, swept them clean of everything dressed in gray.

Crawford's Division lost three hundred in killed and wounded, Ayres's Division two hundred and five, Griffin's Division one hundred and twenty-five, in all six hundred and thirty-four men. But the enemy's right flank was completely broken, leaving between five and six thousand prisoners in our hands; the Fifth Corps alone capturing over three thousand men, with their arms, eleven regimental colors, and one four-gun battery with its caissons. Seven o'clock P.M., camp-fires were burning in every direction, around which gathered groups of men, jubilant over the successes of the day. Retracing its steps over the line of battle, the Fifth Corps bivouacked at night on the White Oak road, near Gravelly Run Church.

CHAPTER VIII.

THE LAST MARCH OF THE FIFTH CORPS.

THE second day of April was Sabbath—a bright, clear day. Called from their bivouac near Gravelly Run Church, whose closed doors reminded us of the wicked times upon which we had fallen, the two divisions of Crawford and Griffin, turning their backs upon Five Forks, at an early hour in the morning were marching in the direction of Petersburg, to open communication with the main body of the army on the right.

The enemy was found in strong position directly across our path, at the junction of the White Oak and Claiborne roads. Miles's Division of the Second Corps, sent to reinforce Sheridan, and that marched in front of the Fifth Corps, at once opened the attack on the enemy. Before the lines of Crawford and Griffin could be formed, General Humphreys, with the rest of the Second Corps, moved down from the right. The connection with the right of the army was now complete, and leaving Miles to act with his own corps, Sheridan countermarched the Fifth Corps to Five Forks, and crossing Hatcher's Run by the Ford road, reached the Southside Railroad without opposition.

A thousand caps went swinging into the air as the troops crossed that great thoroughfare of the Confederate army. The men believed that they had now reached the objective point of the campaign, and with willing hands awaited the order to unsling knapsacks, and commence the work of tearing up the railroad. But instead of a halt, the march was continued at a quick step up the road toward Petersburg. Then, obliquing to the left; and still marching on across Chandler's Run, late at night the Eleventh bivouacked in line of battle north of Sutherland Station, the right of the regiment resting on Namozine road, and connecting on the left with the rest of Baxter's Brigade.

GENERAL WARREN RELIEVED. 393

The absence of General Warren from the head of the column, as it filed out into the White Oak road, early in the morning, was the first intimation to the troops that the general had been relieved of the command. With the splendid achievements of General Sheridan fully acknowledged, and with an admiration of his dashing soldierly qualities second to none, the men of the Fifth Corps have never forgiven him for his hasty action toward their well-tried commander.

The successes that followed the victory of Five Forks—a victory which belongs as much to Warren as to Sheridan—and that culminated in the surrender of General Lee, sunk out of sight many things that might otherwise have come to the surface. Regarded at the time as a freak of temper rather than the dictate of calm and sober judgment, the removal of General Warren remains to this day without the justification of reason or expediency.

The enemy that we knew to be behind the line of earthworks in front of our bivouac, slipped away during the night, and on the morning of April 3d the Fifth Corps, commanded by General Griffin, moved out with its accustomed promptness.

Too busy with the exciting contest in our immediate front to hear the guns that had opened all along the front of Petersburg, it was not until this morning that we knew of the successful storming of its outer defenses, and the compression of our lines around the city. It was while the men were waiting for the order to fall into ranks, that a deep and prolonged cheer came rolling along the line of troops, like the swellings of a tornado, telling that Petersburg and Richmond were both evacuated, and that the whole rebel army was in precipitate retreat toward Danville.

If the quartermaster had gone through the ranks of the Eleventh, and, taking up all the sore feet and stiffened limbs, had issued to each man of the regiment a new pair of legs, they could not have marched forth with a more supple step. The roads over which we moved were the same, in their make-up, that we had been traversing for four long and wearisome years—swamps and woods, varied only by woods and swamps. That day, too, we were marching, at a dog-trot, after Merritt's cavalry; but all fatigue was gone. From his place in the ranks each private soldier could see the end of the rebellion in the capture of Lee's retreating army; and toward that point everything was now made to bend.

Ten o'clock at night we bivouacked at Deep Creek, with the Appomattox River not far to our right. Scores of stragglers from the Southern army, and multitudes of contrabands, who had lost their masters, had fallen into the moving column during the day. Gathered around the camp-fires that the chilly night-air still made pleasant and agreeable, the events of the passing hours were discussed with an interest as absorbing as cabinet ministers could discuss them.

An hour later most of the men had stretched themselves on the ground to sleep. Walking up and down through the ranks of prostrate forms, we found ourselves not alone wakeful with the thoughts of the past and the promises of the future. With heads toward the fire lay huddled together a group of darkies, all on terms of the most friendly intimacy. We came upon them, unobserved, and waited a moment to listen to their talk.

"I feels better to-night than I did after that fight at Gettysburg," said one, whose voice was at once recognized. "That was a mighty warm place, I tell you. It seemed to me as if I'd never git away from thar. I felt as if I wanted to pray, but de colonel's Jim was thar, and de doctor's Andy, and I didn't like to let 'em see me. Then the shells begin to come faster than ever, and dey seemed to say as plain as anything, H-a-r-vey! H-a-r-vey!! So I stretched myself square on de ground, jist as I'm laying now, and I said low to myself, O, Lord, if you please, do de very best you can for Harvey. Jist then I heard an awful hollering. Andy said, 'de Johnnies is gitting whipt;' and it was all true. I felt good then; but I feels a heap better now."

Daylight of April 4th the Fifth Corps was again on the move. The cavalry had divided into three separate columns, and were pushing forward to harass the flank, and cross the front of the retreating Southerners. It was the same hurried march to-day as yesterday; and not until the head of the column crossed the Richmond and Danville Railroad at Jetersville, sixteen miles from the place of starting, was the hard day's work completed.

Throughout the day of April 5th Griffin's Corps remained intrenched at Jetersville. Amelia Court House was five miles to the northeast, and already in possession of the Confederate advance. Next day, turning westward, General Lee marched with rapid haste for Farmville, in the desperate endeavor to place the Appomattox River between himself and his eager pursuers. It was on this morning that Sheridan turned over the Fifth Corps to General Meade. It had followed the cavalry for three days, keeping up with the troopers in all their long and hurried marches, and watching at night in the same line of battle, or resting in the same bivouac.

The Sixth Corps was now pushed to the front. Moving one day on the flank of the army as far to the left as Prince Edward Court House, and the next day hanging on the rear of the retreating rebels, April 9th the Fifth Corps halted at Appomattox Court House.

The 9th day of April, 1865, was Sabbath; just such a calm, clear day as the one that preceded it, on which we moved out from our bivouac near Gravelly Run Church. The two armies of Grant and Lee were at last together, with only the little town of Appomattox between them. But there was no deploying of skirmishers, or movements of divisions into lines of battle, or unlimbering of cannon. The army of General Lee had surrendered; and in a small house, plainly seen low-squatted within a green inclosure, and before whose door an orderly on horseback still held the white flag brought in by Gordon and Wilcox, Grant and Lee were settling the terms of capitulation.

CHAPTER IX.

HOMEWARD BOUND.

The great work done, and well done, the lines of the victorious Federal army began to draw away from the scenes of the surrender, leaving the Fifth Corps behind to carry out the terms of the capitulation and to take charge of the public property. We confess to a feeling of loneliness, as with the disappearance of the last brigade over the hill that bounded our view, the notes of fife and drum, every moment growing fainter, were heard no more.

But the morning came when the spoils of war were all secured, and the last Southern soldier paroled. Then the bugle sounded the order to march. It was the homeward march. One look at the beautiful country around the head-waters of the Appomattox, and, with faces once more toward Richmond, the column moved forward, first to Farmville, and then along the Richmond and Danville pike to the banks of the James. As we crossed the river, Belle Island was in full view, bringing an angry look to the eyes of the men, that at last expressed itself in derisive cheers, as they marched by the doors of Libby Prison and Castle Thunder.

The day before the evacuation of Richmond, the only remaining prisoners confined in Libby were sent down the river for exchange. Among these was Captain James T. Chalfant, of Co. F, captured at the battle of the Wilderness, May 5th, 1864. After nearly a year's experience in the prison-pens of Lynchburg, Macon, Charleston, Columbia, and Charlotte, twice making his escape, and each time recaptured, the captain was the last Pennsylvanian to leave Richmond as a prisoner.

Richmond was now in the rear, and moving over the Peninsula, across the Chickahominy and the Pamunkey, and then across the Rappahannock at Fredericksburg, we

"Nightly pitched our moving tents
A day's march nearer home;"

until one evening, in the last hours of sunlight, the troops looked down from Hall's Hill upon the City of Washington, smiling at the return of peace, but sad and stricken over the death of Abraham Lincoln.

After a few days of rest and quiet came the grand review of the armies of Meade and Sherman by the President of the United States, the Secretary of War, and General Grant. Then followed the work of disbanding; and the ranks of the Federal army were scattered from Maine to Minnesota, each true volunteer forgetting the calling of the soldier in the more peaceful duties of the citizen.

As the State capital had been the rendezvous of the departing regiments, so it now became the gathering place of those returning from the war.

Its best friends would hardly have recognized the old Eleventh, so changed was its organization, had not General Coulter and one or two of the original staff officers remained to prove its identity. One of its field officers—Major I. B. Overmyer—and most of the line officers had been promoted from the ranks. Even the drummer boys had grown up to be men, and came back wearing sword and epaulets.

Those promoted out of our ranks, as well as those in them, did valuable service wherever they were placed. Col. H. A. Frink, of the One-hundred-and-eighty-sixth Regiment, afterward breveted brigadier-general, will be remembered as the efficient provost-marshal of Philadelphia. Assistant Surgeons W. C. Phelps and W. F. Osborne—whose places were filled in the regiment by Drs. John M. Rankin and Charles D. Fortney—became surgeons; the former of the Twenty-second Pennsylvania Cavalry, and the latter of the One-hundred-and-seventeenth Infantry Regiment.

Awaiting our arrival in Harrisburg were men who had been absent from the regiment on detached service, or sick in hospital, sent forward to be mustered out of service with their several companies. There were also a few returned from the prisons of the South, among whom were Captain A. G. Happer, of Co. I, and Lieutenant Freeman C. Gay, of Co. K. Captain Happer was severely wounded, and fell into the hands of the enemy at the battle of the Wilderness. Lieutenant Gay was captured at Gettysburg, and remained nearly two years a prisoner.

More than three thousand men were enrolled in the ranks of the Eleventh during the war. Less than three hundred marched back to Camp Curtin for final discharge. Many of the absent ones, who had been sent home because of disease, or the severities of the campaign, or of honorable though disabling wounds, could have answered to their names had there been a calling of the roll. But the rest are filling graves scattered from Gettysburg to the Appomattox, from Annapolis to Andersonville, and will only answer

"When the general Roll is called."

The Story of the Regiment is not for them. Its pleasant memories or sad reminiscences of marches and bivouacs, and of battles fought and victories won, are only for the living.

"On fame's eternal camping-ground
Their silent tents are spread;
While glory keeps, with solemn round,
The bivouac of the dead."

THE END.

www.ingramcontent.com/pod-product-compliance
Lightning Source LLC
Chambersburg PA
CBHW020741020526
44115CB00030B/726